WORD

AND

FIGURE

WORD

The Language of

AND

Nineteenth-Century French Poetry

FIGURE

Carol de Dobay Rifelj

Ohio State University Press
Columbus

Copyright © 1987 by the Ohio State University Press.
All rights reserved.

Library of Congress Cataloging-in-Publication Data

Rifelj, Carol de Dobay, 1946–
   Word and figure.

   Bibliography: p.
   Includes index.
   1. French poetry—19th century—History and
criticism.   2. French language—Figures of speech.
3. French language—Versification.   I. Title.
PQ433.R5   1987   841'.009   87–1504

ISBN 0-8142-0422-8

For Tony and Claire

Contents

Acknowledgments

Preliminary work for this project was funded by a grant from the National Endowment for the Humanities, and its writing was made possible by a fellowship from the American Council of Learned Societies and leave from Middlebury College. I am very grateful to all these institutions for their support.

An earlier version of parts I and II of Chapter 2 appeared in *Romanic Review* 70 (1979):346-56; a shorter version of Chapter 5 was published in *Kentucky Romance Quarterly* 19 (1982): 365-77; a small portion of Chapter 6, part II, appeared in *Romance Notes* 21 (1980):1-4. I am grateful for permission to reprint them here.

I would like to express my gratitude to the late Paul de Man for his inspiration and counsel. Special thanks go to Christine Froula for sympathetic readings, helpful discussions, and unfailing encouragement. I would also like to thank Nancy O'Connor and Ed Knox for their readings and advice, Tom Copeland for his technical assistance, and the readers and editors at Ohio State University Press for their helpful suggestions.

Preface

Carl Sandburg once defined poetry as "the synthesis of hyacinths and biscuits"(x). But this is a post-nineteenth-century
view of poetry. As an old word for flower, as a precious stone,
or as the standard literary metonym for reddish-gold, *hya-
cinthe* is eminently "poetic." But biscuits? The fact that biscuits have in fact become a part of poetry reflects the change in
poetic diction that occurred during the nineteenth century,
when the introduction of formerly banned terms into French
poetry overthrew the conventional, restricted lexicon and
created new possibilities for poetic expression. Asselineau
wrote that "La fonction du romantisme fut la reconstitution,
la création de la langue poétique et du style littéraire au XIXe
siècle" (quoted in Brunot, "Les Romantiques," 309). French
poetry was long overdue for such a reform: from the seventeenth to the early nineteenth centuries it had distinguished
in a very rigid way between elevated and low diction, the noble
and the *roturier* ("common"). Poetic conventions covered all
the dimensions of what has been defined as linguistic register
and prescribed both acceptable subjects of verse and the language proper to express them.

Those poets who breached this code, using colloquial or familiar words and even vulgar and slang expressions, were
clearly writing in opposition to the accepted canon. Hugo
claimed a revolutionary role for himself in the line beloved of
literary critics and survey textbooks, "Je mis un bonnet rouge
au vieux dictionnaire." But many of the other major poets of

the century had a part in the elaboration of this new poetic language. Gautier praised the richness and range of Baudelaire's language; Verlaine was described as a "grand marieur de mots, l'un de l'autre étonnés" (*Dictionnaire néologigue*); the task Rimbaud set himself was to "trouver une langue" ("La Lettre du voyant"). Of course, each poet developed this poetic program in a different mode, raising different questions about the use of unconventional language in a highly conventional context.

I will not attempt to provide a history of French poetic language, a task already masterfully accomplished by the great historians of the French language. Nor will I try to determine influences among these poets. The object of my analysis is, rather, language in context. I will study the functioning of familiar discourse in individual poems, examine in what ways each poet exploited its stylistic potential, and show how the use of colloquial language can take on a figurative dimension. Intruding into the texture of poetry, familiar discourse becomes a kind of trope: it calls attention to the surface of the work, complicating and interfering with the poem's referential dimension. This renewal of poetic language and the figurative uses it made possible are of primary importance both to these poets and to those who came after them, for whom hyacinths and biscuits, as well as the colloquial, slang, or technical terms referring to them, have become the stuff of poetry.

WORD

AND

FIGURE

ONE

Poetic Language and the Language of Poetry

All languages are rich in semantic and connotative possibilities, and poetry makes the most of them. The major innovators of French poetic language in the nineteenth century had access to many different levels and varieties of discourse. The concept of linguistic register, or language varieties, can help to define more precisely what kinds of language were available to them, to outline the poetic norms according to and against which they were writing, and to determine the rhetorical dimensions involved when they transgressed against those norms.

I. Levels of Language

When we read a passage like the second stanza of Baudelaire's "L'Imprévu" we are struck by the way it juxtaposes different styles:

> Célimène roucoule et dit: "Mon coeur est bon,
> Et naturellement, Dieu m'a faite très-belle."
> —Son coeur! coeur racorni, fumé comme un jambon,
>   Recuit à la flamme éternelle!

But to determine just what brings this incongruity about and what its effects are requires a closer examination. We recognize elements from different categories and different levels of what linguists have termed "language varieties" or "contextual language."[1] *Flamme éternelle* belongs to the language of sermons and the Bible; whereas *flamme* in the sense of "love" or "passion" belongs to the vocabulary of classical French poetry, a sublanguage I will be describing later on. On the other hand, *recuit* and *jambon fumé* belong to the language of cooking, a subject area (despite Sandburg's definition) eliminated from such poetry. These culinary terms lead us to read *flamme* as a cooking fire as well. The phrase *Flamme éternelle*, belonging to the *langue soutenue* of sermons and dramatic and lyric poetry, is associated with written language and formal address. *Très-belle* is also a marker of formality, since the hyphenated form, though correct, was falling into disuse at the time (according to Littré and Larousse). On the other hand, "Et naturellement" is the kind of colloquial expression we associate with spoken discourse. It appears in what is indeed an example of reported speech; but *roucouler* in the sense of "sweet talk" was classified as a familiar term by contemporary dictionaries, and it is the speaker of the poem who uses it. Baudelaire makes much of these various levels and semantic fields. For instance, he plays on the root *corne* in *racorni* to recall the devil, in opposition to "Dieu m'a faite . . . " in the preceding line. Beyond these multiple resonances is the allusion to Célimène from "Le Misanthrope," motivating both the direct quotation and, to a certain extent, the use of familiar language, since comedy was traditionally a less formal genre.

I have already called on several different categories in discussing these lines: semantic fields, levels of formality, differences between spoken and written discourse, genre considerations, and the question of intertextuality. It would be well to sort some of them out, determine their interrelations, and give an idea of the connotations they can carry.

Linguists, especially in Britain, have recently given attention to the different ways the speakers of a language can express themselves. People observe not only syntactical and semantic rules, but also rules relating to the context or situation of their utterances. Unlike geographical dialects or temporal dialects (e.g., Old French, modern French), the relevant dimensions here are those Gregory has termed "diatypes," the possibilities within a particular individual's speech.[2] We would expect great variation, for example, in the utterances of a physician if she were writing an article for a medical journal, comforting a child patient, or making a grocery list. Linguists have established different systems of classifications to describe these variations, sometimes using different terms to refer to the same categories. I will follow the summarizing work of Gregory and Carroll's *Language and Situation*, which describes contextual language in three general, overlapping ways.[3]

First, the dimension of *field* comprises the linguistic features usually correlated with an extralinguistic situation, baseball, say, or the weather. Although subject matter is the most important element here, what we call "subject matter" can be described more precisely. The general field of baseball is treated very differently when one is discussing a game in a bar, making a bet, announcing the batting order to the team, or swearing at the umpire. The second dimension, *mode*, refers to the medium of utterance: a radio sportscast, a newspaper column, a conversation between friends, and the printed program are all modes in which aspects of baseball can be discussed or presented. The major modal distinction is, however, the one between written and spoken discourse. Many of the characteristics of mode are related to another dimension, that of *tenor* (sometimes called "role") covering the relation between speaker and interlocutor. This dimension comprises illocutionary status (the speaker may be questioning, informing, greeting, etc.) and social position, the latter usually correlated with formality or informality of expression.[4]

Obviously, there are interrelations among these categories: we might well expect criticism of an umpire's call to be expressed in the spoken medium and in distinctly informal speech at that. In the sports section of the paper, it would probably be somewhat more formal. If it came up in a law suit brought by an aggrieved player, considerable formality of address would be involved, as well as technical expressions associated with the legal field. When there is considerable predictability of the ways these categories intersect, the sublanguage so formed is called a *register*. Registers may be radically restricted, like the language of bridge-bidding or knitting patterns, or they can have much looser boundaries, like political journalism or sermons or conversations about the weather.[5]

The fact that words and phrases belong to particular registers gives them stylistic connotations. As Kerbrat-Oreccione notes, an expression can give information unrelated to its denotative role: namely, that "la séquence relève de telle catégorie de discours ou registre de langue" (38). For example, part of what *patate* connotes is that it belongs to familiar discourse (16).[6] The importance of this aspect of language to the study of poetry is obvious: poets make use of the various resonances of terms, among them their register-levels. Gautier recognizes this power of words in his preface to *Les Fleurs du mal*:

> Pour les poètes, les mots ont, en eux-mêmes et en dehors du sens qu'ils expriment, une beauté et une valeur propres comme des pierres précieuses qui ne sont pas encore taillées et montées en bracelets, en colliers ou en bagues.
> . . . Il y a des mots diamant, saphir, rubis, émeraude, d'autres qui luisent comme du phosphore quand on les frotte, et ce n'est pas un mince travail de les choisir. (46)

In the stanza from Baudelaire quoted above, the religious and poetic connotations of *flamme éternelle* are highly relevant, as are the status of the familiar expressions and the field marking of *recuit*, both of which undercut these connotations. It is important to remember, however, that the stylistic effects of these "marked" terms depend on their context. There are two kinds of contexts that are important and that intersect here: those established by the text itself and those within the genre (more properly the subgenre) to which it belongs. The interrelations between these contexts are of course of great interest as well: *recuit* is an unexpected term in the genre of love poetry of Baudelaire's time; and, in the context of this stanza, it gains stylistic force through its juxtaposition with *à la flamme éternelle*.[7]

What are the implications of these categories and their connotations for the constitution of a "poetic language"? Some linguists have called literature itself a register, sometimes proposing a further subdivision of linguistic varieties into genres. Gregory and Carroll see literary genres as individually marked registers within literature (45-46). But others have recognized that, on the contrary, in literature we might expect to find elements from all registers.[8] In some periods the combination of disparate registers can itself serve as a marker of poetry. Symbolism and postsymbolism can accommodate strong juxtapositions of registers, as in Laforgue's *blocus sentimental* ("L'Hiver qui vient") or Pound's "a tale for two,/ Pregnant with mandrakes" ("Portrait d'une femme"). But such startling combinations of register are not characteristic of poetry of all periods: Racine could use the oxymoron *flamme si noire* but not the medical expression "*inflammation* si noire." The notion of poetic language as "strangeness," proposed by the Czech formalists and some of their French structuralist inheritors is a postromantic one: in other cultures and ages "poetic" status depends on conforming to the norms of a restricted poetic diction.[9] This is true in particular for French poetry of the eighteenth and early nineteenth centuries, which Bruneau calls "neoclassical" (in Brunot's *Histoire*).

Each age has its own poetic conventions regarding meter, rhyme, syntax, diction, and rhetoric, though they are of course subject to change. I am using "convention" in the sense of the set of expectations and assumptions the reader brings to a text by virtue of her experience with literature.[10] The standardization of these conventions contributes to the creation of poetic traditions. Poetic practice must take the established traditions into account, whether to confirm them or to counter them.[11]

So, although it is true that any word can enter into poetry, at a given time there are words that can properly be called "poetic" because, by convention, they are marked as such.[12] Not only is this true for the neoclassical norm against which the romantics and Symbolists were writing, but they in their turn developed a characteristic poetic vocabulary: Marouzeau points out the romantics' *fauve, farouche,* and *ténèbres,* the "Impressionists' " *languide, remembrances, détresses* (*Précis,* 109). As unconventional language is adopted by poets, it gradually becomes the conventional language, and often, what was first attacked as "unpoetic" becomes the very sign of poetry. Poetry becomes, for example, the "synthesis of hyacinths and biscuits."

The opposition between "poetic" and "ordinary" language has often taken the form of a distinction between high or "elevated" and low diction; between noble and common (in French *roturier*, "plebian"). The first terms of these sets are obviously highly valorized. Aristotle establishes such a distinction in the sections of the *Poetics* called "The basic principles of poetic style":

> The specific excellence of verbal expression in poetry is to be clear without being low. The clearest, of course, is that which uses the regular words for things; but it is low. . . . Impressiveness and avoidance of familiar language is achieved by the use of alien terms; and by "alien" I mean dialectical words, metaphor, lengthening of words, in short anything other than the standard terminology. . . . So, then, poetic expression should have some mixture of this kind in it; the one ingredient, that of foreign words, metaphor, ornamental words, and all the other varieties, will ensure that it is not commonplace or low. (58-59)

The devices Aristotle recommends are those used in his time to set poetic language apart: phonetic alterations of words through metrics; the use of archaisms and literally "foreign" or dialectical terms; and tropes. Such devices were thus part of what constituted contemporary poetic language.[13] Although what counts as "foreign" words varies, the pattern of this opposition can be seen in literature and criticism in other periods and cultures as well.

"Alien" terms may in fact include "everyday language," as in the mixture of styles characteristic of modern poetry. In their otherwise excellent analysis of poetic language, Molino and Tamine attempt to divide poetry into two major groups: the first using standard discourse, a "langue accessible à tous" (whether refined or popular); the second distancing itself from the standard. They put satire, parodies, pastiches, comic verse, *vers de circonstance*, and "poésie lyrique directe" (examples that use refined language), ballads and songs (popular language) into the first category, characterized by a refusal of obscurity and of the "grands mouvements de la rhétorique et du sentiment" (94-96). Yet, not only do many examples of the genres they mention make use of obscurity (much circumstantial verse, for instance) or inflated rhetoric (in fact, it is the common coin of most pastiche); but also the poetry of the other pole, "haute poésie," can certainly make use of the characteristics they associate with the "standard." (They do not describe this pole, but it probably includes tragedy and the heroic ode). The standard language relevant here is the *poetic* standard applicable at the time. As those studying language in context have shown, there are many "standard languages," both within a language as a whole and within any person's idiolect.

Theorists of poetic language have traditionally established a three-level hierarchy of styles. A middle style is introduced between the grand and simple styles; and the three styles correspond to three major divisions of genres.[14] In *Introduction à l'architexte*, Genette has shown how widely genre classifications have varied from age to age and from theorist to theorist. It can be stated, however, that the more rigidly the genres are defined, the more fixed the stylistic constraints tend to be (Enkvist, 54). With potentially wide variation from genre to genre, even at one age, there is not only one "poetic language." Furthermore, at any period, different poets use poetic conventions very differently, and the way they use them can vary from text to text.[15]

The conventions in force at a given period govern the ranges of linguistic register open to a poet. Whether poetry is to be sung, spoken, or read silently is of consequence to its metrics and phonetic effects. Because most French poetry since the Renaissance is in the written medium, syntax and expressions associated with the spoken mode tend to be avoided in verse. The dimension of field is also important. First, at a given period, certain kinds of speech acts (e.g., exhorting, narrating, addressing one's beloved) may be typical or unusual. Second, certain subjects may be common or banned. We may also expect predictability in the dimension of tenor: formal style is often an important part of "poetic diction," and different levels of formality are often associated with particular subgenres. Of course, a particular text may or may not meet the reader's register-expectations (Gregory and Carroll, 72-73). In fact, when poets like those I will be studying play against these expectations, that resistance is itself highly relevant stylistically.[16]

Using the categories of linguistic register can help us both to characterize the poetic discourse belonging to a particular tradition and to distinguish more clearly poetic usage that deviates from its genre-conventions. It is especially useful in studying the language of nineteenth-century French poetry: the poets I am studying resisted the way the theorists and practitioners of French neoclassical poetry had divided up their linguistic world. But before going on to outline the basic characteristics of the neoclassical poetic code, I should mention certain problems that arise in classifying terms: first, with respect to the levels of the signifier and the signified; second, regarding the ways French language levels can be distinguished; and finally, taking into account the ways contemporary dictionaries indicate usage.

In applying the concept of register to poetic texts it is important to distinguish as carefully as possible between the subjects represented and the language levels used in their representation. Kerbrat emphasizes that semantic analysis should disassociate "Les connotations qui ont pour support signifiant l'objet lui-même, indépendamment de toute verbalisation" and "celles qui n'apparaissent que dans le traitement linguistique de l'objet" (73). The difference between *bagnole* and *voiture*, for instance, is a purely linguistic one. The French language offers many examples of language choice varying by formality. Thus, when Baudelaire refers to a prostitute, for instance, he has a wide range of tenors to draw on. The periphrase "célèbre évaporée / Que Tivoli jadis ombragea dans sa fleur" or the synechdoche "Laïs" ("Les Petites Vieilles") or the euphemism "femme galante" ("Le Vin du solitaire") belong to the high style. *Catin*, as in "Au lecteur" and "Crépuscule du soir" belongs to "un langage un peu libre" according to Littré. But in "Le Jeu," Baudelaire uses not only the euphemistic *courtisane* but also the vulgar *putain* to refer to the prostitutes in a casino. Of course, each of these terms carries stylistic connotations; and the language used reflects a certain attitude to what is represented. As Kerbrat notes: "le choix d'un terme de niveau 'élevé' ou 'bas' est un indice indirect du caractère prestigieux ou méprisable que le locuteur prête au dénoté" (102; see also 103). The signifier carries a further message about the signified; in fact, it has another signified.

The situation is complicated in poetry by the fact that certain subject matters are themselves considered "poetic" or "unpoetic." Many of the words introduced into nineteenth-century poetry refer to aspects of everyday, contemporary life, words like *caoutchouc* or *photographe*: there are no other, more "poetic" words that could be substituted for them. Technological expansion in the nineteenth century brought many such terms into the French language. These kinds of expressions had been avoided not because of their level of formality but because of their semantic field; in Kerbrat's terms, not because of their stylistic connotation but because of their denotation. Neoclassical poetry would have used periphrasis to denote such referents. Thus, the nineteenth-century poets championing the literal term rather than periphrasis sought to open poetic discourse to the field of everyday contemporary life as well as to the familiar tenor and the spoken mode. Furthermore, some concepts are only expressed at one level of style. For instance, as Marouzeau notes, *livresque* is unlikely to appear other than in refined usage (*Précis*, 108). So, although technical or scientific terminology, slang, childish expressions, etc., may be classifiable as such by dictionaries, it is often difficult to determine whether it is as signifier or as signified that they are to be analyzed.

A further distinction must be kept in mind, the one between the language of narration and that of reported speech. Traditionally, informality of diction was more acceptable in quotations than in the poet's voice: the distance between the narrator and the speaker assured the former's innocence with regard to what he or she was reporting. A parallel can be seen in the history of the novel: Hugo was proud of having introduced slang into *Claude Gueux* and *Les Misérables*; Sue's *Les Mystères de Paris* was an immense success; but when Zola had his narrator use slang and familiar diction in *L'Assommoir* in 1876, it created a scandal.[17] Needless to say, the code for lyric poetry was even stricter, and marked terms (colloquial, scientific, childish, etc.) stand out in the context of verse.

The question of whether an expression is to be analyzed in terms of its signifier or its signified arises in particular in relation to "vulgar" language. For Matoré, such language refers to extralinguistic reality; it is "grossier" whether the signifier is "populaire" or not (86). Most other linguists, however, use it as an equivalent of "langue populaire" a language level associated with the familiar tenor and the spoken mode (Kerbrat, 25; Marouzeau, "Langue vulgaire," 242; Guiraud, *L'Argot*, 78). Although the divergence between standard and popular language is particularly strong in French (Guiraud, *Le Français populaire*, 10), there are many different ways lexicographers classify usage that differs from the "langue cultivée" or "langue bourgeoise," including *familier, populaire, vulgaire, style trivial*, and *grossier*.[18] Although dictionaries may disagree on the classification or even on the inclusion of a word, it seems clear that there is a scale of acceptability lying between the ranges covered by slang dictionaries on the one hand and lexicons of "poetic" words on the other. We can make the "mode" distinction between speech and writing, covering such pairs as *ça/cela* and many syntactical differences. At the beginning of the nineteenth century familiar or vulgar expressions belong to the spoken language alone; both Littré and Robert oppose the words relating to colloquial usage to "langue littéraire." Therefore, mode, at this period, is largely subsumed under the heading of formality of tenor.

I will be treating three main categories of colloquial usage: familiar language, popular language, and *argot*. The first is usually taken to be the conversational form of the standard language. The classification Popular French, the language of the working classes, is based on sociocultural criteria as well as properly linguistic ones (characteristics relating to the spoken mode and variations from standard grammar). The distinction between popular language and *argot* has a more rigid social definition: the latter was, until the nineteenth century, the secret language used by criminals. Though it was always mixed with popular speech, it was a separate language, not to be confused with the later senses of *argot* as slang in general or technical or professional jargons. Popularized by the 1828 memoires of Vidocq (the criminal turned chief of the investigative police) and Eugène Sue's immensely successful novel, *Les*

Mystères de Paris (1842-46), terms of *argot* began to turn up at all levels of discourse, if only for comic or picturesque effect.[19]

The lines between familiar language and popular language on the one hand and between popular language and *argot* on the other are not clear ones: as Bruneau points out, they vary from one person to another and from one generation to another (*Histoire*, 12:386). These categories appear to be abstractions linguists apply to earlier periods than their own.[20] As Valdman has shown, Standard French and Popular French are fictions, two poles of a continuum that cannot be delimited with precision. Furthermore, all these levels of language are interdependent: they can often be defined only by what they are not. Like all linguistic entities, their existence depends on their diacritical distinction from the other components of the system.

In studying the intrusion of familiar and popular discourse into the poetry of the nineteenth century, it is useful to establish whether an expression was felt to be colloquial at the time.[21] Fortunately, this was the age of the great lexicographers, expecially Littré (whose dictionary was published between 1863 and 1872) and Larousse (*Le Grand Dictionnaire universel* dates from 1866-76). Littré was particularly concerned with recording usage. He gave a large number of quotations from literary sources as illustrations, to the point that he was criticized for writing a dictionary of the French *written* language.[22] But he recognized that these sources do not make up the whole of the French language and that there are problems in determining levels of language: "Cette constatation est oeuvre délicate et difficile. Pour peu qu'à ce point de vue on considère les formes et les habitudes présentes, on aperçoit promptement bien des locutions qui se disent et ne s'écrivent pas; bien des locutions qui s'écrivent, mais qui sont ou dépourvues d'autorité ou fautives" ("Préface," iii). Fortunately, in studying poetry it is written usage that is important, and the precise classification of an expression matters less than the fact of its exclusion from the *langue soutenue* and the effects it can elicit in its context. Also, Littré did not only report on usage; his dictionary created norms for uses: it was the reference work consulted by writers of the time to find out what was or was not acceptable (Chaurand, 145).[23]

Of course, phrases that are popular by virtue of their syntax are not to be found in dictionaries in any case. The individual words in Verlaine's lines, for instance:

> Dis, qu'as-tu fait, toi que voilà,
> De ta jeunesse?

are all perfectly acceptable. It will be important to take note of such constructions. But the use of a popular or slang word in the context of a poem can have great power. Literary scandals caused by the introduction of familiar language tended to center on individual words: *mouchoir* in Vigny's translation of *Othello*; *gamin* in Hugo's *Claude Gueux*, or *torchons radieux* in his "Choses écrites à Créteil." Using familiar diction outside of its normal context can be startling in everyday situations, too; Bally cites the discomfiture of the French people present when the president of a central European literary group complimented Giraudoux on his *bouquins* (239). Because of the particularly restricted nature of traditional poetic language in the nineteenth century, poets were able to make effective use of the stylistic shocks created when rules of formality were broken. To gauge the innovations in their work, we should look at the poetic code that provided its background.

II. *Poetic Diction*

In his 1796 "Cours de littérature," La Harpe discusses how French neoclassical poetry followed Aristotle's prescription to use "alien" terms by means very different from those the Greeks used:

> Chez eux [les Grecs] les détails de la vie commune et de la conversation familière n'étaient point exclus de la langue poétique; presque aucun mot n'était par lui-même bas et trivial. . . . Un mot n'était pas réputé populaire pour exprimer un usage journalier, et le terme le plus commun pouvait entrer dans le vers le plus pompeux et dans la figure la plus hardie. Parmi nous, au contraire, le poëte ne jouit pas d'un tiers de l'idiome national: le reste lui est interdit comme indigne de lui. Il n'y a guère pour lui qu'un certain nombre de mots convenus. (1:297)

Because of these limitations, the work of most poets of his time is monotonous: "c'est qu'il est bien difficile de soutenir un langage de convention dont il n'existe aucun modèle dans la société" (1:298). This *langage de convention* was constructed through a series of restrictions. Its corollary was a set of devices necessary to avoid the two-thirds of the French language La Harpe says it eliminated.

How much of the language was to be excluded varied by genre. Fontanier, for whom poetic language is distinguished by figures and a distinctive vocabulary (as it was for Aristotle), wrote in the 1820s that "Certains genres de poésie s'éloignent beaucoup moins que certains autres du langage commun, soit par le ton et le caractère de leur style, soit par la nature de leur objet" (181). Although there were different systems of genres and different names for the styles corresponding to them, they tended to be grouped into three categories by style: high (ode, epic); middle (tragedy); and low (comedy, satire, *epître*).[24]

The major distinction, however, was between high and low language: through the progressive exclusion of terms and situations reputed to be "bas," their opposite, "noble" language, was constituted. Barthes sees this language as a true *écriture*, "c'est-à-dire une valeur de langage, donnée immédiatement comme universelle" (42). The prestige of the great writers of the seventeenth century served as its foundation. Voltaire, who with most of his contemporaries believed that the French language had now reached its point of perfection, shows the importance of the classical writers in fixing the language in his *Dictionnaire philosophique*: "Il me semble que lorsqu'on a eu dans un siècle un nombre suffisant de bons écrivains devenus classiques, il n'est guère plus permis d'employer d'autres expressions que les leurs" ("Langue française," 19:189). The importance of the classic authors was maintained into the nineteenth century: the dividing point between historical and current usage in Littré's dictionary entries was the seventeenth century.

Not surprisingly, as this poetic language became codified during the course of the eighteenth century, the rules became stricter, until usage found in Corneille or even Racine was no longer possible. These rules covered all the dimensions of register and included both signifiers and signifieds. This poetry's "foreign" words did not include dialectical terms, but rather a category of terms that could really be called "poetic" in the sense that they were to be found only in literature. Such was the prestige and durability of this code that we still think of words like *zéphyr, coursier,* and so on as poetic terms. That these strictures were maintained can be seen from the existence at the beginning of the nineteenth century of several dictionaries of poetic language, explaining which terms to use in which genres. Words excluded from such lexicons, then, and some that were banished to the fable, verse tale, and so on, could not be "poetic," could not constitute a poem. In addition, many "low" words that had no equivalents in the high style, their fields considered intrinsically unacceptable, were banned from poetry: details of everyday life, especially contemporary life, the entire spectrum of the life of the lower classes, and technical fields like medicine or botany. Even in reported speech, characteristics associated with the spoken mode were avoided: conversations could be recorded only in the high style. Even the "genres familiers" (light poetry, satire, and so on) were expected to restrict themselves to the language of polite conversation.[25] In his *Art poétique,* Boileau criticizes the writers of burlesques (a short-lived parodic genre) for speaking *le langage des halles,* counselling: "Quoi que vous écriviez, évitez la bassesse:/ Le style le moins noble a pourtant sa noblesse" (lines 78-79). As for the dimension of tenor, all informality was forbidden. There were to be no intrusions of familiar speech, let alone popular language or slang.

The problem facing neoclassical poets was, of course, how to write anything interesting when so many subjects and so much of the language was forbidden to them. Their solutions were the devices we now associate with neoclassical style. Because these devices were increasingly standardized they have lent themselves easily to parody and ridicule.[26] They are of three major types: synonyms, rhetorical figures, and epithets. A poet wanting to refer to, say, chocolate could do so: he could consult Carpentier's *Gradus français, ou dictionnaire de la langue poétique* and find a term equivalent to chocolate in the high style: *cacao.* Such terms are the so-called *synonymes de style,* terms with equivalents in more casual genres. They were often words no longer in common use. Thus, Carpentier recom-

mends *labeur* for *travail*, *époux* for *mari*, and *s'acheminer* for
marcher. Another way to add elegance by simply substituting
another equivalent was to use the name from classical mythol-
ogy associated with the referent: thus, a bereaved mother was
Niobé, the moon, *Diane*.

Tropes offered many other possibilities, especially personification, euphemism, synecdoche, and periphrasis. The importance of such tropes can be seen in Delille's definition of
poetry as "une métonymie continuelle" (quoted in Bruneau,
12:23). Synecdoche was very common, usually involving the
general term for the particular and the material for the name
of the thing. Thus, *la chaudière* became *le bronze*, *peigne* became *l'ivoire* or *l'écaille*, and so on. The major trope was, of
course, periphrasis, and standard phrases were adopted. Thus,
Carpentier gives "Le temple d'Hermès" or "le sanctuaire
d'Hermès" as equivalents for the word *laboratoire*, and a gun is
"un cylindre homicide." Often, periphrases combined several
figures: rather than saying that a woman was pregnant, the
poet, according to Carpentier, should write: "Elle porte en son
sein [metonymy] le fruit [metaphor] de leur union [euphe-
mism]."

Finally, it was possible to use a forbidden term when it was
surrounded with enough prepositional phrases or adjectives
to raise its style sufficiently. The standard example was Racine's use of *chiens* ennobled by its epithet, *dévorants*. It was
this much-discussed phrase that gave rise to Hugo's boasting
that he had removed the common noun's *collier d'épithètes*.
These epithets became standardized, too, and were listed with
appropriate words in the poetic dictionaries.

Neoclassical diction did not disappear with romanticism.
Many of the romantics carried on the standard diction (Lamartine and Vigny notably), whereas the Symbolists made it
a part of their mixed language. Traces of it still appear in
twentieth-century poetry.[27] There were, of course, reactions
against this code. At the end of the eighteenth century Delille
and his school introduced a great number of words relating to
country life and agriculture into what was considered a new
genre, "descriptive poetry."[28] In the early nineteenth century,
romantic theorists and practitioners sponsored the incorporation of exotic and picturesque words into verse and prose.

Thus, there was a redefinition of "foreign" words, this time including literally foreign words. Various attempts were made to introduce the tenor and the field of everyday life into verse, notably Sainte-Beuve's "Joseph Delorme" poems and Desbordes-Valmore's intimist verse.[29] Among others, Coppée and du Camp continued this tendency; and the middle years of the century saw a great increase in such experimentation, until, according to Cressot, thousands of words had entered literary language (3).

The major poets of the nineteenth century, including Hugo, Baudelaire, and Verlaine, were engaged in creating a new poetic language in opposition to the old. They recognized that the language of the canon, because of the very fact that is was an established language, was now "commonplace." The passage from La Harpe quoted above links restricted diction to "images . . . hardies," an association already indicated by Aristotle. But the figures of neoclassical poetry had themselves become canonical. The limitations of the poetic language had led to extensive use of periphrasis and synecdoche, that is, to a proliferation of figures to avoid the *mot propre*, which was seen as the ordinary. By the nineteenth century, it was the use of the *mot propre* or even *malpropre* that was "hardi." Its concomitant was again striking figure, used to set off a language no longer fully distinct from that of the informal role or the spoken mode. In the 1880s the Decadents made a mixture of familiar and exotic diction part of their program, and the consequent "strangeness" noted by critics was yet another way of setting apart poetic language from "les mots de la tribu." A pattern emerges here, of the estranged becoming familiar and the commonplace becoming strange, opening up the simple opposition proposed by Aristotle. With these developments, too, the relationship between diction and figure becomes an issue.

III. Word and Figure

"Je nommai le cochon par son nom" is Hugo's claim in "Réponse à un acte d'accusation." There are a good many assumptions lying behind this statement, among them that there is one true word for a thing and that referential language is pref-

erable to figurative language. Genette sees the basic characteristic of figurative discourse as the possibility of a simpler way
of saying what the figure expresses in a roundabout way (*Figures*, 205-21). Hugo's statement represents a rejection of such
indirection and of rhetoric as such. At the same time, it is a
repudiation of neoclassical diction: *cochon* is a provocative
word against the background of the contemporary literary
code. The introduction of familiar language into poetry has
often been linked with a rejection of rhetoric. Lines like Hugo's "Plante là toute rhétorique" ("Genio libri") and Verlaine's
"Prends l'éloquence et tords-lui son cou" ("Art poétique")
enunciate and illustrate such a view. Yet it has been observed
that, in trying to resist rhetoric, nineteenth-century literature
paradoxically reaffirms it.[30] I will examine Hugo's claims and
the value he accords to literal language in the chapter on his
work, but the refusal of rhetoric associated with nineteenth-
century poetry bears closer examination here. First, the search
for simplicity of expression represents a continuity, not a
break, with classical theory; second, familiar language does
not stand in simple opposition to rhetoric; and finally, language levels themselves have a figurative dimension.

An important strain of seventeenth-century theory stressed
the importance of clarity and simplicity over ornament, following the classical ideals of order and purity enunciated by
Malherbe and codified by Boileau. Bouhours, for example,
wrote: "la langue française hait encore les ornements excessifs;
elle voudrait que ses paroles fussent toutes nues, pour s'exprimer plus simplement" (quoted in François, 1:332). An important purpose of periphrasis was to avoid technical language, to use terms that everyone could understand. Of course,
there were conflicting tendencies like the ideal proposed by
Du Bos: poetry as "une suite continuelle d'images" (quoted in
Barat, 15). As periphrases became more complicated they
turned into riddles, like Chénier's periphrase for paper: "un
albâtre docile / Au fond des eaux formé des dépouilles du lin"
(quoted in François, 2:96). Nonetheless, as Foucault says:

> Toute la littérature classique se loge dans le mouvement
> qui va de la figure du nom au nom lui-même, passant de la
> tâche de nommer encore la même chose par de nouvelles
> figures (c'est la préciosité) à celle de nommer par des mots

> enfin justes . . . Le romantisme croira avoir rompu avec
> l'âge précédent parce qu'il aura appris à nommer les
> choses par leur nom. A dire vrai tout le classicisme y ten-
> dait: Hugo accomplit la promesse de Voiture" (134).

The conflict between simplicity and ornament, the latter
tending toward obscurity, finds echoes in the nineteenth century. When Brunetière wishes to defend the literary language
of his time from "la déformation de la langue par l'argot" he
maintains two incompatible positions: the classical ideal of
"une langue qui soit immédiatement entendue de tout le
monde," and the vision of a literature that begins only when
"les choses de la pensée cessent d'être en quelque sorte accessi-
bles à tout le monde" (944, 943). Like neoclassical poetry, the
poetry of the nineteenth century accommodates both the vision of a language for "tout le monde" and the special, her-
metic languages of a Nerval or a Mallarmé. Mallarmé's prizing
of suggestion rather than naming itself carries on one aspect of
neoclassical theory, echoing Rivarol's injunction: "la poésie
doit toujours peindre et ne jamais nommer" (quoted in Barat,
19).

In neoclassical poetry tropes served to ennoble language not
only because of their ornamental value, but also because words
unacceptable in their literal senses were often considered appropriate to poetry in their figurative meanings. For example,
Carpentier finds *acier* familiar in the literal sense but noble in
the figurative (standing for weapons or instruments made of
steel or iron): "ce mot paraît alors appartenir à la langue poétique."[31] Of *indigent* he writes: "En prose il ne se dit que des
personnes, mais en vers il est beau en parlant des choses." This
capacity of "noble" language was what led Gautier to describe
the neoclassical attitude as an "horreur du mot propre"
(quoted in Bruneau, *Histoire*, 12:49). But it would be wrong to
associate figurative with poetic and literal with familiar language. On the one hand, by the beginning of the nineteenth
century standard *synonymes de style* and periphrases had lost
a good deal of their figurative power: as dictionaries like Carpentier attest, they came to be the only terms to use. In this
way they came closer to literal expression. On the other hand,
familiar and popular language is by no means lacking in fig-

ures.[32] In fact, just as some terms become elevated when used in their figurative sense, so many others become familiar: *ordure* or *gueule* or *espèce de*, for example. "Fig. et fam." or "Fig. et pop." are common designations in Littré.

When poets came to use many such terms, they had varied effects. An example might be the expression *tas de*. In Baudelaire's "Le Cygne": "Je ne vois qu'en esprit . . . Ces tas de chapiteaux ébauchés et de fûts," *tas de* is used in its literal sense, as a pile of physical objects. But when Hugo called the officials of the Second Empire "ce tas de laquais" and "ce tas de bourreaux" in "La Force des choses" (*Châtiments*), *tas de* is figurative. Its familiar status contributes to the strength of the insult. In "Voix de l'orgueil" (*Sagesse*), Verlaine uses the expression in the following lines:

Voix d'Autrui; des lointains dans des brouillards.
   Des noces
Vont et viennent. Des tas d'embarras. Des négoces,
Et tout le cirque des civilisations
Au son trotte-menu du violon des noces.

Here, in conjunction with the enjambments, the broken-up sentences, and the old-fashioned, lightly comic term *trotte-menu*, *tas de* helps to establish a casual tone. The rhythm is that of the spoken mode, countering the regularity of the alexandrine line. Incongruous semantic fields are brought together: wedding parties and negotiations, circuses and civilizations. The added resonance of the slang sense of *cirque* enhances the effect of this striking contrast. The extreme informality and familiar tenor of *Des tas de*, contrasting with the term *civilisation*, destabilize the stanza's level of formality. Conflicts in register are characteristic of Verlaine's style, an important aspect of his "imprécision." In Rimbaud's "L'Orgie parisienne," *tas de* functions in ways related to Hugo's and Verlaine's use of the term. It appears in a line describing the Parisians returning after the fall of the Commune: "Tas de chiennes en rut mangeant des cataplasmes." The familiar expression contrasts with the medical term *cataplasme*. Their incongruity underlines the incoherence of the revolting image expressed in this line and the violence of the insult it carries. We can conclude from these examples not only that familiar expressions are often figurative, but also that their familiar status gives them stylistic connotations, connotations that can be put to use in very different ways. We can also see from lines like these how far we have moved from neoclassical decorum in poetic diction.

The fact that levels of formality have stylistic connotations means that their use can produce figures rather than eliminating them. If, as Genette claims in *Figures*, figure exists in the gap between what is said and what might have been said, then diction, too, has figurative possibilities: if another signifier is possible—*je m'ennuie* for *je m'emmerde, femme de mauvaise vie* for *putain*—there comes into existence another kind of figure, a figure of register. The gap between the two terms can be read as parody or humor or satire or opposition to poetic tradition or in many other ways. In the neoclassical tradition, just as *voile* for ship carries the message "I am poetry," so does *coursier* for horse. When poets begin to use *cheval* or *bidet* or *canasson* instead, their message is different, but not less important.

Studying language varieties makes us aware of the many ways speakers of a language can express themselves. The pig does not have just one name: even simple reference can involve a good many terms, among them the more elevated *porc*. On the other hand, words have many meanings and many uses: *cochon* used in addressing a person is both familiar and figurative, and it is usually used for insulting rather than referring. As poets introduced familiar language, slang, technical words, and so on into their work, they opened new possibilities for stylistic effects and for figurative expression, possibilities that have become an important part of modern poetry.

The poetic program Hugo enunciated in his line "Je mis un bonnet rouge au vieux dictionnaire" was developed in very different modes by Hugo himself, Banville, and Baudelaire, and it culminated in the striking lexical inventiveness of the work of Rimbaud, Verlaine, and their successors. Both Corbière and Laforgue also use striking diction, but this aspect of their work has been studied extensively, and I will not treat them in detail.[33] Nor will I deal with other minor poets working in the same direction or the Decadents who followed. This development was at its height between 1850 and 1880, by when the new poetic vocabulary had for the most part been established.[34]

In studying these poets, I will examine only their verse. Prose poetry responds to very different stylistic exigencies, genre conventions, and reader expectations. In fact, the prose poem offered freedom from genre constraints lessening conflicts with the established codes.[35] Verse, on the other hand, had to contend with the conventions of diction that its form led readers to expect. It was the interaction with these conventions that made possible many of the new effects this poetry created.

As the example of *tas de* shows, familiar diction has a different role to play in the work of each of these poets. Those roles can tell us something about the way each uses language in his poetic universe. They also raise different theoretical questions, about the relationship between literal and figurative discourse, about the concepts of "lofty" and "low" subjects and styles, and about the ways familiar diction can be naturalized, either by genre considerations or by a correspondence between the signifier and the signified. Such problems are not only interesting from a theoretical point of view: they inform the poems themselves. It is through their work that these poets established a new model both for poetic language and for the language we use to discuss it.

TWO

Victor Hugo: Responding to "Réponse"

In "A André Chénier," Hugo wrote:

> Oui, mon vers croit pouvoir, sans se mésallier,
> Prendre à la prose un peu de son air familier.
>
> *Les Contemplations*, 1, v

His poetry and drama have often been considered in the light of this and similar statements. The connotations of *mésallier* show that we have to do with a discussion of what is noble (and thus what has a place in verse) and what is considered "low." It is Hugo who is usually given the major credit for enlarging French poetic vocabulary, and it is certainly his texts that are most often cited in the context of discussing the perceived "revolution" in poetic diction in nineteenth-century France. Indeed, it is his work that has codified the very language we use to talk about this change. The only French text holding a place similar to that of Wordsworth's "Preface to the *Lyrical Ballads*" in English literature is Hugo's "Réponse à un acte d'accusation," from *Les Contemplations*: it is the text regularly cited in discussions of the changes in poetic diction brought about by romanticism. In his history of the movement, Gautier writes of the "secret du style romantique" and those who criticized its "mâles poètes et le vigoureux prosateur (Hugo)": "C'est cette veine de langage qui leur déplaît dans les poètes modernes et chez Hugo en particulier" (*Histoire*, 122). In studying this "veine de langage," I would like first to show how Hugo set the terms in which the problem of diction was to be discussed throughout the nineteenth century and beyond; then, to examine in more detail the poetic manifesto that set out to oppose the neoclassical manner, "La Réponse" itself; and finally, to explore in some of Hugo's other work two of the questions this poem raises: the use of the literal term rather than periphrasis and the mixing of styles in lyric verse.

I. The Fortune of a Literary Manifesto

Hugo was responding to no particular accusation in his "Réponse": many critics of the time were hostile to his "familiar" style. One went so far as to call it "le râle de l'agonie universelle"; and though others opposed this view, then and more recently, it is Hugo who is usually blamed or credited by critics with the perceived shift in poetic diction.[1] It should be remembered that Hugo himself went through several stages with regard to poetic diction, both in theory and in practice. In his 1824 preface to what would become *Odes et ballades*, he claimed for Boileau and Racine the merit of having "fixed" (immobilized) the French language; and in the 1826 preface, he maintained, "Un écrivain qui a quelque souci de la postérité cherchera sans cesse à purifier sa diction . . . Des fautes de langage ne rendront jamais une pensée, et le style est comme le cristal, sa pureté fait son éclat" (Pléiade, 1:275n; 282). It is significant that in the former of these prefaces, he set up the analogy between poetics and politics that will be at the foundation of the "Réponse" in order to talk about the "battle" between the romantics and the Classics; but here Hugo the royalist rejects any association of romanticism with revolution: the former may be the result of the latter, he asserts, but it is not its expression.

By the 1827 "Préface de *Cromwell*," however, Hugo felt that languages were not fixed, but in constant flux; and in the 1834 *Littérature et philosophie mêlées*, he stated that each age has its own language and linked linguistic change to historical and social developments. The "langue propre" of the nineteenth century was a "langue poétique" (*O.C.*, 5:33). In the 1856 *Contemplations*, the "Réponse," its "Suite," and "Quelques mots à un autre" make the assertion that this language has been found, and found by Hugo himself. Although in "Réponse" he claims that others have better furthered the cause, he also writes "Alors, brigand, je vins," responding to Boileau's famous line "Enfin Malherbe vint" in *L'Art poétique*.

The elevated language of poetry had been known at least since Ronsard as "la langue noble," opposed to "low" language; and it was Delille who first called the latter *roturier* ("low-class"), thus making explicit the resemblance of this classification to the social order. This link between politics and style was noted in 1806 by Bonald as well, who saw in it a "nouvelle preuve de la distinction des deux sociétés; distinction aussi fondamentale en littérature qu'en politique" (1005). It is this concept that is thematized in "Réponse," and it is the pronouncements of this poem that have been taken by critics as affirming and as proving that Hugo altered the diction of poetry in France.

Not only do critics almost always refer to this work when discussing either French poetic practice in the nineteenth century or many other works of Hugo, but, from the first, critics have used or transposed expressions from the poem to describe the change in diction they have perceived. Already in 1872, Banville writes that nine-tenths of French words "exiled" from poetry were "délivrés" by Hugo (*Petit Traité*, 59). He quotes the famous lines beginning "Je fis souffler un vent révolutionnaire," but the poem was echoed already in the idea of imprisonment (as in "le bagne lexique") and subsequent liberation. In an 1876 article, Naquet first describes Hugo's achievement in what is more or less a paraphrase of the poem, goes on to quote the well-known section beginning "Quand je sortis du collège," and concludes: "Voilà quelle fut cette Révolution que Victor Hugo a accomplie. . . . Ou . . . Victor Hugo est dans le vrai contre Racine, c'est la langue moderne qu'il faut adopter, ou bien, il nous faut continuer la langue des auteurs classiques. . . . (Ou) Racine et Louis XIV, ou Victor Hugo et la Révolution. Nous sommes pour Victor Hugo et la Révolution" (180). It is remarkable to see what extent Hugo's poem had codified the ways it was possible to talk about the question.

Later critics have followed suit. Bruneau in the classic *Histoire de la langue française* also accepts Hugo's characterization of his influence as a "revolution" and merely transposes the words of the text: "Mais Victor Hugo allait bientôt libérer la légion sépulcrale des vieux mots damnés" (12:54). More recent students of the French language, too, have repeated these received ideas, these received phrases.[2]

Hugo himself, discussing poetic language in *William Shakespeare* (1864) reverts to the language of his earlier poem: "En France . . . la littérature tendait à faire caste. Etre poète, cela revenait un peu à être mandarin. Tous les mots n'avaient pas droit à la langue. . . . Sortons, il en est temps, de cet ordre d'idées; la démocratie l'exige. . . . Sortons du collège, du conclave, du compartiment du petit goût, du petit art, de la petite chapelle" (*O.C.*, 12:276). The echos of the poem in this quotation are obvious; even the words "sortons du collège" recall the opening of the often-quoted section, "Quand je sortis du collège, du thème."

It should be noted that some critics have taken Hugo at his word regarding the dating of the poem as well as its import. It is now generally considered to have been written in 1854; and its predating to 1834 has been explained in various ways: as a means to antedate Hugo's adhesion to liberal views (in this regard see "Ecrit en 1846"); as a setting of the text in the context of the romantic battles of the 1830s; or as a revisionist reaction to Janin's history of French drama, which appeared in 1854. It was also in the 1830s that Hugo's plays had evoked the most vehement criticism of his irregular division of the alexandrine line and his "low" diction. But in any case, the historian of literature may have found it a neater picture of the century to have the battle over diction won in the 1830s by the "Romantics"; the text is not so useful, not such an event, published just a year before the *Odes funambulesques* of Banville and *Les Fleurs du mal*, both of which, as we shall see, make use of contrasts and dissonances in diction. Through this poem then, Hugo has indeed accomplished a revolution, at least in the way we talk about poetic diction.

II. "Réponse"

It should be asked to what extent Hugo carries out, in this poem itself, the "revolutionary" precepts he enunciates. We would expect a poem of the *ars poetica* genre to be to some extent self-referential. Although it is clear that it self-consciously violates certain of the precepts of the neoclassical code for the composition of poetry, it is interesting to see what becomes of these innovations in the texture of the poem. I will look first at the prosodic rules Hugo infringes, then at his most important —or at least most famous—claim, that of renewing poetic vocabulary, and finally at the relationship he seeks to establish between this kind of diction and figurative discourse.

Hugo lays claim to several innovations: the freeing of the alexandrine from its rules, the liberation of rhymes, and most importantly, a rejection of the neoclassical diction, rhetoric, and division into genres. With respect to the rhythm of this and other Hugo texts, it has frequently been noted that many of the innovations for which he spoke out had been accomplished already by Delille and his school at the end of the eighteenth century. We do see in this text a certain amount of suppression of the *césure*, as in lines 7-8:

> Toute cette clarté s'est éteinte, et je suis
> Le responsable, et j'ai vidé l'urne des nuits.

The enjambement between these verses and the trimeter of the second line are striking examples of the points he wishes to make. But in general the verses are quite regular, even in the section where he discusses the transformation of the alexandrine:

> Le vers, qui sur son front
> Jadis portait toujours douze plumes en rond,
> Et sans cesse sautait sur la double raquette
> Qu'on nomme prosodie et qu'on nomme étiquette,
> Rompt désormais la règle et trompe le ciseau,
> Et s'échappe, volant qui se change en oiseau,
> De la cage césure, et fuit vers la ravine,
> Et vole dans les cieux, alouette divine.

All of these lines may be divided into hemistichs; most have the classic four accents, and two (the third and sixth) are perfectly symmetrical. Enjambements and *rejets* are to be found elsewhere in the text, and it is curious that Hugo rejected the self-referentiality one might expect from such a passage, that here, at least, he should not escape from "la cage césure."

As for demolishing "la bastille des rimes," it is difficult to determine just what is meant by such a declaration. The rhymes in this poem are extremely rich; they are correct for the eye as well as for the ear; and they follow the rule of alternation between masculine and feminine rhymes. On the other hand, as Banville noted, the introduction into poetry of various kinds of words formerly considered inappropriate—and words like *madrépores* or *mob* would be among them—created the possibility of much richer and more varied rhymes. Banville also considered that this expansion of vocabulary relieved the necessity for distortions in syntax, inversions in particular, and Hugo claims to bring peace to syntax. Inversions, however, are frequent in this poem: "De la chute de tout je suis la pioche inepte," for example. Nonetheless, a more casual tone has indeed entered serious poetry in lines like:

> En somme,
> J'en conviens, oui, je suis cet abominable homme;

a tone brought about by the broken line, natural syntax, the enjambement, and conversational lexical elements (*en somme*, *oui*).

Before going on to examine the ways Hugo uses such elements, we should note that it is not clear where in the poem the subject is lyric poetry and where it treats the language of the theater. Of course, Hugo maintains that he has reformed both, but he alludes primarily to theatrical diction. It is especially his dramas that had aroused such vigorous denunciations at the time the poem is set; it is in *Hernani* that a king is heard to ask the time; and it is in his plays that he most strikingly breaks up the alexandrine verse. Further references to the theater in this poem include allusions to *Phèdre* and *Athalie* and to the Paris conservatory of music and drama. The word *conservatoire* is important for its incorporation of the concept of conservatism as well. And although he claims here to have released the ode from its conventions, his own *Odes et ballades*

of the 1820s, as the preface quoted above indicates, were rela-
tively conventional.

Although it is clear from this text that Hugo has introduced
many words from fields formerly excluded (that is, words that
evoked milieux or thoughts considered unseemly, like *cadavre
fumant*, *cochon*, or *ânerie*), and that he uses a more natural
syntax, it is also evident that he does not descend below the
bounds of the middle style or at least of the lowest acceptable
genre in point of style, the satire. The line "j'y fis entrer le
chiffre" is justified in this poem where the words "quatre-vingt-
treize" appear, but the impact of using this date is mitigated by
its historical prestige. On the level of the signifier, despite the
polemical tone and claims, there are almost no words that
would be classified as familiar, let alone vulgar, according to
the dictionaries of the time. So the words that "Vaugelas . . .
/ Dans le bagne Lexique avait marqués d'une F" (for both *for-
çat* and *familier*) are still in jail. The only exceptions are the
expressions *tas de*, *bastringue*, and the childish terms *papa* and
toutou. Pejorative words and expressions of insult abound:
ânerie, *croquant*, *mâchoire*, etc., but these had all been used
by such writers as Saint-Simon, La Fontaine, or even Malherbe. There would certainly be a good number of slang or
even familiar terms equivalent to *grimaud* or *catin* or *maraud*
(or even *nez* and *mâchoire*); and so, a certain amount of censor-
ship has been imposed. The language of the *gueux*, the poor, is
not in fact included. Hugo prided himself on his introduction
of popular language and slang into his novels, especially *Le
Dernier Jour d'un condamné* and *Les Misérables*, where there
is a section on *argot* that amounts to an essay on the subject. In
this novel there is also an allusion to his innovation in an earlier work: "Ce mot, *gamin*, fut imprimé pour la première fois
et arriva de la langue populaire dans la langue littéraire en
1834. C'est dans un opuscule intitulé *Claude Gueux* que ce mot
fit son apparition. Le scandale fut vif. Le mot a passé" (*Les
Misérables*, pt. 3, bk. 1, chap. 7). That he refrains from including such language in his poetry in general and in such a polemical work as "Réponse" in particular, shows that he is still to a
certain degree bound to the conventional distinctions between genres.

Moreover, when in this text Hugo turns from his claims of

liberation to a description of the new poetry, his diction becomes markedly more elevated. After line 191 precise numbers become *au front triple* or *millions d'ailes.* Conventionally "poetic" words (*l'azur, lyre, zénith et nadir*) reappear at the moment when "la muse reparaît." "Low" expressions, then, are excluded from the subject of poetry, which is still called "sacrée." The poetic revolution described in this text, then, is announced and furthered, but not completed.

In "Réponse" Hugo thematizes the ways in which poetic diction had been considered and makes them part of the poem's figural structure. Thus Delille's division of language into noble and "roturier" becomes the evocation of a revolt compared in all points to the French Revolution: it has a taking of the Bastille, proclamations, executions, a terror, even reminiscences of the "Marseillaise" (throughout the text, but especially in the line " 'Aux armes, prose et vers! Formez vos bataillons!' "). This extended metaphor represents more than a stylistic device: Hugo reveals a belief in a metaphoric relationship between history and art. As he says in "Réponse": "L'idiome, / Peuple et noblesse, était l'image du royaume." And he writes in *Littérature et philosophie mêlées*:

> Nous l'avons déjà dit ailleurs et plus d'une fois, le corollaire rigoureux d'une révolution politique, c'est une révolution littéraire. Que voulez-vous que nous y fassions? Il y a quelque chose de fatal dans ce perpétuel parallélisme de la littérature et de la société. L'esprit humain ne marche pas d'un seul pied. Les moeurs et les lois s'ébranlent d'abord; l'art suit. (*O.C.* 5:29)

So not only is there a link between the two, but it is a necessary, a causal link. It is thus by a kind of metalepsis that he expresses the desire to influence the course of French history and thought itself through his writings: as he reminds us in this poem, "Qui délivre le mot, délivre la pensée." We can see in this conception of literature a motive for writing polemical, political pieces like "Ecrit en 1846" or *Les Châtiments.*

What Hugo seeks is to make his words actions. In "Réponse" he turns them into people through their personification as the men and women of the Revolution, and he makes them act in lines like "Les préjugés . . . Se dissolvent au choc de tous les

mots flottants / Pleins de sa volonté, de son but, de son âme."
The catachretic power of language, the moment where figure
and action join, is alluded to explicitly in a parody of the creation of light, the performative "j'ai dit à l'ombre: Sois! / Et
l'ombre fut." It is clear that in the optic of this poem, language
is not just described in terms of the revolution; it is to become
a revolutionary force itself. The poem, then, is not merely an
account of the French revolution nor of the Romantic reform
in poetic diction; it represents a political act. Its success (at
least its success as literary polemic) may be gauged by the critical reaction outlined above.

The tying together of literature and society in a forward-
moving progression leads to the thematic contrast between old
and new in this poem. It is presented in explicit references to
the old order and, on the lexical level, in archaisms (*anciens
vers françois, force mots*). Furthermore, it is central to the very
structure of the poem, which takes on an historical or narrative movement, summarized by the words *progrès saint* and
"Le mouvement complète ainsi son action." The movement alluded to is not only that of historical development and change,
but also the movement of the tropes that parallel it, its
tropisms.

The other metaphor traditionally used to describe language
unsuitable for poetry, linked with the metaphor of social class,
is the pair *bas / élevé*, another thematic contrast developed in
this text. Hugo presents himself as accused of the "chute" of
everything, reminiscent, of course, of the Fall, an idea carried
out through references to God and the evocation of *Genesis* in
lines 4-5 and in the allusion to the tower of Babel. In the old
order, noble words are said to be "montant à Versaille," in contrast to the "genres *bas*," that were *dégradés*, the etymology of
this last word completing the idea of a lowering.

The poem reverses this order of things: "sur le sommet du
Pinde" (the mountain of the muses), "on dansait Ça ira"; and
damned words are "tirés de l'enfer." By the same token, the
"spirals" of periphrases are crushed, and good taste is "foulé
aux pieds." The ending relates an apotheosis of poetry that
rises "à l'éternité par les degrés du temps," assisted by the
flight of the muse and joined by the Revolution. It might seem
paradoxical that it is by descending into the "profondeurs du

langage insondable" (already an oxymoron) that the Revolution raises up "la foule dégradée," but this final image makes explicit this turning upside-down, this "revolution," and it further joins together the two revolts, the political and the linguistic or poetic. In the lines "J'ai . . . mêlé, confondu, nivelé sous le ciel / L'alphabet, sombre tour qui naquit de Babel," the idea of a leveling of social class is tied to even the smallest elements of poetic language (as "dévastateur du vieil ABCD" had shown earlier); and the words *sous le ciel,* enlarging the perspective, show that the whole system has its basis in a kind of transcendence. This is not another paradox: as the last section makes clear ("Et Dieu le veut"), the wheeling movements of the Earth exist as motion only with respect to the fixed point represented by God or Heaven.

Interwoven in these metaphorical networks are the related pairs of light / darkness and large / small or free / restricted. The light / dark imagery parallels that of height / depth: Hugo presents himself as accused of bringing darkness, but this situation is reversed in the course of the poem, as signaled by the line "J'ouvris les yeux." By the end the new poetry is described as moving freely in light, as having "regards éclatants" and a flight that is an "ouragan d'étincelles." Thus the shadow of the poem's beginning becomes divine light of reason and beauty in another inversion of imagery.

The contrast between Hugo and his adversaries is cast throughout the poem as that between the petty and the enormous; and because he is a "monstre énorme," he is presented as too large for the categories and restrictions of the neoclassics; he "overflows." The imagery of liberation is tied to this concept of breaking out of boundaries: prisons, jails, "bornes," images of circles are opposed by the many references to freedom and motion, like "Je bondis hors du cercle et brisai le compas." In the following verses:

"Voyez où l'on en est: la strophe a des bâillons,
L'ode a les fers aux pieds, le drame est en cellule,"

several strands of imagery interact: *fers aux pieds* indicates obstacles to movement, *en cellule,* a closing-in, and *bâillons,* the incapacity of speech imposed on writers. Opposed to such images are evocations of the movement of the masses, the many indications that poetry and theater have been freed, like "sa langue est déliée," references to great size (*immense, énorme, déborde*), and the claim, "J'ai mis tout en branle."

Thus, the metaphors of this poem are linked to each other, they have metaphorical relationships among themselves, generating the movement of the text in their continual shiftings and intermeshings. It is surprising, then, that a text so dependent on metaphorical articulation should be at the same time a text that disparages figurative language. But such is the case: reform in poetic diction is presented, both explicitly and implicitly, as a rejection of the metaphoric in favor of the literal. In this Hugo was reacting against the "horreur du mot propre" that Gautier saw in the restrictions of neoclassical diction (Bruneau, *Histoire*, 12:49) and the consequent overuse of periphrasis. Hugo reacts against such fastidiousness by including "la vie abjecte et familière" (line 53) in lines like "j'ôtai du cou du chien stupéfait son collier / D'épithètes" and expressions like *bagne, terroriste, rustre*, and so on. But Hugo enlarges his criticism to figurative language in general. His declaration, "Guerre à la rhétorique," is amplified by lines like "Syllepse, hypallage, litote frémirent" and the description of the pursuit of Dumarsais, author of the *Traité des tropes*. Tropes are seen as under the protection of the Academy, the literary establishment. This point of view is clear, too, in the lines:

> Je massacrai l'albâtre, et la neige, et l'ivoire;
> Je retirai le jais de la prunelle noire,
> Et j'osai dire au bras: Sois blanc, tout simplement.

In other words the metaphoric term, which had become conventional, is replaced by the literal color word. But in this connection, it must be noted that the words *jais* or *albâtre* were terms that had lost a good deal of their figurative status: they had become in a sense, if not the literal words for black or white, at least the "proper" terms, the only possible terms. The gap between what is said and what could have been said which Genette sees as the prerequisite for the existence of figure is somewhat diminished with the virtual elimination of the original term (*Figures*, 208-11).

The style Hugo opposed to periphrasis is called explicit and "honnête," that is, there is a conception of figure as deceitful, in contrast to the truth of the literal, which somehow attains nature. This concept can be seen in the lines:

> J'ai dit à la narine: Eh mais! tu n'es qu'un nez!
> J'ai dit au long fruit d'or: Mais tu n'es qu'une poire!
> J'ai dit à Vaugelas: Tu n'es qu'une mâchoire!

Here there is a clear repudiation of both metonymy (*narine* for *nez*) and metaphor (in the next line); while the *mais, tu n'es que* form implies a discovery of truth. But the third line undermines the first two: the word *mâchoire*, in the sense of a man without intelligence or wit, is of course figurative. The same contradiction can be seen in the lines,

> le mot propre, ce rustre,
> N'était que caporal: je l'ai fait colonel;
> J'ai fait un jacobin du pronom personnel,

where the *mot propre* itself is personified.

"Je nommai le cochon par son nom" is another instance of the elevation of the *propre*, implying again that each thing has a name, and its own, correct name.[3] All of this presupposes a ground in nature, in a real world to which words can be said to refer. Words that denote, then, are a means of apprehending the world, whereas figurative language is opaque. The stability this concept gives to the reeling world evoked by this text can be seen in the final lines, where Hugo claims that art is the "porte-voix" of God. It is in the *Suite* to this poem that Hugo makes explicit the connection between the word, *le verbe*, and God, but it is evident here also, as the words *Et Dieu le veut* make clear. This idea of Hugo's poetry being somehow more true-to-life has been carried on by critics. Bruneau writes, "Ce qui frappe, quand on examine les corrections de Vigny, de Lamartine et de Hugo, c'est que l'expression simple remplace souvent dans leurs vers l'expression figurée. . . . La révolution romantique a donc été, à ce point de vue, un retour au naturel" (*Histoire*, 12:46, 48). This is an echo of lines like "Sois blanc, tout simplement" from the poem "Réponse," but it is remarkable that Bruneau should find Hugo's language "simple."

Of course, it is impossible for Hugo to rid his discourse of figures, even of those he mentions in a deprecatory way. He makes use of syllepsis in line 216, "Sa langue est déliée ainsi que son esprit," in which the word *déliée* means at once "loosened" (as "loose tongue") and "liberated." An example of hypallage might be the line "populace du style au fond de l'ombre éparse," where the word *éparse* seems to modify *ombre*, whereas it would be more logical for the populace to be scattered. When Hugo writes "Je pense . . . avoir un peu touché aux questions obscures," *un peu*, in its contrast with what follows, certainly qualifies as a *litote*, or understatement. *Emphase* is a question of degree, but this poem has at least its moments of grandiloquence. Hugo may avoid the kind of periphrasis that obviates the need for concrete nouns, but he still uses expressions typical of neoclassical verse like *l'azur* and set phrases like *la marche du temps*. And he clearly does not avoid figure. Indeed, at times his metaphors seem to stumble over each other, as in the lines: "L'Alphabet,/Sombre tour qui naquit de Babel," or the description of the French language as a salon where the literal word changes from a corporal to a colonel and where the participal, a slave, becomes a hyena. Hugo claims to have "écrasé les spirales" of periphrasis, but his figures multiply in a dizzying whirl. Thus it is again surprising to find that the movement portrayed in the poem is said to "complète ainsi son action": as the word *révolution* shows, the movement it "describes" is continuous and unending. And indeed, motion is not halted in the poem after these words. Rather, the Revolution is portrayed as vibrating, entering, and teaching at the same time as it is called a lantern and a star in the sky, images of stability by which people can be guided. For the stars in the sky are themselves in constant revolution. Thus, the end of the poem controverts rather than confirms the concept of a transcendent, immobile poetry, a revolution completed.

It would be wise, then, rather than taking Hugo at his word, to take the poem at its words. Although it seems to oppose rhetoric, it can only exist—as can any language—as figure. Indeed, even the literal is described by means of tropes. The assimilation of the Revolution to all aspects of human life in the last section accomplishes on a metaphorical level the fusion of linguistics and politics implied by the *noble / bas* classification of words and the central metaphor of the poem. History itself becomes literature: "Dans le mot palpitant, le lecteur la [la Révolution] sent vivre . . . Elle est la prose, elle est le vers, elle est le drame; / Elle est l'expression, elle est le sentiment." But the totalization effectuated here seems dispersed by the centrifugal force of the fragmented metaphors used to describe it: the accumulating figures of lines 215-25 seem themselves to dissolve "au choc de tous ces mots flottants." These figures are supported by air, as the imagery of floating, flying, and breathing would suggest, not by any direct, referential relationship with nature or reality. The line "Elle entre aux profondeurs du langage insondable" is logically a paradox; that the Revolution should make Liberty enter man through his pores is inconceivable: only words make it possible.

In the history of French language and literature, a restricted poetic lexicon has been tied to stylized periphrasis. But freedom in diction, in fact, implies a greater range of possible figures. The standard neoclassical metonymies and metaphors give way, as in this poem, before the introduction of striking metaphors like those mentioned above, or "L'imagination, tapageuse aux cent voix, / Qui casse des carreaux dans l'esprit des bourgeois." The pattern found in this poem, a rejection of rhetoric leading to its reintegration at another level, is one to be seen repeatedly in the work of philosophers as well as poets. In this respect Hugo resembles writers as different as Locke, Nodier, or Mallarmé. It is not surprising that critics, like several of those quoted above, should also have followed this pattern.

We have seen in the introduction that the enlarging and the restriction of poetic diction or language in general are two poles of a controversy that has traversed French culture at least since du Bellay. Both points of view are present in the work of Victor Hugo. Whatever the truth of his claims in "Réponse à un acte d'accusation," the poem has come to represent the side supporting vocabulary expansion and a general lifting of rules. Thus the poem itself is an example of the power of language; it is effective rhetoric, in the sense of persuasion; and its words seem to have obeyed his—or their own—injunction: "Soyez / La fourmilière immense, et travaillez!"

III. *The Poetics of the* mot propre

It is of course impossible to treat the whole of Hugo's production, even within a limited perspective. On the other hand, it is a critical commonplace to say of a particular poem or group of poems that it is in this work that Hugo realizes the aims set forth in "Réponse." I would like to look at some of these works to see how he carries out the precepts enunciated in "Réponse" regarding the *mot propre*, i.e., the rejection of neoclassical periphrasis and valorization of the literal.

It was periphrasis on which Hugo concentrated in the attack on neoclassical tropes he mounted in "Réponse," and there are reasons for his choice. It was by means of periphrasis that "low" expressions could be avoided in literary works. Among the uses of the trope that Dumarsais points out (154-55), the first ("Par bienséance, . . . pour envelopper les idées basses ou peu honnêtes") and the third ("pour l'ornement du discours, . . . la périphrase poétique présente la pensée sous une forme plus gracieuse ou plus noble") depend on the distinction between noble and low expressions Hugo denounced in his poem. Periphrasis was also an easy—and a common—target. Voltaire, for instance, criticized a poet for not saying right out, "le roi vient" (quoted approvingly by Fontanier, 362). The most famous mocking of the device is probably Molière's in "Les Précieuses ridicules," but he is by no means alone. Theoreticians of rhetoric all warn against its overuse or misuse (See Dumarsais, 156; Fontanier, 362-63; Morier, 299-300). Thus, Hugo's derision of "le long fruit d'or" is itself conventional; it arises from a long tradition of caricaturing preciosity.[4]

But as I have already suggested in discussing "Réponse," there is a deeper reason for his concentrating on this figure: his belief in the coincidence of the word and the thing. This concept can perhaps be seen most clearly in the poems he wrote about the "book of nature," poems like "A André Chénier," "La Vie aux champs," and especially "Je lisais. Que lisais-je?" (all from the *Contemplations*). In this last poem we find the lines:

Le monde est l'oeuvre où rien ne ment et ne dévie,
Et dont les mots sacrés répandent de l'encens.

If the world is a book, then Hugo's words can reproduce it perfectly; his poetry can mime the universe. But periphrasis goes around the word: it is the very figure of deviation. Hugo is committed to the correspondence theory of truth, to the direct expression of the world through language. Hence the importance of the literal.

His introduction of the "real words for things" can be seen especially in the works in which he treats scenes from domestic life. Bonald had pointed out that the general rule delimiting what was acceptable and what was not in the high style came down to the distinction between the public and the domestic spheres, the latter involving "détails familiers" which had to be avoided (1005-8). Hugo was among the first to turn his attention to that sphere as a subject for serious verse, as he announced in the preface to *Les Feuilles d'automne*: "Ce n'est point là de la poésie de tumulte et de bruit; ce sont des vers sereins et paisibles, des vers comme tout le monde en fait ou en rêve, des vers de la famille, du foyer domestique, de la vie privée, des vers de l'intérieur de l'âme" (*Oeuvres poétiques* 1:715). Such poetry naturally tended to incorporate elements from the semantic fields that had been proscribed. Thus we find in this collection references to particular objects from everyday life in lines like "Table toujours servie au paternel foyer" (I), "Dans l'alcôve sombre" (XX), or "L'autre jour, il venait de pleuvoir, car l'été,/Cette année, est de bise et de pluie attristé/ . . . J'avais levé le store . . ." ("La Pente de la rêverie"). This last example shows the way such elements are commonly associated with prose syntax. Brunot (in Petit de Julleville, 7:731) points out that *laver*, perfectly acceptable when used figuratively, was familiar in the line from "La Prière pour tous," "Comme un pavé d'autel qu'on lave tous les soirs." Although not "familiar" as a dictionary classification, *laver* was a term that could be considered surprising both because it came from the domestic sphere and because of this literal use, showing the link between the detail of everyday life and the rejection of periphrasis.[5] Such usage can be found throughout Hugo's poetic career and especially in works where he treats interior scenes or the "simple life" as in *Les Chansons des rues et des bois*. As he wrote in *Les Voix intérieures* XX: "La vie aux mille soins, laborieux et lourds,/ Se transfigure en poésie!" It will be useful to look at two such works, "A des oiseaux envolés" (from *Les Voix intérieures*) and "Les Pauvres Gens" (from *La Légende des siècles*) to see what role these elements can play in the functioning of particular texts.[6]

"A des oiseaux envolés" is an interesting example because of the many devices Hugo uses to create its poetic effect and because of the claims it makes about poetry. In this poem the poet calls to the children he has evicted from his study for having put some of his verses into the fire in their play. Examples of conversational speech combine with natural syntax to give a casual tone and the impression of spoken discourse, as in expressions like *Voilà tout, Belle perte! en effet!*, and *oh non!—dicter des vers? / A quoi bon?* and in the following lines:

Il pleuvait ce matin. Il fait froid aujourd'hui.
Un nuage mal fait dans le ciel tout à l'heure
A passé. Que nous veut cette cloche qui pleure?
Puis on a dans le coeur quelques remords. Voilà
Ce qui nous rend méchants.

Here the two enjambements and the simple syntax combine to create a prose rhythm. The diction is likewise both simple (there is not a word that goes beyond the vocabulary of a very young child) and colloquial ("Que nous veut cette cloche," "Un nuage mal fait," and so on).

There are many mentions of the particular accoutrements of the poet's study: his table, his chair pushed against the wall, "mon grand fauteuil de chêne et de tapisserie," pencils, crayons, and the books and various objets d'art displayed around the room. This emphasis on the concrete detail will be examined further in the context of the realism of "Les Pauvres Gens"; here the objects are important especially because they are explicitly opposed to poetry. Indeed, the poem is, in large measure, about the opposition of poetry to everyday life. Not only have the children already destroyed some of the poet's verses, his other children ("embryons près d'éclore"), but they continue to be opposed to his work when he calls them back to his study. He tells them to go on distracting him, to bump his arm, to cast shadows on the book he is reading, and even to throw more verses into the fire. The children's charm, beauty, and grace are contrasted with his verses, "boiteux, difformes,

gauches . . . corps hideux . . . vers laids." Furthermore, the
the burning of the poems is opposed to a serious crime they
might have committed instead, breaking one of the china
vases: "Quel crime? quel exploit? quel forfait insensé?/Quel
vase du Japon en mille éclats brisé?" There is a series of references to fine porcelain throughout the poem, all preceded by
the first person possessive adjective ("mes tasses de Saxe,"
"mon vieux Sèvres," "mes vases de Chine"), until at last to woo
the children back he makes the sacrifice of letting them touch
"Mes gros chinois ventrus faits comme des concombres." (It is
the Bible, however, that is presented as the ultimate treasure).
So poetry is one pole of a dichotomy with domestic life (represented by children and fine china) at the other extreme.

When the poet claims to value the latter more than the
former, the reader cannot avoid the feeling that Hugo protests
too much. We cannot accept as fully ironic "Belle perte, en
effet!" the description of his poetry as ugly, nor the opposition
between the useless poetry of Hugo and the beautiful verses of
Méry, "qui demain s'envoleront aux cieux." These works he
would not let his children touch. Méry's "birds" (or his children: "les vers nouveau-nés") are his verses; Hugo's birds are
his own children: "des oiseaux envolés." Had Hugo chosen a
more serious candidate as his rival, it might not be so difficult
to accept his modesty as sincere. Hugo cannot even bring himself to characterize Méry as great: he calls him "le poète char-
mant." Furthermore, the opposition between family and poetry can hardly stand up when it appears in a poem. At least we
know Hugo has not allowed his children to burn the lines we
are reading.

In fact, this poem brings together the two spheres it seems to
contrast, linking them on several levels. First, the lines "Toute
ma poésie,/c'est vous, et mon esprit suit votre fantaisie" explicitly unites the children with the poet's work. Moreover,
the children are presented as able to approach directly the
"poem of nature," again a kind of poetry opposed to his own:

Ce livre des oiseaux et des bohémiens,
Ce poème de Dieu qui vaut mieux que les miens.

If the poet wants to follow their fantasy, it is to approach their
direct access to this true poetry. Indeed, he wants to carry to

the realm of domestic life the direct representation of nature he believes poetry capable of attaining.

The highly rhetorical nature of this poem (both in the sense of figure and as relation to the reader) precludes our seeing in it the destruction of rhetoric "Réponse" called for. But it does not diminish what he has accomplished in this poem: through his introduction into verse of the subjects, the objects, and the language of everyday life, he has made those elements the carriers of poetry. In this text his children have become his poetry, not because these pretty creatures seem like "real" children to us (in fact, they don't), not because he can give us direct access to their lives, but because he has made poetry out of them. In the opposition children/poetry, poetry has won.

This poem has often been compared to the fifteenth poem of *Feuilles d'automne* and "Le Pot cassé" from *L'Art d'être grand-père*. The former opposes poetry to children as in this text and claims that rather than being a distraction they serve to enrich the poet's work. But there are no familiar expressions and almost no details of everyday life. Even the line cited by Brunot (in Petit de Julleville, 731-32) as examples of the *mots proscrits ou suspects* Hugo introduced into verse, "Ebranlez et planchers, et plafonds, et piliers!" ends in a word evocative of grander constructions than a bourgeois house. The same attitude is taken in "Elle avait pris ce pli" (*Les Contemplations*), where the daughter's morning visits give the poet new strength. The point of departure for "Le Pot cassé" is a broken china vase, but there is no opposition established between poetry and the family. On the other hand, in this late work the diction is free enough to admit *water-closet* in a description of paradise.

Of course, there are many other instances of the poetry of ordinary life in Hugo.[7] But the question we should ask is the extent to which such poetry's use of concrete details represents the rejection of the figurative in favor of the literal advocated in "Réponse." A text that can help us to answer this question is "Les Pauvres Gens." Its title alone makes it clear that Hugo is claiming to depict a class of society usually absent in poetry and leads us to expect the introduction of lexical elements appropriate to the milieu and probably inappropriate to serious verse.

The poem begins as follows:

Il est nuit. La cabane est pauvre, mais bien close.
Le logis est plein d'ombre et l'on sent quelque chose
Qui rayonne à travers ce crépuscule obscur.
Des filets de pêcheur sont accrochés au mur.
Au fond, dans l'encoignure où quelque humble vaisselle
Aux planches d'un bahut vaguement étincelle,
On distingue un grand lit aux longs rideaux tombants.
Tout près, un matelas s'étend sur de vieux bancs,
Et cinq petits enfants, nid d'âmes, y sommeillent.
La haute cheminée où quelques flammes veillent
Rougit le plafond sombre, et, le front sur le lit,
Une femme à genoux prie, et songe, et pâlit.
C'est la mère. Elle est seule. Et dehors, blanc d'écume,
Au ciel, aux vents, aux rocs, à la nuit, à la brume,
Le sinistre Océan jette son noir sanglot.

It is obvious that Hugo bases his picture on a series of concrete details calculated to give the reader an impression of the household and its inhabitants in much the same way as a realist novelist might do. Particular elements carry particular sorts of information: the adjectives *pauvre, humble, vieux* reinforce the title; the net hanging on the wall gives us the profession of the husband; the gleaming of the dishes indicates the cleanliness of the family; the praying wife, their piety. The bed with its long curtains would seem to be a gratuitous detail, a kind of "effet de réel" were it not that Hugo needs the curtains to hide the children in the bed to prepare for the "surprise" (though it is doubtful that readers are in fact surprised) of the poem's last line: "Tiens, dit-elle en ouvrant les rideaux, les voilà!"

Several remarks should be made about these elements. First, they are primarily carried by nouns: *cabane, filet, bahut*, and so on. Second, like all realist details, they are typical. As Aragon pointed out about "Souvenir de la nuit du 4" (*Châtiments*), (a work he sees as fulfilling the "credo du réalisme en poésie" of "Réponse"), the top in the child's pocket is "le détail qui fait croire au tout, le détail *typique* du réaliste" (*Hugo*, 46, 54). Aragon goes on, however, to make a further point about such details: "Pas un mot qui ne soit la description des choses telles qu'elles sont, qui ne suppose l'existence des choses indé-

pendamment de celui qui les dit" (48). But if the motivation of
elements like those in the first section of "Les Pauvres Gens" is
so easy to recuperate, it is just because they are not simply
brute facts. Rather, the relation between even these simple
nouns and their referents is accomplished by a detour, by figure. It is their figurative quality that invests them with their
meaning. They are metonymic in nature: the net is a metonymy for the husband's profession, the "humble vaisselle" is
another metonymy for their poverty; its gleaming is a synecdoche for the objects in their room, all, we are sure, equally
clean despite their humbleness. Indeed, the dishes themselves
can be taken as a synecdoche for the lives of these "pauvres
gens": humble but shining.

This is in fact the message carried by the poem's language
levels as well. Another look at the first lines of the poem shows
that, though everyday objects are mentioned, the diction used
to describe the scene, though simple, has no trace of familiarity, let alone vulgarity. Words like *cabane* and *logis*, for example, are perfectly acceptable.[8] The allegorizing of the "Océan"
in the last lines of this section prepares the richly metaphoric
descriptions of the sea in the rest of the poem, where the language, far from incorporating colloquial elements, in fact includes "noble" words like "Dur *labeur*." The reported speech
of the fisherman and his wife later in the poem does include
colloquial rhythms and expressions: "Tiens!" "cinq enfants sur
le bras," "c'est gros comme le poing," and so on. At one point
the husband refers to the orphaned children as "ces chiffons."[9]
But even here there are examples of higher diction and expressions we would not expect in this milieu. As he considers
adopting the children of his dead neighbor, the fisherman says
"Ce sont là des accidents profonds"; and he imagines that
"C'est la mère, vois-tu, qui frappe à notre porte." It is instructive to contrast Hugo's reproduction of popular speech in "Les
Pauvres Gens" with Corbière's in "La Balancelle." Other than
some familiar syntactical constructions and the use of *chiffons*, Hugo's fisherman speaks mostly in standard, even somewhat elevated French:

"Je suis volé, dit-il; la mer c'est la forêt.
    —Quel temps a-t-il fait? —Dur. —Et la pêche?—Mauvaise.

> Mais vois-tu, je t'embrasse, et me voilà bien aise.
> Je n'ai rien pris du tout. J'ai troué mon filet.
> Le diable était caché dans le vent qui soufflait."

Corbière's sailors, on the other hand, speak a tongue rich in popular constructions, *argot*, and sailors' terminology:

> —Bon! Si j'aval' ma gaffe avant toi, faut pas s'rendre.
> —J'sais ça z'aussi bien q'vous. — Oui, mais faut m'foutre le feu
> Dans la soute à poudre, et . . . Ta main, pilote, adieu!

Though reduced in its use, in "Les Pauvres Gens" noble diction is still a sign of nobility, not of social class but of character.

This kind of raising of low subject-matter to a higher level, where it can be treated in a dignified style, is frequent in Hugo. Gély has shown how in many of the *Contemplations* "toutes ces choses familières . . . se révèlent 'choses cosmiques' " (*Intimité*, 419). The eye of the dying horse in "Melancholia," for instance, is "plein des stupeurs sombres de l'infini, / Où luit vaguement l'âme effrayante des choses." In other words they do not remain familiar objects; they turn into greater things, like the holes in the beggar's cloak that become constellations. Concrete details turn into figures.

We can conclude that, at least in these texts, the rejection of periphrasis and the inclusion of concrete details from everyday life did not lead to the elimination of figurative discourse any more than "Réponse" accomplished the rejection of rhetoric it called for. On the contrary, we have seen that such details play an important role in the figural structure of these works. Furthermore, the language level of these texts cannot be said to be very low: very few words would be classified as familiar at the time. What Gély discusses even in the *Contemplations* is "images familières," not familiar language. That is, there are elements from the field of everyday life, but informality of tenor is infrequent. We should not undervalue the importance and the novelty of Hugo's turn to the domestic sphere nor the freedom from periphrasis that it entailed; but it is to other works, most often later works, that we should look in order to find more frequent and striking uses of colloquial diction.

IV. "Les mots en liberté"

In the neoclassical hierarchy, both songs and satirical verse had a less stringent code of vocabulary usage. The stylistic motivations of familiar language in these genres will be the subject of a section of the chapter on Verlaine. But Hugo also extended the limits of the constraints governing them, and he used the very breaking of these rules as a stylistic device. I would like to examine some of the ways he puts into practice in such works the liberation of language he claims in "Réponse" to have accomplished. It is in *Les Chansons des rues et des bois* (1865) that he exploited the possibilities of the song and in *Les Châtiments* (1853) and *Les Contemplations* (1856) that he created his most famous polemical pieces, "Réponse" among them.

Calling a work "songs" suggests that we are not to take these poems too seriously. They might be comparable to songs meant to be sung like those of Béranger, noted for their use of popular language.[10] A literary antecedent is the "littérature poissarde" (written in vulgar language), which had a vogue in the eighteenth century. Hugo alludes to this light genre when he refers to its creator, Vadé, in describing the "temple" of nature where the poet has been worshipping:

> Ce temple qu'eût aimé Virgile
> Et que n'eût point haï Vadé.
>
> ("Clôture")

The theme and practice of emphasizing the *mot propre* are important in *Les Chansons*:

> O fils et frères, ô poètes,
> Quand la chose est, dites le mot.
> Soyez de purs esprits, et faites.
> Rien n'est bas quand l'âme est en haut.

As these lines from "Réalité" show, the use of the literal expression is tied to a program of mixing styles; in effect, Hugo sets out to accomplish in lyric poetry what he had done earlier for the *drame*. Pronouncements of this intention appear often in this collection in lines that echo those above: "Rien n'est haut ni bas," "du fond de toutes les proses/Peut s'élancer le vers sacré" ("Le Poète bat aux champs"); "Mêle les dieux, confonds les styles" ("Genio libri"). This poetic program is the major theme underlying several of the pieces, and it provides the motivation for the many instances of familiar words and expressions.

It is in this collection that we find in Hugo the contrasts in diction that are a central characteristic of Baudelaire's style and that will be pushed to such an extreme in the poetry of Rimbaud and Corbière. Hugo does not just slip occasionally into the familiar style in the manner of Musset; he very consciously juxtaposes literary and classical allusions with elements of everyday, contemporary life and with familiar or even popular terms.[11] In "Le Poète bat aux champs," the line

> Bergers, plantons là Tortoni

combines the traditional characters of pastoral poetry with both an allusion to a Parisian café popular at the time and the familiar expression *planter là*. The poetic value of the familiar is the subject of the poem, whose first section ends with the lines: "Amis, le corset de Denise / Vaut la ceinture de Vénus." In keeping with this tenet, the poem includes words like *guinguette*, *voyous*, *gamineries*, and the "mot très familier" (according to Littré), *ces calembredaines-là*. Chronology and stylistic level are mixed in another text when the poet tells us the genie of his book to:

> Cours, saute, emmène Alphésibée
> Souper au Café de Paris.

and

> Que ton chant libre et disant tout
> Vole, et de la lyre de Thèbe
> Aille au mirliton de Saint-Cloud.

It is in this poem, "Genio libri," that Hugo enunciates his program most clearly, echoing "Réponse" once more and again mixing allusions and language levels: "remue / L'art poétique jusqu'au fond. / Trouble La Harpe, ce coq d'Inde, / Et Boileau . . . Plante là toute rhétorique." He finishes the poem by combining a traditionally poetic sentiment with a prosaic rhythm and an intrusion from everyday life:

> Pourvu qu'on sente la rosée
> Dans ton vers qui boit du café.

The combining of poetic styles and the suppression of the distinction between high and low that these poems present are an important aspect of the "genius" of this book, and Hugo is able to explore their possibilities in a variety of texts. The third part of "Clôture," "Le Poète est un riche," for instance, reverses the hierarchy rich / poor: nature is the true source of wealth, and there, "le poète est propriétaire." This theme motivates the use of vocabulary of commerce and finance, a conceit appearing in virtually every stanza and including terms like *appartements meublés, à crédit, rentes*, and *payé comptant*. One of the last stanzas shows the effects to be elicited from striking contrasts in diction:

> Quand les heures font leur descente
> Dans la nue où le jour passa,
> Il voit la strophe éblouissante
> Pendre à ce Décroche-moi-ça.

Hugo begins with what is in effect a periphrase for the evening, incorporating the noble word *nue* and the "poetic" epithet *éblouissante*, only to end with *Décroche-moi-ça*. Referring to a secondhand clothes dealer's shop, this term (with various spellings) is classified as popular in the *Larousse du XIXe siècle*, and it appears in the slang dictionaries of Delvau, Larchey, and Delasalle. In these lines, then, high and low are confused stylistically as well as thematically.

In "Choses écrites à Créteil," Hugo returns to the subject of what a poet can or cannot say, with interesting consequences. The speaker in the poem makes clear his rhetorical stance vis-à-vis the implied reader, beginning with "Sachez," continuing "je vous le déclare," and ending with "je vous le dis." Indeed, the title makes it clear that the poem's subject is not only what happened at Créteil, but also what the poet has chosen to write about it. What he in fact writes is clearly set against the conventions of verse. He affirms that he addressed the young woman he saw by the water as "O lavandière! / (Blanchisseuse étant familier)." In doing so he recognizes distinctions in diction while simultaneously flounting them: however improper the latter word may be, he has seen fit to use it in this line of poetry. The poem's central metaphor is the comparison of nature to clothing, in particular, to the sort of clothing the girl is washing in the stream. As a consequence stylistic juxtapositions abound, like the comparison of "ces nippes" to "Les blancs cygnes de Cythérée," or the contrast between the last three words and the rest of the following lines:

L'aube et la brise étaient mêlées
A la grâce de son bonnet.

What is mixed in these lines are not only the referents of these expressions, but also the stylistic milieux in which we would expect the terms used here to be found. This combining of stylistic markers is parallel to the elimination of social distinctions the speaker claims when he tells the young woman that " 'Les rois sont ceux qu'adorent celles/Qui sont charmantes comme vous;' " and " 'Si vous vouliez, je serais prince'." The poem's first stanza contains the most such juxtaposition of this sort and the one, if we are to believe Hugo's note, that caused the most uproar: "j'ai vu . . ./Une fille qui dans la Marne/Lavait des torchons radieux." The epithet does not appear to have been able to raise the language level high enough to suit Hugo's critics: *torchon* evoked milieux that were just too common. In a note he wrote but did not publish, Hugo describes the reaction:

> quelle audace! quelle folie! je pouvais faire remarquer que j'avais dit cela dans un sourire. que c'était prendre ce sourire bien au sérieux. mais point. est-ce qu'il y a des circonstances atténuantes à *torchons radieux? Torchons radieux! Torchons radieux! Torchons radieux!* Pendant deux mois, dans beaucoup de journaux, il n'y eut guère que ce mot. (*Oeuvres poétiques*, 3:786-87)

This critical reaction has a certain irony: this poem, whose subject is at least in part what a poet can or cannot write, ends with singular discretion: "L'idylle est douce,/Mais ne veut pas, je vous le dis,/Qu'au delà du baiser on pousse/La peinture du paradis." What is shocking about this text and others in the collection, then, is not their licentiousness but the informality of their language and their use of referents from milieux considered low. The program of raising the most common subjects to the level of poetry did not, it appears, meet with universal success.

It is important to recognize, however, that this program was neither confined to *Les Chansons* nor without other resonances in Hugo's work. The collapsing of the distinctions between high and low subjects and discourse follows naturally from the Hugolian vision of oneness in the universe. The line "rien n'est haut ni bas" is echoed in "Rien n'est haut et rien n'est infime" from "Egalité" or "Rien n'est ni tout à fait mort ni tout à fait vivant" from "A Albert Dürer"(*Les Voix intérieures*). The link between this conception of nature and the mixture of poetic styles can be seen in the poem from *Les Contemplations*, "Unité," where the sun, "cette fleur des splendeurs infinies," is contrasted to the humble daisy. The last two lines describe the daisy looking up at the sun,

> Le grand astre épanchant sa lumière immortelle.
> —Et moi, j'ai des rayons aussi!—lui disait-elle.

The nobility of the former is marked by noble diction, including a neoclassical periphrase, the lowness of the latter by spoken syntax. Diction equals place in the universe; and both kinds of distinctions are to be erased.

But there is a fault in the logic of this unification, this leveling: in order to articulate it, Hugo needs the very distinction he sets out to eliminate. The poetic effect of "Unité" depends on our recognition of the differences between the two stylistic levels used. Furthermore, except for instances like this poem and texts with particular targets for attack, it is not in his philosophical poems that Hugo uses such diction. Even in the *Chansons*, as Ward has pointed out, the public, philosophic poetic voice gradually takes over from the private one. Familiar language does not seem to be so appropriate to such subjects as neutral, if not markedly noble discourse, for in these poems the diction is more elevated. "Au cheval," the final, visionary poem in the collection, includes words typical of neoclassical verse like *aquilon, astres*, and *azurs*; and the horse is described in the periphrase "le dételé du char d'Elie." Thus, we find again in this collection the structure of "Réponse": strong, low diction in passages thematizing the reversal of high

/low divisions, followed by higher diction as the poet turns to his vision of the future. Hugo implicitly concedes this point in one of the *Chansons*, whose title, "Paulo minora canamus," admits the distinction between genres. The poet puts aside "pour un instant" "Tous nos grands problèmes profonds" to treat of humble flowers, little birds, and Jeanneton, the washerwoman. The language here makes it clear that the high/low opposition has not been banished: when "Meudon remplace Denderah," "J'en descends; je mets pied à terre;/Plus tard, demain, je pousserai/Plus loin encor dans le mystère/Les strophes au vol effaré." In fact, he does return to such subjects and such images later in the collection. Nonetheless, for Hugo, the light genre of song does permit language he rarely uses in serious verse; and it is for this reason that these works so often thematize as well as practice a rich and varied scale of poetic diction.

Not only in "Réponse" and its "Suite" but also in others of the *Contemplations* Hugo's target is the restrictions in poetic diction, and his weapons include the very words of his text. "A André Chénier," "Quelques mots à un autre," and, especially "A propos d'Horace" make use of language from a wide variety of registers, and the lowness of their diction seems to vary directly with the violence of the attack. These poems can be read, however, in the context of the other genre that traditionally had a looser code of conventions, the satire.

Satire is a genre at which Hugo excels, and it is in such verse that we find some of his most striking innovations in poetic language. A look at satires such as Boileau's shows that the genre could admit references to particular amounts of money, allusions to food as specific as "une langue en ragoust de persil couronnée," and insults like "Filoux effrontez" (21, 36). Boileau approvingly puts in the mouth of a rejected poet the same claim to using the literal expression that Hugo makes in "Réponse," (where Boileau was one of the main targets): "Je ne puis rien nommer, si ce n'est par son nom./J'appelle un chat un chat, et Rolet un fripon" (14). On the other hand, he has been careful, he tells us in his preface, not to "laisser échaper un seul mot qui pust le moins du monde blesser la pudeur" (63). Bruneau defines the language traditionally appropriate to the satire as that of "la conversation soignée" (72-73). Now,

"soignée" is certainly not the term we would want to apply to
the following lines from "Eblouissements" (*Les Châtiments*):

> A ce ramas se joint un tas d'affreux poussahs,
> Un tas de Triboulets et de Sancho Panças.
> Sous vingt gouvernements ils ont palpé des sommes.
> Aucune indignité ne manque à ces bonshommes;
> Rufins poussifs, Verrès goutteux, Séjans fourbus,
> Selles à tout tyran, sénateurs omnibus.
> On est l'ancien soudard, on est l'ancien bourgmestre;
> On tua Louis Seize, on vote avec de Maistre;
> Ils ont eu leur fauteuil dans tous les Luxembourgs;
> Ayant vu les Maurys, ils sont faits aux Sibours;
> Ils sont gais, et, contant leurs antiques bamboches,
> Branlent leurs vieux gazons sur leurs vieilles caboches.
> Ayant été, du temps qu'ils avaient un cheveu,
> Lâches sous l'oncle, ils sont abjects sous le neveu.
> Gros mandarins chinois adorant le tartare,
> Ils apportent leur coeur, leur vertu, leur catarrhe,
> Et prosternent, cagneux, devant sa majesté
> Leur bassesse avachie en imbécillité.

It is impossible to do justice here to the range of language levels, the variety of objects of derision, the intensity of invective
that Hugo attained in his polemical pieces. But a look at this
passage from the poem can indicate something of Hugo's technique and the role language levels play in it.[12]

First, Hugo portrays his targets, those who support and ben-
efit from the Empire, as physical and moral wrecks. He compares them to fools, Sancho Panza, and Triboulet (François I's
fool); he shows them as old, feeble men with nothing to do but
talk about the good times they used to have. To do so, he uses
the vocabulary of illness (*cagneux*, *poussifs*, and so on). Such
terms are used to denigrate the historical characters alluded-
to, like Rufin, who have already been presented as despicable
characters. This language culminates in the line "Ils apportent
leur coeur, leur vertu, leur catarrhe," where the shock of the
last word comes not only from its contrast with the meanings
of the words that precede it (and whose form in the line is
identical), but also because of its status as a medical term. Its
incongruity is underlined by the oddity of its spelling. These

are the kinds of effects that Rimbaud will achieve in his invective verse, in "Les Assis" in particular.

The names of the people mentioned in these lines, as so often in Hugo, lose some of their status as proper names: they lose their ability to refer uniquely both when they are used in the plural ("les Maurys," "un tas de Triboulets") and when they are modified by adjectives, as in "Ruffins poussifs."[13] Another kind of confusion of reference occurs in the line "Gros mandarins chinois adorant le tartare": here the unlikely combination of characters compresses the technique used throughout this passage, where contemporary figures are used along with literary and classical allusions, where *poussahs* rub shoulders with *bourgmestres*, the foreign origin of the words underlining their incongruity. Hugo seems to attack his opponents with a barrage of unrelated names.

Low language has a particular role to play in such a passage. Hugo plays such expressions off against words like "leur vertu" and "sa majesté" as he did the medical term *catarrhe*. He chooses terms from the whole spectrum of French usage. Forty lines earlier, he had used the word *grinche*, from Parisian *argot*, perhaps the first appearance of *argot* in modern French poetry (Pléiade, 2:1107). Here, the low language varies from a familiarity in tone in lines like "On tua Louis seize, on vote avec de Maistre" or "du temps qu'ils avaient un cheveu" to the more properly familiar *soudard*, *un tas de*, and "ils ont *palpé* des sommes" to the next lowest level, the popular expressions *caboches*, *bamboches* for amusements, and *gazons*. This last term refers either to a wig or to the few hairs left on a bald head, and is listed in both Delvau and Larchey's dictionaries of slang. *Bamboches* is especially striking in its stylistic contrast with its epithet, the anteposed *antiques*. The perceptibility of such terms as antithetical to the pretentions of Hugo's targets, who claim to be other than the former soldiers and bourgeois that they are, plays a considerable role in the effectiveness of his satire.

Gaudon points out the novelty of the use of these slang and popular expressions in his very effective analysis of the combined effects of syntax, rhythm, and image in *Eblouissements* (*Temps*, 175-77). But he sees the introduction of such language in *Les Châtiments* as "une nouvelle application de la théorie du mot propre" (167; see also 168). This is the same opinion Sainte-Beuve expresses, with a pejorative impulse, when he writes that Hugo came to "attacher une vertu excessive au mot propre et . . . pousser quelquefois les représailles jusqu'à prodiguer le mot cru" (quoted in Gély, *Intimité*, 206). Yet when we look at the popular expressions introduced in this section, we find that they are figurative, not literal. *Un tas de* and *palper* are standard French in their literal senses. A *bamboche* is literally—and perfectly acceptably—a marionette; *faire des bamboches*, meaning "se livrer à toutes sortes d'amusements et de plaisirs" (Littré) is figurative and popular. Likewise, the etymology of *caboches* combines *bosse* and the derivations of *caput*, whereas the metaphor embedded in *gazons* is obvious. Hugo himself claimed that figurative language depended upon popular language: "Le langage figuré est essentiellement le langage populaire. Les métaphores sont des filles de carrefours; il y a émeute d'images" (*Notes de travail pour William Shakespeare, O.C.,* 12:351). Here the revolutionary class is not rioting to assert the rights of the *mot propre* as in "Réponse." We do not need to assert the priority of popular language as Hugo does in this note to recognize its figurative dimension and to see it at work in his texts.

In his songs and in his satire, Hugo has certainly gone beyond the bounds of these genres as they existed at the beginning of the nineteenth century, where, according to Bruneau, the limits of familiarity did not exceed the terms that "l'honnête homme emploie dans la conversation" (*Histoire,* 12:72). On the other hand, in these genres no more than in "Réponse," Hugo's use of such language did not bring about a reduction in figurative language. Indeed, as the above quote shows, he himself was aware of the links between the two; and he was able to exploit them to the fullest in texts such as the ones we have studied.

We will see again in Baudelaire's work the importance of details of everyday life; and Rimbaud will carry on the use of medical terminology and slang in his poetry of invective. We should not consider Hugo as a "source" for these poets, or even as a precursor: as mentioned earlier "Réponse" was first published in 1856, the same year as the *Odes funambulesques,* a year before the first edition of *Les Fleurs du mal* and after many of them had already been published; *Les Chansons des rues et des bois*, published in 1865, followed the 1861 edition of the *Fleurs du mal* and preceded by only a year *Les Poèmes saturniens*, which include texts like "Croquis parisien" and "Monsieur Prudhomme." Nonetheless, as the critical reaction to "Réponse" shows, Hugo set the agenda for the way poetic diction was discussed in the nineteenth century and since; and the questions about figurative language he raised in that text and the others I have studied are those informing the work of the other major poets of the time.

As we have seen, Hugo's emphasis on the literal follows from one of the basic tenets of his thought, his belief in the power of language to mime the order in the universe: "Comprenez que les mots sont des choses" ("Suite").[14] This logocentrism both presupposes that there is such an order and valorizes denotation as the foundation of language. One of its consequences is the often-noted importance of nouns and naming in Hugolian rhetoric, an importance manifested in the predominance in his poetry of nominative syntax, condensed metaphors formed by the apposition of two nouns, accumulations of proper names, and extensive use of enumeration, as well as in the rejection of periphrasis studied above.

But just as there is a tension between stylistic "democracy" and the poetic means necessary to express it, there is an incompatibility between the vision of oneness in the universe (articulated, as we have seen, through diction as well as direct statement and other figures) and the priority of naming, whose function is to distinguish. It is for this reason that we find in Hugo both an affirmation of the power of language to name the world and the breakdown of the proper noun's capacity to refer. Furthermore, as Gaudon has noted ("Mesure," 230) and as the passage from "Eblouissements" shows, the very devices of accumulation and enumeration Hugo uses to fill up his poetic universe lead to a kind of excess that puts meaning itself into question.

THREE

Banville the Funambulist

Certain of the *Chansons des rues et des bois* and *Les Châtiments* show one of the more obvious results of the collision between elevated and familiar diction in poetry, its comedy. The master of such comic possibilities is surely Banville. His satire does not have the violence of Hugo's polemical attacks, but what it lacks in bite it makes up in humor. Baudelaire pointed out that the very excess of "bouffonnerie" in Banville destroys its bitterness, "et la satire, par un miracle résultant de la nature même du poète, se déchargera de toute sa haine dans une explosion de gaieté, innocente à force d'être carnavalesque" (2:167).

Banville was very conscious of his role in creating "une nouvelle langue comique versifée, appropriée à nos moeurs et à notre poésie actuelle."[1] The importance of his work and, at the same time, the subversive power of this new poetry were widely recognized, especially after the publication of the *Odes funambulesques* in 1857.[2] What Banville saw as appropriate to his time was "la chanson bouffonne et la chanson lyrique," pointing to a joining of dimensions traditional genre distinctions prohibited ("Préface," 6:8). On the other hand, he did not make great claims for these pieces. He called them "des fantaisies plus que frivoles" and excuses himself for republishing them in book form. In fact, he did not sign the first edition. Banville maintained in practice as well as theory the distinction between such poetry and his serious works; as Verlaine points out, "dans ses merveilleuses oeuvres purement lyriques," Banville avoided "les à-peu-près et les calembours, exquis dans les *Odes funambulesques*" (Letter quoted in Stephan, 53).

Although he saw rhyme as the main instrument of his new comic verse, Banville was able to draw humorous effects from his diction as well, and in so doing, he introduced a good number of familiar expressions into poetry. It was here in fact that he was a major innovator (from 1846 on, when the first of the *Odes* were published) for unusual rhyme was a major stylistic device in traditional satire. Banville created comic effects both through discordances between subject-matter and treatment and through the juxtaposition of disparate registers in the same text. It is useful to look in some detail at this too-neglected work, not only to rediscover some of its charm, but also to see the workings of discordant style in a vein very different from those of Hugo or Baudelaire. Many of these pieces have lost their relevance and even their humor as their targets have been forgotten, but some of them retain interest because they allow a glimpse of a new, intermediate style, neither satirical nor somber, ironic, yet good-humored.[3]

I. *"Où sont les plâtres de Dantan?"*

The phrase I have used for the title of this section, taken from the "Ballade des célébrités du temps jadis," shows one of the major sources of Banville's humor: the contrast between an established lyrical form (and its corresponding diction) and a contemporary or banal subject. Such contrasts are especially sharp in poems written in the archaic verse forms that Banville renewed—virelais, rondeaux, and so on—but they appear throughout his comic verse. In "La Ville enchantée," for instance, various landmarks of contemporary Paris are described in long, elegant periphrases. Banville's *Odelettes* function in a similar way; he defines the odelette as "une manière de propos familier relevé et discipliné par les cadences lyriques d'un rythme précis et bref" ("Préface" to the *Odelettes*, 2:101). A corresponding and opposite method of disjoining subject and treatment is the trivialization of a traditionally lyrical subject.[4]

A good example of the first of these procedures is the poem

"Monsieur Coquardeau," subtitled "Chant royal." Its subject is a Gavarni character, the type of the bourgeois (like Monnier's "M. Prudhomme," to whom he is compared in the third line):

> Roi des Crétins, qu'avec terreur on nomme,
> Grand Coquardeau, non, tu ne mourras pas.
> Lépidoptère en habit de Prudhomme,
> Ta majesté t'affranchit du trépas,
> Car tu naquis aux premiers jours du monde,
> Avant les cieux et les terres et l'onde.

The mock nobility of these lines is created in large measure by their rhetorical flourishes: the series of apostrophes, the capitalization of *Crétins*, the interjection "non, tu ne mourras pas," the inversion, the metaphor in the third line, and the measured rhythm of the sixth. Conventionally noble terms like *trépas* and *onde* contribute to this effect, and even the technical term *lépidoptère* has an elevated ring in this linguistic milieu. The familiarity of *crétin* is all but submerged in it, too. The humor is created by all this expense of rhetoric on the insignificant subject: "Grand Coquardeau" is virtually a contradiction in terms. Such a text, exactly contemporaneous with the publications of *Les Contemplations*, is based on a caricature of precious language as "Réponse" was; but here the target is different: its subject is the bourgeois, not poetic language. Despite the difference in object and tone, however, Banville's poem indirectly offers a critique of the neoclassical style: it undermines its rhetorical and lexical conventions by sapping their usual power to confer "nobility" on a text.

Similar effects can be found in the parodies of other poems, Hugo's in particular. One section of the *Odes* is called "Les Occidentales," and it includes poems like "V . . . le baigneur" (based on "Sara la baigneuse"), describing a paunchy old doctor in his bath.[5] Banville points out that the poems of this section are "rigoureusement écrits en forme d'odes, dans lesquels l'élément bouffon est étroitement uni à l'élément lyrique" (6:331). This combination creates the tone of whimsy for which Banville is justly noted. But it is the lyric element, or at least, traditional lyrical devices themselves that are often the point of the parodies, as in the following lines from "Le Critique en mal d'enfant":

> Il invoquait les Muses, l'une
> Ou l'autre, et leur disait : "Erato, mon trésor!
> Thalie! ô Melpomène à la chaussure d'or!"
> Il disait à la Lune : "O Lune!"

By showing how the critic misuses apostrophe, classical allusions, and neoclassical diction, Banville foregrounds these devices; and their usual connotations function ironically. An especially clear instance of the dismantling of traditional figures occurs in the following lines from "L'Odéon": " . . . ce rire usité / chez les hommes qu'afflige une gibbosité." The convoluted periphrase, when translated, turns out to conceal the familiar expression "rire comme un bossu" (Fuchs, 191).

The other side of this procedure is the intrusion of "unpoetic" elements and language in descriptions of traditionally poetic subject matter like a beautiful woman, the poet's muse, or the arrival of spring. Such elements include references to food like *rôtis cuits à point, sorbets à la neige* or the refrain in "Le Flan dans l'Odéon."[6] We also find illnesses and their remedies (ulcers, chlorosis, tuberculosis, emetics, and cataplasms) and unattractive bodies, like the description of Dr. V . . . or the line "Ils pendent en lambeaux comme de vieilles gorges" (from "Académie royale de musique"). What is most improper to allude to in poetry seems to be what is closest to bodily functions, and Banville clearly takes pleasure in flouting the interdictions against such lexical fields. As he notes proudly in his preface to the *Odes*, "la borne idéale qui marque les limites du bon goût y est à chaque instant franchie" (6:5). (Even in this comic verse, however, Banville holds back from the explicitly sexual and scatalogical elements that Rimbaud will use in satirical and more serious poetry alike.) Related to the evocation of the body are the mentions of clothing and makeup, not clothing described in vague, ethereal terms, but the precise item, a corset, a detachable collar, face powder, sometimes including the object's brand name. Items of apparel often appear as the accoutrements of the people caricatured, but they are used in other contexts, too, as when the poet describes tenors "qui durent un an, comme la crinoline" ("Académie royale de musique").

The beginning of "L'Amour à Paris" shows how the introduction of the paraphernalia of everyday life can create tensions within these texts:

> Fille du grand Daumier ou du sublime Cham,
> Toi qui portes du reps et du madapolam,
> O Muse de Paris! toi par qui l'on admire
> Les peignoirs érudits qui naissent chez Palmyre.
> Toi pour qui notre siècle inventa les *corsets*
> *A la minute*, amour du puff et du succès!

Peignoirs érudits shows in condensed form the stylistic shocks created by juxtaposing elements from conflicting registers. These juxtapositions are the framework on which the poem is constructed. Inverted syntax, apostrophe, traditional epithets and metaphors, and the subject matter (an invocation to the poet's muse) tell us to read the poem in one way; but the references to clothing, to the dressmaker Palmyre, and to the two contemporary caricaturists make a traditional reading impossible. *Corsets à la minute* is incongruous in an address to the muse not only because it refers to underclothing, but also because it is the antithesis of the eternal: this kind of corset was a novelty in 1846, when the poem was written. Besides, in his note to the poem Banville points out that at the time, these corsets were considered "pernicieux": only women of questionable morals wore them (6:316-17). The language is likewise of its time: the fashionable anglisicm *puff*, meaning deception, has itself gone out of style.

This poem shows clearly how everyday elements can fix the poems in their period. So do the many allusions to the artists, actors, demimondaines, and Parisian characters of the day. These people appear not only as subjects of satirical attack, but as figures from the passing scene or just people whose names are good for a joke. Thus, the phrase "plus de collet" in "La Tristesse d'Oscar" brings forth "pas même un collet née Révoil" (as Louise Colet signed her works); and there is a rondeau to a woman called Désirée Rondeau: "son nom créait ici une nécessité absolue" ("Commentaire," 6:363). Many of the objects that came into use in the nineteenth century also find their place in these texts: broughams, rubber erasers, theater gaslights, photographs, and so on. So do many anglicisms like *steam-boat, twine, gin,* and *spleen,* used not for exotic effect, but as a reflection of fashionable speech and the anglophilia of the time. Its accent on the evanescent, on fashion, lends this verse much of its lightness of tone: it is a refusal of the realm of Poetry, the eternal. Although this attachment to its time makes many of these verses hard to follow or inconsequential today, it is also what makes them novel.

The other major component of this comic treatment of traditionally serious themes is the use of familiar language. Popular and familiar expressions like *par exemple, mamelu, marmots, pingres,* and *tartines* for an author's work appear throughout the *Odes.*[7] These terms are complemented by terminology from special registers, especially the language of journalism and theater slang. Usually, such language is used to puncture a more conventionally lyrical mood that has been established by the use of the staples of neoclassical diction. *Lyres, astres,* and *clairons* are just as abundant in these poems as more familiar language. In fact, it is usually the conjunction of the two kinds of language that creates the humor of these verses. So it is not sufficient to divide Banville's comic verse into two categories, serious subject/frivolous language and vice versa. They are often intermingled: even in the "Chant royal" to M. Coquardeau, the familiar term *crétin* was used; and the title *Odes funambulesques* itself contains the kind of contradiction in connotation that is so central to this collection. In addition, the contrasts in tone this mixing of styles establishes can carry significance beyond its humor.

II. *"Bonsoir, chère Evohé"*

Contrasts in diction appear from the first poem of the collection, "La Corde roide," on. Its second stanza includes the lines, "J'ai comme un souvenir confus / D'avoir embrassé la Chimère. / J'ai mangé du sucre candi / Dans les feuilletons du lundi: / Ma bouche en est encor amère." Such combinations of registers appear frequently in the *Odes,* often in startling collocations like *ces culs-nus d'Amours.* A look at a stanza from "La Tristesse d'Oscar" shows some of the levels at which this mixing of styles occurs. The poem mocks a successful publicist who is afraid that his resemblance to a famous actor will hurt his political career.

Il rayonne, il est mis comme un notaire en deuil.
Et cependant toujours parmi l'or de son oeil
　　　　Brille une perle lacrymale;
Il erre, les regards cloués sur les frontons,
Triste comme un bonnet, ou comme des croûtons
　　　　De pain, à l'Ecole normale![8]

Disparate fields of discourse are brought together: the Ecole normale, tympanums (as on temples or churches), a notary in mourning, gold and pearls. On the level of formality, the noble expressions and constructions, like *rayonner* and *parmi* with a singular noun, are deflated by the use of the colloquial phrase *triste comme un bonnet*. *Lacrymale* is an intrusion from the register of scientific discourse. Such elements are in tension with the verse form (adapted from Hugo's "La Douleur du Pascha," according to Banville) and the grandiloquent tone it creates. The main rhetorical figure here is the simile, but rather than elevating the style, the similes link the character with distinctly common things: a nightcap, the notary's clothing, and food—very poor food at that. They are one of the first instances of the subversion of the word *comme*, a feature that other nineteenth-century poets and, later, the Surrealists will adopt. On an intertextual level, beyond the allusion to the *Orientales*, the poem's title obviously recalls Hugo's "Tristesse d'Olympio"; and a further tension results from the contrast between the very different subjects of the two poems. Banville has marshalled quite a panoply of devices and a wide range of registers and allusions to create the comic effect of these lines.

Another level of comedy arises through the device Banville sees as the major source of his humor, rhyme, enriched in these poems by the use of unconventional vocabulary. In his *Petit Traité de versification française*, Banville calls attention to the increased possibilities for rich and varied rhyme provided by an expanded poetic lexicon, and he makes full use of them throughout the *Odes*. Foreign words, technical terms, and proper names often have unusual sounds whose humorous potential is realized when they appear at the end of lines like: "Bugeaud veut prendre Abd-el-Kader:/A ce plan le public adhère." Thus, we get rhyming words like *dodécahèdres, topinambou*, and *madopolam/Cham*, as well as internal rhymes like "Shakespere expire." When used in short verses, rhymes come up more frequently, and in forms like the rondeau and the triolet they are repeated several times, offering a frequency in sound-repetition that can be funny in itself. The rondeau to Arsène Houssaye does not even mention his name but begins "Où sait-on" and rhymes "en veste de Lami-Housset" with "Plus d'une encor fait voir au blond Arsène/Où c'est." Such effects are obviously heightened by mixing allusions to disparate sources and stylistic levels:

> Le beau Tassin, en matassin,
> N'est pas de ceux dont on se fiche.
>
> . . . .
>
> On eut pris pour un faon, Tassin
> Quant il figurait dans *La Biche*

Using unconventional expressions like the popular *on se fiche* as rhyming words calls attention to them. Banville's rhymes often bring together elements from very disparate registers, fields, and tenors, like the familiar term *godiches* rhyming with *colonnes-affiches* or *Ajax* with *clairon de Saxe*. In the following lines from "Eveil,"

> Lesbienne rêveuse, éprise de Phyllis,
> Tu n'as pas, il est vrai, célébré S......,

the rhyme allows Banville a word he hesitates to print. But leaving it blank and rhyming it with a Greek name make it all the more striking.

These examples show the way Banville mixes classical and contemporary elements in his blending of linguistic registers. As we have seen, Hugo will put this device to good, but very different use in his *Chansons*. Thus, Banville describes a theater "Où passent à la fois Cléopâtre et Lola." In one of the rondeaux, "Junon, Pallas, Vénus au bel orteil,/Même Betti, le cèdent à madame/Keller." Colloquial language plays an important part in this deflation of the traditionally noble classical allusion, as in "L'Amour à Paris": "Ah! nous avons vraiment les femmes les plus drôles/De Paris! Périclès vit chez nous en exil,/Et nous nous amusons beaucoup. Quelle heure est-il?" In Banville the results are obviously very funny. They can also create a tone of fantasy, as in the description of Paris in "La Ville enchantée":

> Il est de par le monde une cité bizarre,
> Où Plutus en gants blancs, drapé dans son manteau,
> Offre une cigarette à son ami Lazare,
> Et l'emmène souper dans un parc de Wateau.

Beyond their comedy such descents in style often carry a more serious message: one of the major themes of this collection is the decline of contemporary France. This decline is seen in the lack of appreciation of the arts by an uncomprehending public, in the arts themselves, and in the period in general, dominated by the crass, unappreciative bourgeois.[9] As Banville writes in the first satire of "Evohé," "Eveil": "Vois, le siècle est superbe et s'offre au satirique." It is often shifts in diction that mark the difference between an ideal past and present mediocrity. In "Académie royale de musique," the poet salutes the Opéra in a long passage of neoclassical verse, ending in the lines: "O temple! clair séjour de la danse et du luth!/Parnasse! palais d'or! grand Opéra, salut!" The next lines destroy the illusion of the Opera's grandeur, both in what they describe and in their prose rhythm: "Le cocher s'est trompé. Nous sommes au Gymnase./Un peuple de bourgeois, nez rouge et tête rase,/Etale des habits de Quimper-Corentin." The passage that follows incorporates allusions to contemporary life like the men's sideburns and the newspaper a woman is reading, pejorative similies ("Un notaire ventru saute comme un pantin"; "sa gorge a l'air d'une maison"), and familiar expressions like ce sujet for the notary's wife, tendrons for the young girls an old banker pursues, and rats for the dancers at the opera. Diction, then, is used to reflect value. What it describes and inscribes is in fact a change in values: the triumph of the bourgeois (like those described in this poem) leads to the fall of poetry. Thus, in this age "L'artiste ne peut guère, avec son luth divin,/Réaliser assez de rentes" ("A un ami"): the register of finance has come to replace that of high art in Banville's verse as well as in life. This point is made especially clearly in "La Corde roide": "Quittons nos lyres, Erato!/On n'entend plus que le râteau/De la roulette et de la banque." In "Eveil," Banville opposes his poetry, in the person of his muse,

to the productions of other poets, including two writers of semi-
obscene verse:

> Tu n'as . . .
>
> . . . . . .
>
> Ni fait de Giraudeau ton souteneur en titre;
> Ni dans des vers gazés, qui font rougir un pitre,
> Fait éclore, en prenant la flûte et le tambour,
> Un édit paternel pour les filles d'amour.

Anticipating Baudelaire these lines bemoan the prostitution
of art.

In lines like these, Banville extends his sense of decline to
the subject of love. He goes on:

> Lorsque Antoine est mangé, Cléopâtre vers Londre
> Vole comme un oiseau, sur l'aile du steamer,
> Et, de Waterloo-Road affrontant la rumeur,
> Puise à ces fonds secrets que, pour ses amourettes,
> La perfide Albion avance à nos lorettes. (1859 edition)

Here, the classical allusions, *Albion* for England, and the convoluted periphrase of the last lines are countered by the contemporary steamer and the familiar expressions *lorette* and
"Antoine est *mangé*" (*Antoine est à sec* in the 1873 version).
The fifth satire, "L'Amour à Paris," is a longer development of
the same theme. In the passage from this poem quoted above,
the contemporary Parisian muse is a very superficial one, with
her corsets and stylish peignoirs. She has sold out: the muse
and love have become what Parisian style dictates through its
caricaturists and its fashion houses. In a theme Baudelaire de-
velops too, the modern world is presented as one defined by its
products. Ideal poetry and the language of ideal poetry, we are
led to conclude, cannot survive in such circumstances.

III. *"De son vil échafaud"*

When Banville uses traditionally elevated diction and its opposite in this way, he is not propounding the kind of leveling
in style Hugo proposes in "Réponse" and practices in the *Chansons*. On the contrary, even as Banville breaks down traditional distinctions, he reinforces what they stand for. Baude-

laire points out that the recurring term (what Guiraud would call a *mot-thème*) in Banville's verse is *lyre*. For Baudelaire, Banville is the absolutely lyrical poet. Looking at Banville's diction confirms both the importance of this term and what it implies. The word *lyre* is part of the neoclassical poetic lexicon: if the poet and his muse have to lay down their lyres, or their *lyres*, it means the end of poetry.

This emphasis on lyricism is related to Banville's opposition to realism. This is one of the recurring themes in the *Odes*, despite the many references to contemporary life they contain. In "Réalisme" the poet exclaims "Regardez ce que font ces imbéciles-là!" In "Bonjour Monsieur Courbet!" (based, of course, on Courbet's painting with the same name), the poet finds that his beloved countryside has been ravaged: the trees are twisted, the colors are ugly. He asks Cybèle what has happened, and she explains that Courbet has passed through. Sure enough, he hears the leaves and grasses calling " 'Bonjour, Monsieur Courbet le maître peintre!/Monsieur Courbet, salut! Bonjour, Monsieur Courbet!' " Here again, the descent from lyricism is marked by a descent in poetic language, in expressions like those just quoted, the phrase *les astres rabougris*, and the descriptions of the destroyed landscape.

Banville, then, seems very much tied to the conventional divisions into genres and the diction corresponding to them. But there are some texts that gesture towards new possibilities, among them the last piece in the *Odes*, "Le Saut du tremplin." This poem has become one of Banville's most famous both because it departs from the satirical tone of the rest of the collection (and so can be taken more seriously) and because it is one of the first instances of a conceit that was to have a long posterity, the image of the poet as clown.[10] The poem presents an acrobatic clown who is able to jump higher than all the others. But he wants to go still higher, and he asks his springboard to push him up to where he can no longer see the vile crowd below him, "Jusqu'à ces sommets où, sans règles,/Embrouillant les cheveux vermeils/Des planètes et des soleils,/Se croisent la foudre et les aigles." In the last lines of the poem and the collection, he jumps so high "qu'il creva le plafond de toiles/Au son du cor et du tambour,/Et, le coeur dévoré d'amour,/Alla rouler dans les étoiles."

Clearly, the central contrast here is again that between the real and the ideal worlds. One of the groups of people the clown wants to escape are "des réalistes en feu"; and he is obviously himself the figure of the misunderstood romantic poet. When he speaks to his springboard, "Cet émule de la Saqui / Parl[e] bas en langue inconnue," and it will be up to posterity to rediscover him, "sa plaie au flanc." Banville says this poem expresses "l'attrait du gouffre d'en haut" (6:385), and it is, not surprisingly, through the metaphor of height and depth that he articulates his vision.

The language he uses parallels this opposition: "low" language tends to be used for "low" subjects, whereas elevated language expresses what is literally and figuratively elevated. Some of the devices used in the more satirical pieces, like rhymes with unusual words and references to contemporary figures still appear in this text: *Madagascar* rhymes with *car*, *qui* with *Saqui* (Madame Saqui was a famous acrobat). The phrases *en vérité* and *selon tous les principes* appear when the clown is described early in the poem, and the other acrobats call him " 'ce diable-là'." But by and large, a more conventional diction is used. Such language translates the poet-clown's aspirations and his search for the ideal world: "Jusqu'à ces éthers pleins de bruit / Où mêlant dans l'affreuse nuit / Leurs haleines exténuées, / Les autans ivres de courroux / Dorment, échevelés et fous, / Sur les seins pâles des nuées."[11] When the clown turns his attention to the bourgeois in his audience, there is a corresponding drop in the poem's stylistic level:

> Frêle machine aux reins puissants,
> Fais-moi bondir, moi qui me sens
> Plus agile que les panthères,
> Si haut que je ne puisse voir
> Avec leur cruel habit noir
> Ces épiciers et ces notaires!

Conventionally poetic devices in these lines include the periphrase denoting the springboard (part of an extended apostrophe covering six stanzas), the inversion of nouns and adjectives, and "poetic" epithets like *agile*. Even the fifth line is ennobled by its syntax. When *Epiciers* and *notaires* appear in the last line, with the connotations these professions have, these terms are out of place in their linguistic surroundings. High language, then, equals high subjects and vice versa.

On the other hand, there are some indications of a breaking-down of this structure. The subject of the poem, an acrobatic clown, is hardly a noble one, and the first line of the text ("Clown admirable, en vérité") is a kind of stylistic paradox. A springboard is an unlikely subject to be addressed in an apostrophe, too; and its response to his plea is not the discourse of a noble shade, but its propelling him up to the sky. As the clown addresses his springboard, the nobility of his language transmits his growing elation until he cries out " 'Plus haut! plus loin! de l'air! du bleu!/Des ailes! des ailes! des ailes!' " But the last stanza includes a surprising feature, a repetition that gives it a colloquial tone, as though the poet were addressing a child: "Enfin, de son vil échafaud,/Le clown sauta si haut, si haut." In these lines the word *haut* itself is brought down; spoken language is adequate to express the poet-clown's ultimate apotheosis.

The image of the clown himself points the way to an aesthetic no longer tied to genre distinctions: his face may be "barbouillé de blanc," but his soul is that of a poet. He is the figure of a new sensibility that can find the lyrical in what is usually considered base. It is thus in a poem like this one rather than in those where he criticizes his society overtly that Banville foreshadows the work of the later Hugo, Baudelaire, Verlaine, Rimbaud, and Mallarmé. In most of his satirical work, Banville reinforces the distinctions between acceptable and unacceptable language even as he accomplishes an expansion of the poetic lexicon: he needs these distinctions to create his mock heroic style. True, in doing so, he foregrounds neoclassical diction and rhetoric and thereby demystifies them and exposes their arbitrariness. But the shocks in diction are there to create laughter; through their comic effect they may contribute to a text's social or artistic criticism, but they do not figure it. Only when the familiar discourse works with, not against, the lyrical elements is there the glimpse of a new level of style. In his preface to the *Odes'* sequel, *Les Occidentales*, Banville professes himself "content d'avoir fait pressentir le parti immense que la langue française pourrait tirer de l'élément bouffon lié à l'élément lyrique" (7:3). It is in poems like

"Le Saut du tremplin," with their whimsical, fantastic texture, that he is able to realize the new kind of lyricism such linkings can create.

We have seen some of the same devices in Banville as in Hugo. Both use striking contrasts in diction, a caricature of precious style, and names of contemporary figures in incongruous linguistic settings. But in Banville there is no discernable poetic program of mixing styles or introducing everyday elements into serious verse. Nor do we find Hugo's biting satire and political criticism. We will see much of the same vocabulary in Baudelaire as in Banville, references to contemporary life and medical terms as well as familiar language. We will also find the contrasting structure of poeticization of the banal and deflation of conventional rhetoric and diction. But again there is no place in Banville's sunny, lighthearted world for what we will find in Baudelaire. As Baudelaire writes, "dans ses oeuvres, vous n'entendrez pas les dissonances, les discordances des musiques du sabbat, non plus que les glapissements de l'ironie, cette vengeance du vaincu" (2:168). Banville's work shows us how the same structures, when used in comedy, carry different messages. The polemical power and the dark vision these shifts in diction can connote are, in his work, defused by laughter.

FOUR

Baudelaire:
De Quelle Boue?

"J'ai pétri de la boue et j'en ai fait de l'or," a line from one of his unfinished poems, is a succinct statement of Baudelaire's poetic method. A variation on it, "Tu m'as donné ta boue et j'en ai fait de l'or," was to have been the last line of the "Projet d'épilogue" for the second edition of the *Fleurs du mal.* The matter on which Baudelaire works his verbal alchemy is not only the subject matter of his verse, evil, say, or contemporary Paris (the epilogue is addressed to Paris), but also the verbal matter from which he fashioned his works. His vocabulary includes, along with the diction he inherited from neoclassical and baroque verse, the language of the streets he was among the first to depict. The ways such language is transformed into poetry or rather, the way such language transforms poetry will be the subject of this chapter. Among the issues raised by Baudelaire's poetry are the creation of a self-contradictory, oxymoronic style, the question of the "tragic seriousness" with which he treats the everyday, the charges of "prosaism" that have been leveled at his work, and the problem of "realism," especially in relation to the *Tableaux parisiens.*

The position of Baudelaire in the opening up of poetic language in the nineteenth century has elicited almost contradictory commentaries. Valéry praises his poetry's pure melodic tone "qui la distingu[e] de toute prose" (611), whereas, Thibaudet criticizes his "défaillances de langue" (*Intérieurs*, 58). His restricted vocabulary is often contrasted with Hugo's, yet Baudelaire himself admired the range of the latter's language: "J'ignore dans quel monde Victor Hugo a mangé préalablement le dictionnaire de la langue qu'il était appelé à parler; mais je vois que le lexique français, en sortant de sa bouche, est devenu un monde, un univers coloré, mélodieux et mouvant" ("Réflexions sur quelques-uns de mes contemporains," 2:133). It was the extension of poetic vocabulary that Gautier praised in Baudelaire's own style:

> reculant toujours les bornes de la langue, empruntant à tous les vocabulaires techniques, prenant des couleurs à toutes les palettes, des notes à tous les claviers. . . . On pense bien que les quatorze cents mots du dialecte racinien ne suffisent pas à l'auteur qui s'est donné la rude tâche de rendre les idées et les choses modernes dans leur infinie complexité et leur multiple coloration (17-18).[1]

Underlying criticisms of Baudelaire's "défaillances de style" is often an implied correspondence between vulgar language and incorrect grammar, both in turn related to Baudelaire's immoral life. Degradation in morals is seen as leading to degradation in language, as when Trahard explains the weakness of Baudelaire's style by his physical and moral state:

> miné dans son corps et hanté par la peur d'une fin lamentable, il mène de surcroît une vie désordonnée qui l'épuise . . . érotisme, luxure, drogue, stupéfiants, opium . . . comment ne serait-il pas détraqué? . . . Lui manque également l'esprit d'ordre indispensable au poète. (133-34)

Thus, the problem of the relation between the poem and reality is reduced to a simple cause/effect relation between the poet's life and his work. We shall see that this same parallelism is drawn in the cases of both Verlaine and Rimbaud. But even if such a correlation could be proved, it does not explain how such diction functions in his work. We will have to look in more detail at the ways in which Baudelaire transforms the reality and the language of everyday life into the "gold" of his poetry.

I. Oxymoronic Style: From Mud to Gold

In "Fusées" Baudelaire writes: "le mélange du grotesque et du tragique est agréable à l'esprit comme les discordances aux oreilles blasées" (*O.C.*, 1:661). One of the most obvious and

most often remarked-on aspects of his style is his alliance of
disparate elements, his tendency to oxymoron. It can be seen
most clearly in titles like "Horreur sympathique," "Madrigal
triste," in joinings like "aimable pestilence," and in the basic
structuring of poems like "Réversibilité" and "L'Héautonti-
morouménos." The oxymoron has as its nature the joining of
two contradictory elements, but theorists often assert that
they are only seemingly separate. The *Princeton Encyclopedia
of Poetry and Poetics* points out that this figure "reveals a
compulsion to fuse all experience into a unity" and notes its
frequency in religious poetry (596). Cellier links its use in
Baudelaire to the passage from "un univers tragique à un paradis, de la dualité à l'unité," and sees a mythical transcendance (related to the "correspondances") in the oxymoron's
conciliation of opposites (5, 7-9).[2] Fontanier discusses the figure under the heading of "paradoxisme," and he, too, emphasizes its conciliating power. But whereas Preminger and Cellier point out its mystical aspects, Fontanier emphasizes its
underlying rationality: though it could not be taken literally
"sans absurdité," "ce n'est pourtant pas sans un peu de réflexi-
on que l'on peut bien saisir et fixer ce qu'il donne réellement à
entendre" (137). He goes on to analyze a series of examples of
the figure, showing how they can be understood despite their
apparent logical inconsistency: "Faites bien attention aux cir-
constances, et déterminez bien le sens des deux mots, vous ver-
rez que c'est très-possible" (138). His explanations all seek to
bring within the realm of the logical, the reason-able, these
seeming threats to rationality. He is very much aware of their
danger, however: the use of these expressions requires "la jus-
tesse des idées qui les rapprochent"; otherwise we would be
left with "pur galimatias . . . un bizarre et monstrueux ac-
couplement de mots discordans et vides de sens" (140). The
strength of his language reveals his fear that language will go
awry, out of control, that the animal will emerge (*accouple-
ment*), destroying reason by leading to the loss of meaning altogether. This figure is a monster, an assemblage of disparate
parts engendered by an unnatural union.

This attraction to/fear of the irrational appears in Baudelaire's repeated use of the figure. The urge towards rationality
is always thwarted by the oxymoron, which must resist the

transcendence of its contradictions in order to exist as figure. "Paradoxisme" can be seen not only in the oxymorons in Baudelaire's verse, but in an "alliance de mots" from disparate registers as well. There is a kind of stylistic paradox in lines like "Ma pauvre muse, hélas! qu'as-tu donc ce matin?" ("La Muse malade") or " 'Amour . . . Gloire . . . Bonheur!' Enfer! c'est un écueil!" ("Le Voyage"). Baudelaire makes full use of the stylistic potential of such juxtapositions.

In "Tu mettrais l'univers entier dans ta ruelle," for example, a series of contrasts on various levels culminates in the interlocking oxymorons of the famous last line:

"O fangeuse grandeur! sublime ignominie!"

The first line of the poem expresses a paradox: the entire universe is put in the woman's "ruelle"; then the "machine . . . en cruautés féconde" is characterized as a "*salutaire* instrument"; whereas the concept underlying the whole poem is the paradox of the impure, cruel, blind animal who is used to "pétrir un génie." In such a poem it is not surprising to find that traditional rhetorical devices (apostrophe, hyperbole, personification of nature), the euphemism of *ruelle*, inverted syntax, and archaisms like *appas* should be countered by the expression "Comment n'as-tu pas honte?" and the stylistically disparate line:

Tes yeux, illuminés ainsi que des boutiques.

Thus, paradoxes in diction double the poem's underlying oxymoronic structure.

The far-reaching implications of such language can be found in "Au lecteur." As the first poem of *Les Fleurs du mal*, it gives the reader an idea of what to expect in Baudelaire's language as well as in his thematics. Not only does it show the range of his vocabulary, (including terms from such diverse registers as the archaism "*travaillent* nos corps," the zoological term *helminthes*, the exotic word *houka*, and the popular or vulgar *ribote*), but also, it shows how elements from different registers are juxtaposed. Others have examined the poem in detail and pointed out some of the stylistic effects created by such juxtapositions; I would like to concentrate on the ways diction helps to create the dissonances in Baudelaire's style that I have called oxymoronic.[3] First, the rhetorical figure itself is the basic trope underlying the poem: not only the obvious "aimables remords" and "monstre délicat," but also the *"plaisants dessins"* of rape, poison, etc., the descent *"sans horreur* à travers des ténèbres *qui puent,"* and the line "dans un bâillement avalerait le monde" are instances of "paradoxisme." These are paralleled by stylistic discordances. The line that sums up the central idea of the attractiveness of evil,

> Aux objects répugnants nous trouvons des appas;

combines the two: the paradox created by the joining of *répugnants* and *appas* is overlaid with the incongruity of the noble term *appas* in such a context.

There is a further incongruity in the way this philosophical poem contains not one but many references to food, a semantic field marked as distinctly unpoetic. *Alimenter*, *nourrir*, and *une vieille orange* are obvious examples, but *grassement* carries similar connotations, and helminthes are intestinal worms. Thus, the word *riboter*, conflicting stylistically with the rhetorical second half of the line:

> Dans nos cerveaux ribote un peuple de Démons,

is doubly inacceptable and doubly appropriate here as both a popular word and one that refers to an excess of eating and drinking.

Given its "unnatural" unions of terms and stylistic levels, we should not be surprised to find monsters in this poem. The first to appear are the "peuple de Démons." Though likened to intestinal worms, they are to be found in our brains, in a rhetorical figure that is monstrous in a different way from oxymoron, catachresis.[4] Another catachresis, or forced (mixed) metaphor, occurs in the next lines:

> Et, quand nous respirons, la Mort dans nos poumons
> Descend, fleuve invisible, avec de sourdes plaintes.

Here Death is both a river and a creature emitting muffled (literally, "deaf") cries: a hypallage within a catachresis. Monsters seem to beget monstrous language as well as vice versa. The list of beasts of prey in the eighth stanza is followed by a list of their attributes ("glapissants, hurlants," etc.), here assigned to "monstres" in general.

This series of accumulations culminates in the image of *Ennui*, who could swallow the world in a yawn—again an oxymoron and again an allusion to eating. The final phrase describing it, "monstre délicat," repeats this structure, ending the text (before the famous last line) in both another oxymoron and yet another reference to eating in *délicat* (in the sense of "fastidious" or "finicky"). This gradated series ends in the address to the final monster, the reader himself, a two-faced creature whose contradictory spiritual attributes have been the subject of the poem. In the final line, the like and the unlike—the poet and, however unwittingly, the reader—are linked in the words "—mon semblable—mon frère." Chantavoine, a turn-of-the century reader, found this line, "agressif et peu engageant" (30). In one sense, however, it is as engaging as it is possible to be: the poem's language has effectuated the linkings that make it impossible to escape its conclusion. It would be a mistake, however, to take this text's "oxymoronic" style as a means to a higher transcendance or to try to show how the two poles of poetic language cancel each other out. Their poetic effect depends on the tension between them and the stylistic "monsters" they create. The resultant discordance, far from being a weakness, gives the poem its power.

It is in a different way that "Le Monstre," one of Baudelaire's last poems, makes use of discordance in diction. Not surprisingly, given its title, it contains his most concentrated use of "low" expressions. He recognized both its shock value and its disparities in style in a letter to Mendès regarding its possible publication in the *Parnasse contemporain*: "Je vous préviens que la pièce intitulée *Le Monstre*, si toutefois vous osez l'imprimer, a maintenant quinze ou seize couplets, avec un certain air archaïque qui en sauve un peu la crudité."[5] As the critical editions point out, in this poem Baudelaire is imitating the "poèmes satyriques" of the baroque period, works that parodied and ridiculed the lyrical style of love poetry. He could be describing their method and his when he writes in a review of Cladel's *Les Martyrs ridicules*: "La disproportion du ton avec le sujet, disproportion qui n'est sensible que pour le sage désintéressé, est un moyen de comique dont la puissance saute à l'oeil . . . surtout dans les matières concernant l'Amour, véritable magasin de comique peu exploité" (*O.C.*, 2:185). Comic devices begin in this poem with its subtitle, "Le Paranymphe d'une nymphe macabre," with its juxtaposition of *nymphe* and *macabre* and the play on words: a *paranymphe* was a speech praising theological and doctoral candidates at the end of their examinations. Other puns include "Je suis diablement affligé" (line 66), and the lines:

> Je préfère tes clavicules
> A celles du roi Salomon,

alluding to a book of magic attributed to Solomon. An editor's note in *Les Epaves* calls attention to this last one: "Voilà un calembour *salé!* Nous ne *cabalerons* pas contre."

The basic comic structure, typical of the genre, is the deflation of the traditional devices of love poetry. Parts of the woman's body, usually praised extravagantly, are held up to ridicule here with a virulence that prepares the way for Rimbaud's "Vénus anadyomène" and "Mes petites amoureuses." Thus, her "front de guerrière . . . ne pense et rougit que peu"; her eyes, far from lighting up his life, "semblent de la boue"; her skin is "brûlante et sans douceur, / Comme celle des vieux gendarmes." A related device is the juxtaposition of caressing tones and insults, as in: "Tu n'es plus fraîche, ma très chère" or "ce lustre abondant / Des choses qui sont très usées."

The introduction of terminology related to food adds another incongruous element to the text: a kind of sign of the un– or, rather antipoetic, it serves to further disparage the usually elevated subject. "Bouilloner," perfectly acceptable in its figurative sense, becomes literalized via the expression "bonne chère" and leads to the characterization of the woman as an old pot in the lines:

> Le jeu, l'amour, la bonne chère,
> Bouillonnent en toi, vieux chaudron!

Both *piments* and *salières* have culinary senses; and the woman's collarbones (not the part of the body love poetry usually celebrates) are contrasted with the melons and pumpkins other lovers might favor. Furthermore, in a letter to Malassis asking for information about the "giraumont" Baudelaire makes it clear that such allusions were to be taken as signifying the grotesque: he asks whether the term (referring to a kind of pumpkin) could be applicable to "toutes les tumeurs comme seins, fesses, et généralement à l'obésité" (23 janvier 1866, *Correspondance, 2:577*. So when he likens the woman to a thing (and worn-out things at that) the poet is merely making explicit the process of dehumanization the poem as a whole operates.

But if this text represented nothing more than a crude form of humor it would not be very interesting, and it would not explain its title. What is monstrous in this poem is the combination of attraction and repulsion it expresses. The line, "Des choses qui sont très usées," is followed by "Mais qui séduisent cependant." Expressions like *certes, mais, cependant, pourtant*, and *malgré*, are used throughout the poem to articulate this paradox. It is summed up in line 39, where the parallelism in structure makes the contrast all the more obvious: her lips are bitter (the opposite of the usual "sweet as wine"), yet they are an Eden "Qui nous attire et qui nous choque."

The poem's frequent disparities in diction serve to convey this ambivalence. Archaisms like *narguer* and the language of love poetry are opposed by familiar words like *tendron* and *caravanes* (in the sense of "une vie aventureuse et dissipée" [Littré]) and the popular expressions *salières* (for the hollows behind a thin person's collarbones) and *dèche* ("poverty"). Baudelaire's diction falls to its lowest level in the vulgar term *cas* and the word *cancan*, which Littré classifies as "très-familier et même de mauvais ton." Such terms underline the oxymoronic structure of the poem. In lines like:

> Ta carcasse a des agréments
> Et des grâces particulières;

it is the language-level of the term *carcasse* used to refer to a woman's body that creates the paradox. "Ma vieille infante" inverts this procedure by deflating the elevated term, and this time it is an oxymoron besides.

As in "Au lecteur," linguistic paradoxes in "Le Monstre" point up thematic ones; and again the poem ends in an oxymoron and one that refers to a monster: the woman he loves is a "monstre parfait." It is followed by yet another *paradoxisme*, one englobing the rest of the poem:

Vraiment oui! vieux monstre, je t'aime!

In this last stanza, the poet underlines one paradox with another while denying it is a paradox: he says he is seeking "la crème" of evil (another alimentary reference as well as another oxymoron) and therefore that he is "très logique" in loving the monster. And indeed, in "Le Monstre" there is a kind of logic, though it is not clear whether for Baudelaire as a man repulsion led to attraction or vice versa. As a poet he was able to raise the attraction for the ugly to a new kind of beauty. The woman's eyes "semblent de la boue": from this mud he is able to fashion his poem, breaking down the distinction between the vulgar and the noble and accomplishing the program he sets forth in "Le Peintre de la vie moderne." In this essay the prostitutes he proposes as models for the artist are "exemples d'une fatuité innocente et monstrueuse" (monstrous because of the mixture we have been studying). "Parfois elles trouvent, sans les chercher, des poses d'une audace et d'une noblesse qui enchanteraient le statuaire le plus délicat, si le statuaire moderne avait le courage et l'esprit de ramasser la noblesse partout, même dans la fange" (*O.C.*, 2:721). What Baudelaire says we will find in Guys' drawings of prostitutes is what can be found in his own poetry: "rien que l'art pur, c'est-à-dire la beauté particulière du mal, le beau dans l'horrible" (722).

II. "Aesthetic Dignity": From Gold to Mud

In an important and influential article, "The Aesthetic Dignity of *Les Fleurs du mal*," Auerbach studies this mixture of styles, demonstrating how Baudelaire created a new poetic style, "a mixture of the base and contemptible with the sublime, a symbolic use of realistic horror."[6] Though his object is to show how Baudelaire treated traditional subjects in new ways, what his essay reveals is how difficult it is to separate treatment from subject matter. His point of departure is a discussion of the fourth "Spleen" poem ("Quand le ciel bas et lourd"). He begins by showing how, through the alexandrine line, allegorical figures, and "grave rhythm," Baudelaire establishes the dignified style appropriate to his subject, "deep despair," and then how he introduces "things that seem hardly compatible with the dignity of the sublime": the sky compared to a pot lid, the trappings of horror stories, the medical term *cerveaux*, and the images in the last stanza. But as Auerbach proceeds in his analysis of the poem, his subject subtly changes. It turns out that rather than treating a lofty subject in trivial terms, Baudelaire has done the reverse: "He was the first to treat matters as sublime which seemed by nature unsuited to such treatment" (154). The subject of the poem, which had been "deep despair" (worthy of the poem's "lofty tone"), is now an untraditional subject, "gray misery." The stylistic contradiction has shifted to that between this "lofty tone" and the lowness of both the subject matter and "many details" (153).

When we look at the elements that, according to Auerbach, constitute both this tone and its other pole, we find that they combine without distinguishing them many different aspects of discourse, from rhythm to rhetoric to diction. Furthermore, when he goes on to treat Baudelaire's love poetry, the "harsh and painful disharmony" he finds is at the subject level only: he is referring to the contradiction between the simultaneous hatred and attraction the poet expresses. Questions arise, too, with respect to his comments on the poem's diction: he makes too much perhaps of the use of *cerveaux* and *hurler*, both of which had a long tradition of figurative use. On the other hand, though he finds the image of the bells compared to "des esprits . . . qui se mettent à geindre opiniâtrement" as contributing to an "absurd hubbub" (152), he does not note the fact that *geindre* was a familiar term, the only word in the poem that would be inacceptable because of its informality in tenor alone.

What Auerbach's essay reveals is how these levels, which I have been trying to distinguish, tend to influence each other, how they begin to shade into each other. Their interrelationship can be seen in the second "Spleen" poem ("J'ai plus de souvenirs"), which I will look at more closely and also in another aspect of Baudelaire's poetry that Auerbach calls to our attention, the accent on the physical. Auerbach points out this aspect of Baudelaire's work when he studies the carnal nature of his love poetry, but the physical—and even the medical—are important elements in Baudelaire's verse as a whole. "Une charogne" will provide a starting point for the examination of such discourse.

The second "Spleen" is a poem that exhibits a kind of heterogeneity at many levels, and an examination of these levels shows how they are interrelated. First, on the level that particularly concerns us here, the lexicon of the poem draws on many different vocabularies, including the commercial terms *bilans* and *quittances*, the familiar word *fouillis*, the mythological sphinx, the allusion to Boucher, and the exotic *Saharah* (spelled with an extra "h"). On a syntactic level, there is a remarkable shifting of pronouns from *je* to *tu* via an *il* implied by the copula joining the *je* with the cemetery and the boudoir.[7] On the level of the signified, there is a series of collections of heteroclite objects: the secretary with its bills, verses, etc.; the pyramid, itself likened to a *fosse commune*, where corpses are thrown in pell-mell; the bedroom with its hodgepodge of objects.[8]

None of these things seems to have more importance than any of the others. Indeed, a kind of equivalence is established: love letters and bills are interchangeable. The fourth line makes the connection explicit:

> Avec de lourds cheveux roulés dans des quittances.

Not only does this verse imply a mercenary relation between the lovers, but it also makes it seem impossible to distinguish between the hair and the receipts. That all these objects should be in the plural is another way of making them lose their particularity. Everything in this world seems to be equivalent to everything else. The phrase *à tiroirs* contains a similar implication in the sense of *tiroir* as an intercalated tale in a novel: such digressions (and often digressions within digressions—containers within containers) are joined by only the thinnest of links to the main story. Each of the objects in the poem could tell a story, but their stories—the stories of the poet's life—are unrelated; there is no logical thread linking them.

The text as a whole is structured as a series of similes and metaphors, likewise lacking logical connections between them. The poet's brain is first a secretary, then a pyramid, then a cemetery, then a bedroom, and so on. Indeed, it must be so, because spleen, as presented in this poem, is just this loss of proportion, a loss of the capacity to distinguish that leads to "morne incuriosité." Hence the play on *plus* and *moins* and the echo between the first, isolated line:

J'ai plus de souvenirs que si j'avais mille ans

and lines 17-18:

L'ennui, fruit de la morne incuriosité,
Prend les proportions de l'immortalité.

Not only are the poem's images seemingly perfectly contingent, but the similes themselves show another kind of interchangeability, as in the line:

Où comme des remords se traînent de longs vers

Adam among others has pointed out the oddity of the use of "comme des remords" rather than "comme des vers"; both the meaning of *comme* and the normal functioning of similes are put into question.

In this context, then, *fouillis* is important at several levels: because it means a jumble of unrelated things and because its status as a familiar term doubles this meaning. But this plurivalence indicates another dimension to the poem: an interrelatedness both on each of these levels and between them that counteracts the arbitrariness so important to its theme and its structure. There are links between the apparently unrelated images, including the container/contained structure of the images, the associations with death and dissolution, and the play on the word *souvenir* in the first line that generates the first section of the poem. The image of the pyramid is a good example of the ways each element can be tied to others:

C'est une pyramide, un immense caveau,
Qui contient plus de morts que la fosse commune.

The pyramid is one in a series of containers in the poem, and of course what a pyramid contains is both a corpse and a collection of objects that had surrounded the person in life. Furthermore, the pyramid as a shape evokes the idea of things piled up, accumulated, and thus it is related to both the accumulations of objects and the image of the snow piling up. Moreover, the term prepares us for the images of the Sahara and the sphinx that will appear later in the poem. One could go on to every one of the other words in the lines just quoted and make similar connections, but the point should already be clear: not only do elements in the text reinforce and complement each other, but it seems possible to recuperate them in the poem's overall structure.[9] This is the point of Jauss's "second reading" (161-70) in his masterly commentary on this poem, the phase he calls "interpretation." His goal is always to bring its disparate elements together to form a coherent whole, "the harmony of a coherence of meaning" (*Toward an Aesthetic*, 161). Although I would agree that the reader of poetry does follow a trajectory like the one he outlines in her deciphering of a text, I think it is important that *this* poem contains elements that work against such incorporation.

Auerbach had tried to show in the fourth "Spleen" "the contradiction between the lofty tone and the indignity both of its subject as a whole and of many details" (153). But our analysis of the second "Spleen" shows that it is not always easy to tell what is the whole and what is a detail. There are certainly incongruities in the poem, incongruities of diction among them. But incongruity itself is the subject matter here. At the same time, the sense of an incapacity to discriminate that pervades the poem acts as a counter to the reader's unifying tendencies: the series of images, however closely linked, could in principle continue spinning off indefinitely. Indeed, in a sense they do continue—in the three other poems also entitled "Spleen," in the section "Spleen et idéal," in the elastic collection *Les Fleurs du mal*. This metonymic confusion between the container and the contained repeats at a macrotextual level the structures of this poem and defeats our attempts to effectuate a metaphoric linking of all its parts. Its intricate orderings—as in the lines on the pyramid quoted above—get out of hand through the very multiplicity of their linkings and their resonances, miming the lack of order that (at one level) is the poem's structure as well as its theme.

Another text that points up the difficulty of distinguishing part from whole is "Une charogne." Its stylistic incongruities are perhaps the most obvious of all those in Baudelaire's work, and they have elicited a good deal of commentary. The poem was considered shocking by his contemporaries, and time has not dulled the effect of its startling juxtapositions. Here is the tenth stanza:

> —Et pourtant vous serez semblable à cette ordure,
> A cette horrible infection,
> Etoile de mes yeux, soleil de ma nature,
> Vous, mon ange et ma passion!

But when we speak of juxtapositions, are we speaking of the poem's language or the relation between the signifier and the signified? There seem to be at least three kinds of clashes in style. One is on the level of diction alone. In the stanza quoted above, *infection* is incongruous as a medical term, in contrast to the conventionally lyrical—exaggeratedly so—language of the poet's address to his beloved. But it is also incongruous because of its semantic field: an infection is not what one expects in the context of passion. *Ordure* functions in the same way without being a technical term. There is yet another kind of discordance, of which a good example occurs in the sixth stanza:

> Tout cela descendait, montait comme une vague,
> Ou s'élançait en pétillant;
> On eût dit que le corps, enflé d'un souffle vague,
> Vivait en se multipliant.

If one did not know that "tout cela" referred to the putrescences flowing from a carcase, there would be no evident conflict in register: the discordance here arises from the lack of proportion between the signified and the signifier.

The whole poem is built on these oxymoronic clashes in style, including clashes between terms ("la carcasse superbe"); ironic touches, like the dog looking for another *morceau* (a delicious morsel) of the carcase; and incongruous expressions like *cuire à point*, another culinary term. The last lines show how the poem's richness of association serves to defeat our efforts to classify its language:

> Alors, ô ma beauté! dites à la vermine
> Qui vous mangera de baisers,

> Que j'ai gardé la forme et l'essence divine
>   De mes amours décomposés!

The word *décomposés* clashes with the rest of the stanza (except for the word *vermine*) in many ways. On a thematic level, it forms a contrast with the divine, unchanging world of forms. Its concreteness contradicts the abstract noun it modifies, *amours*, (thereby making us aware again of the physical—and perishable—reality of the woman the poem addresses). Finally, as a technical term, it is out of place not just in the company of "essence divine" and so on, but in poetry *tout court*. On the other hand, it takes its place in the series of clashes in diction that have constituted the poem; and it completes the series of allusions to art: his loves are "*dé*composés"; the poet will reconstitute them, he will make them into compositions.

And on yet another level, these incongruities of style can be recuperated, like those in "Spleen," in a larger structure; they take their part in the development of the theme of transformation—one of the major themes of Baudelaire's poetry—that underlies this text. What is dead is shown to be bursting with life; what is commonly considered repugnant is shown to be beautiful. The language of the poem mimes these transformations in the series of images in stanzas six through eight, where the carcase is compared to a wave, a "souffle vague," music, running water, wind, and grain being winnowed. This text, then, accomplishes the transformations, the recomposition it describes. Because of this overarching theme it is able to accommodate its discrepancies. But only partially, as both the contemporary reaction and its continuing power for the reader attest: the poem is gripping to the extent that we cannot erase its contradictions. That the last word should be not one of reconstitution but of destruction and that is should be an "unpoetic" term are emblematic of its refusal to be assimilated in a redemptive vision of art.

Rimbaud is usually considered the innovator in the introduction of technical terms in French poetry, but it was Baudelaire who prepared the way. Mitchell has mentioned the extensive use of medical terms in Baudelaire and its place in Baudelaire's poetics of the transformation of the ugly into the beautiful ("Heart," 155). Such terminology is a part of Baudelaire's accent on human physical reality, a semantic field usually eliminated from poetry. In a sense the body is what is most *propre*; and in Baudelaire it calls forth the most precise terms, from the "pieuses entrailles" of "Le Mauvais Moine," to *gerçures, cancres, chloroses, phtisique, miasmes, hydropique, calenture*, and many more. But the example of "Une charogne" shows how the very preciseness of this language, its very removal from the realm of euphemism and periphrasis usually to be found in poetry leads it to play an important role in the figural structure of the texts in which it appears. In "Une charogne" this preoccupation with the physical manifests itself on many levels: the lingering examination of the carcase in all its sensuous actuality, the linking of the abstract idea of love to its physical aspect, and the use of the scientific terms *infection* and *décomposés*. Its angle of vision is revealed in the last stanza, in the literalizing of the expression *manger de baisers*: the language of love has become the language of destruction, as the poetic ideal of love has been reduced to the physical, and as the language of love poetry has itself been radically transformed.

In this section I have been examining the ways in which Baudelaire renews the traditionally "high" subjects of poetry by introducing elements from the low style. I will go on in the next section to look at the other side of this verbal alchemy: his poeticizing of the banal. But it should be clear how these categories tend to shade into each other, even trade places with each other, as in the contrast between the purely contingent and the metaphorically linked elements in "Spleen." In "Une charogne" references to putrefaction reinforce the traditional *carpe diem* theme, but the language typical of poetry treating that theme is deflated by these same images and by discourse inappropriate to the subject. But this language itself is reappropriated in the creation of a new kind of beauty. This is what Jauss sees as Baudelaire's "move away from the Platonic concept of the beautiful, a turn which was so decisive for the development of a modern poetics" (*Aesthetic Experience*, 243; see also 43). Baudelaire's poetry puts into question the very concepts of "lofty" and "low" subjects and styles.

III. The Poetic and the Prosaic

The confusion of terminology about terminology pointed up by Auerbach's essay is related to that revealed by the conflicting senses of the word "prosaic" as it has been used by literary critics. Baudelaire's work has often been accused of "prosaism," but that charge has several different targets. The word *prosaic* can mean both "pertaining to prose . . . having the character, style or diction of prose," or, on the other hand and very differently, being "commonplace, dull, tame" (*O.E.D.*). Realistic elements—that is, elements like those to be found in the realistic novel of the time, are also often felt to be "prosaic" in the first sense, partly because of their association with that genre. But it must be remembered that such devices are anything but commonplace or dull when they intrude into the well-defined realm of poetry. Paradoxically, critics who have referred to Baudelaire's "prosaic" qualities in the second sense (or who wish to defend him from such a charge, like Valéry) are discussing what might also be considered his ultra*poetic* aspects: that is, the conventional neoclassical rhetorical devices and diction often found in his poetry. These judgments reveal the fluidity of the concept of the "prosaic": what in one age was quintessentially poetic has become just the opposite by the time of Valéry and Thibaudet.

In both senses, when Baudelaire's style is described as "prosaic," the term is clearly pejorative. Defining the "prosaic" is at the same time but negatively to determine what is truly—or what should be—poetic. Though what they exclude may differ, critics seem to demarcate the boundaries of the "poetic" by defining what it is not. Yet it is curiously difficult to see just what is meant by "prosaïsme" as it is used by Baudelaire's critics. To the extent that it implies a lack of "nobility," it is related to the distinctions between levels of language that concern us here. Cuénot, in his study of Verlaine's style, puts in the same category the "mots familiers" and "termes prosaïques" that he feels Verlaine got from Baudelaire (76). This is the sense in which Trahard uses the term when he writes, "Baudelaire entremêle parfois des vers de haute volée à des vers prosaïques," giving as one of his examples "pour faire épanouir la rate du vulgaire" from "La Muse vénale" (122). But he

also uses the term to mean "platitudinous" or "banal." Sometimes he seems to relate it to homely elements (as in the first
O.E.D. meaning), sometimes to lines that have the rhythm of
spoken language ("Mon berceau s'adossait à la bibliothèque,"
for example). Sometimes, as in the line "Dans tous les hôpitaux
et dans tous les palais" from "Le Soleil," it is not clear just what
reproach he is making. Likewise, in the list of examples of
"gaucherie prosaïque" that Henri Peyre gives in his article
"Sur le peu d'influence de Baudelaire," it is far from obvious
what qualities are shared by the line "Car le tombeau toujours
comprendra le poète" ("Remords posthume"), the same line
Trahard criticizes from "Soleil," and the entire poems "Les Bijoux" and "J'aime le souvenir." The *Petit Robert* classifies as
obsolete the uses of *prosaïsme* and *prosaïque* referring to poetry that is like prose (and thus, "qui manque d'élévation"). In
Baudelaire criticism the expression "vers prosaïque" is anything but obsolete, but it has lost precision as a theoretical
concept. Even supposing agreement about its meaning, as
Thibaudet notes, what one critic criticizes as "prosaic" will be
admired by another (*Histoire*, 324). His example is the last line
of "Le Cygne," and he proposes a possible justification for the
"platitude" of the last line in a coincidence between its style
and the situation of the swan lost in the dust of Paris. On the
other hand, his own language reveals where he stands on the
issue: he says the language of the poem has come down from
poetry "pour s'abattre dans la prose"; and he concludes his discussion by claiming that Baudelaire "ne connaissait pas sa
langue et la grammaire de sa langue comme Gautier" (324-25).

Thibaudet was among the first to point out that what was
new in Baudelaire's verse was the way its art depended on dissonance, on the incorporation of "une prose nue et . . . une
poésie pure" (*Histoire*, 324). Baudelaire's poems are remarkable in the way they play these two kinds of prosaism—the
traditionally rhetorical and the everyday—against each other.
A good example of the tension between the two appears in "La
Muse vénale," whose central preoccupation, according to Antoine Adam in his edition of *Les Fleurs du mal*, is "effets d'an-
tithèse et de dissonance" (284). These effects are brought about
by a contrast between both the subject and the diction of neoclassical verse and commonplace elements and vocabulary.

The first stanza sets up this opposition (though it was signaled already in the title):

O muse de mon coeur, amante des palais,
Auras-tu, quand Janvier lâchera ses Borées,
Durant les noirs ennuis des neigeuses soirées,
Un tison pour chauffer tes deux pieds violets?

The personification of January, the two inversions in the second line, the mythological figures (the muse and Boreas), the archaism *amante*, the traditional situation of the poet addressing his muse, all these devices put us securely in the realm of conventional poetry. Indeed, *Borées* in the plural, denoting north winds, shows how the frequent use of this mythological character in such verse had turned it into a common noun. The last line, with its simple words and "prosaic" (in the sense of humble) "tison," clearly brings us down to earth from such realms. This pattern reappears in inverted form in the following lines from the next stanza:

Sentant ta bourse à sec autant que ton palais,
Récolteras-tu l'or des voûtes azurées?

The neoclassical periphrase and ultrapoetic terms in the second line contradict the familiar expression *à sec*, making the answer to the questions posed in this stanza an obvious "no." The words "épaules marbrées" carry in themselves the text's contrast between the high and the low styles. *Marbrées* can be taken as comparing her shoulders to marble in the traditional device of comparing parts of a woman's body to precious materials. In this way it turns her into a statue, reminding us of statues of muses. The term also takes its place in the network of imagery relating to riches (palaces, gold, and so on) in opposition to the homely elements of the coal, the shutters, and the expression "gagner ton pain." But in another sense, and in a very different register, *marbrées* can be taken as meaning her shoulders are mottled with cold. "Etaler tes appas" is another stylistic oxymoron: it confronts the term *étaler*, carrying its connotations of merchandising, with the noble word *appas*.

The poem culminates in the line:

Pour faire épanouir la rate du vulgaire.

Faire épanouir la rate is itself a familiar expression, carrying a connotation of vulgarity that effectuates a coincidence of sense and register. This verse epitomizes the way the familiar expressions serve to bring down the level of the subject matter (the poet's muse) parallel to the lowering of the noble that is thematized in the poem. Rather than allowing the poem to end on the pathetic note of "ton rire trempé de pleurs qu'on ne voit pas," familiar language gives the poem its bite, in a kind of stylistic shock.

This harsh note can be explained in part by the fact that what we have here is not a descriptive poem about a woman or a comment on poetic inspiration, but a text about poetry and language itself. *Vénal* has two interrelated senses, both appropriate here: "for sale" (the muse as prostitute), and "interested in money" ("amante des palais"). Of course the hypotext here (in the Riffaterrean sense), is the romantic situation of the artist forced to prostitute himself in order to survive in a venal, capitalistic society. The cliché that expresses this idea is "une plume vénale," which generates the vocabulary of money appearing throughout the text. It also leads to the images of the falseness the muse is required to take on, like the author who must repeat the opinions of others. Indeed, "chanter des *Te Deum* auxquels tu ne crois guère" applies more clearly to the poet than to the muse as a woman. In this line language is presented explicitly as a medium of exchange, reflecting the exchange of money for poetry that is the basis of the poem and that gives it its structure. The extent to which the text is dominated by substitutions can be seen in the tercets, where the muse (already a substitution for the poet), who has been transformed into a prostitute, is metamorphosed into first, an altar boy (quite a change here) and then, a clown. Both these last transformations are necessary for her to "gagner [s]on pain": that is, they take their place in what is already a system of exchange. But the exchange-rate is clearly not a favorable one, as the degeneration in both image and language reveals: we move from palaces to a shuttered room, from "l'or des voûtes azurées" into night; and the poetic style descends from the first words "O muse de mon coeur" to the last, "vulgaire." Rather than making gold out of mud, this poem transcribes a transformation of gold into mud.

"Prosaism" in all the senses described above can be found in this poem: on the one hand, instances of familiar language and elements from everyday life, on the other, conventional poetic vocabulary and rhetorical figures. The way these devices interact is central to its meaning; a contrast between "high" and "low" underlies the text. Yet the poem puts into question the concept of the prosaic as "qui manque d'élégance, de distinction, de noblesse" (Robert, *Dictionnaire*): in its language the prosaic and the noble are juxtaposed; in the word *marbrées* they are combined; and in the series of comparisons used to describe the muse they are shown to be interchangeable. Baudelaire seems to be making this very point in one of the *Fusées*, "Il n'est même pas de plaisir noble qui ne puisse être ramené à la Prostitution," a remark followed closely by another: "Qu'est-ce que l'art? Prostitution" (*O.C.*, 1:649). The poet as prostitute becomes a kind of pure signifier in a system of exchanges, leading to a multiplication of similies that fail to accomplish a union of the poem's disparate elements.

The interchangeability of the poetic and the prosaic provides the motivation for both the thematics and the stylistics of "Le Vin des chiffonniers." Especially at the beginning of the poem, we find a mixture of "prosaic" elements and neoclassical figures and language. The former include gas lamps, the setting in the *faubourgs* (worker's neighborhoods that were appearing at the outskirts of Paris); the characters of the ragpicker, his old soldier friends, and the police spies; and, on the level of the signifier, the familiar expressions *grouiller* and *un tas de*. On the other hand, in the line:

Vomissement confus de l'énorme Paris,

the noble epithets, the inversion of subject and adjective, the personification of Paris, all serve to eliminate the possibility of our taking *vomissement* in its literal sense, despite the fact that drunkenness is the poem's subject. Similarly, in the first stanza the worker's quarter is likened to a "labyrinthe fangeux," the mythological allusion heightened by the noble epithet.[10] This phrase is typical of the movement of the poem, whose subject is the transformation of the prosaic into the poetic, the "solennelle magie" that wine effectuates in the lives of the poor. The poet foretells a literal changing of the city's mud into gold: "Le vin roule de l'or, éblouissant Pactole" through "frivolous Humanity." The second stanza shows how this transformation is accompished at a stylistic level:

> On voit un chiffonnier qui vient, hochant la tête,
> Butant, et se cognant aux murs comme un poète,
> Et sans prendre souci des mouchards, ses sujets,
> Epanche tout son coeur en glorieux projets.

In the third line, *ses sujets* turns what was a ragpicker into a king, and at the same time it elevates the diction from the level of *mouchards*, a "terme de dénigrement" according to Littré. To a certain extent, the simile "comme un poète" has the same function. But here, as so often in Baudelaire, the simile does not refer the reader to a commonly-held set of assumptions about a second entity. Rather, it puts in doubt our standard preconceptions about both ragpickers and poets. We can turn the simile around: the poet is like the ragpicker because, by his own "solennelle magic," he is able to make poetry from the stuff of ordinary life. The power of transformation this poem thematizes and exhibits thus undermines the separation of these two worlds. This is the poetic process Baudelaire describes in his essay on Banville: "Mais si vraiment! le poète sait descendre dans la vie; mais croyez que s'il y consent, ce n'est pas sans but, et qu'il saura tirer profit de son voyage. De la laideur et de la sottise il fera naître un nouveau genre d'enchantements" (*O.C.*, 2:167).

IV. Modernity, Realism, and the Tableaux parisiens

The passage I have just quoted from the essay on Banville on the poet and life is echoed in "Le Soleil," where the sun is described in the following manner:

> Quand, ainsi qu'un poète, il descend dans les villes,
> Il ennoblit le sort des choses les plus viles.

"La vie" has become "les villes": in other words, life (at least contemporary life), means urban life. In *Les Fleurs du mal*, it is especially the *Tableaux parisiens* that deal with "choses modernes," as Gautier puts it. Part of their "modernity" is just their subject: life in the city was a subject still very uncommon in verse. "Le Soleil" also raises the question of how this new subject should or can be treated when the speaker describes himself as "trébuchant sur les mots comme sur les pavés." Because they introduce fields like prostitution and crime as well as many aspects of more ordinary Parisian life, in the *Tableaux parisiens* we find a high incidence of everyday words and expressions, the vocabulary to be heard in such milieux. There are also many terms that call up unpleasant or repugnant images, terms such as *s'empêtrer*, *puer*, or *ordure*, which are often classified by critics as vulgarisms or *trivialités*. The "descente" into life/the city, then, is paralleled by a lowering in language level.

Brooks has discussed the ways in which artists of the modern (in particular Baudelaire and Balzac) are concerned with the "accessory": in the context of nineteenth-century urbanization and industrialization, "life has come in some measure . . . to be determined by the life of the commodities, of the made things which man surrounds himself with" (11). The stylistic consequence of this orientation is an emphasis on the particular; and in poetry we can expect a turn to the precise term, the *propre*, which since Hugo was contrasted with classical periphrasis and with rhetoric in general. Indeed, Baudelaire's texts do incorporate references to elements of contemporary life, like buses, tugboats, and coal. Such elements have led to their characterization as "realistic" poems, because of the importance of detail and physical reality usually ascribed to realist prose.

But, in discussing the novels of Balzac, Baudelaire emphasizes rather the way the novelist was able to transcend the particular:

> Son goût prodigieux du détail, qui tient à une ambition immodérée de tout voir, de tout faire voir, de tout deviner, de tout faire deviner, l'obligeait d'ailleurs à marquer avec plus de force les lignes principales, pour sauver la perspective de l'ensemble. . . . De cette étonnante disposition naturelle sont résultées des merveilles. . . . qui peut se vanter d'être aussi heureusement doué, et de pouvoir appliquer une méthode qui lui permette de revêtir, à coup sûr, de lumière et de pourpre la pure trivia-

lité? Qui peut faire cela? Or, qui ne fait pas cela, pour dire la vérité, ne fait pas grand'chose. (2:120)

The metaphor of the purple of nobility transfiguring triviality reveals that Baudelaire saw in Balzac a fellow practitioner of verbal alchemy. The "wonders" Balzac worked were not the way he represented the details of everyday life but the ways in which he transformed them. This process of transformation, which I have been studying in others of the *Fleurs du mal*, can be seen especially clearly in the *Tableaux parisiens*.

In the first place, as Stierle has shown, these poems do not present an overview of Parisian life as their prose predecessors in the *tableau de Paris* genre had done. They concentrate on eccentric elements of city life rather than on "the present moment of modernity" (359). Furthermore, they are not descriptive poems: as has frequently been pointed out, details and people in the city function as starting-points for the poet's reverie that is the real matter of the poem.[11] The first poem of this section, "Paysage," presents a speaker able to transcend the outside world and to create his own: "faire / De mes pensers brûlants une tiède atmosphère"; and in all these poems ("Les Petites Vieilles" as much as "Rêve parisien") it is transcending concrete reality that is important: "Tout pour moi devient allégorie." The program that Baudelaire sets out for artists at the end of the "Salon de 1845" reveals this position: "Celui-là sera le *peintre*, le vrai peintre, qui saura arracher à la vie actuelle son côté épique, et nous faire voir et comprendre, avec de la couleur ou du dessin, combien nous sommes grands et poétiques dans nos cravates et nos bottes vernies" (2:407). This passage shows not only the importance of contemporary life as a subject for painting, but also the way it should be transformed: through such works of art, the people of the time will appear "grands et poétiques."

The poetic diction that arises from such a conception of the modern and the poetic is, as may be expected, a mixed one. Colloquial and technical language contrast with more traditional discourse. The function of this diction is multiple: more than just serving as a sign of the "real" or the "contemporary," familiar discourse plays various roles in the thematic structure of these poems. For example, "Le Soleil" makes use of scientific or medical terminology in its dichotomies of city/and poorhouse/palace, demonstrating how the poet can "ennobli[r] le sort des choses les plus viles." In "Le Cygne" familiar expressions like *bric-à-brac* and *baraques* and references to the construction of the *nouveau Carrousel* and to the street cleaning services help establish the contrast between modern Paris and classical antiquity or the Paris of former times that is central to the poem. Verlaine will set up a similar juxtaposition in his "Croquis parisien." The famous first lines of "Les Sept Vieillards":

> Fourmillante cité, cité pleine de rêves,
> Où le spectre en plein jour raccroche le passant!

incorporate a striking use of vulgar diction, the verb *raccrocher*, from the language of prostitution. The appearance of such a term serves to create a rupture in the text parallel to the shock attributed to the speaker at the sight of the specter.

The techniques used to destabilize the tone of poems like "Une Charogne" and "La Muse vénale" appear frequently in the *Tableaux parisiens*. Contrasts in diction in "Les Petites Vieilles" contribute to the image of the "monstres disloqués" as well as to the ambiguity of the speaker's attitude towards them, the kind of attraction and repulsion we saw in "Le Monstre." "Danse macabre" uses a mixture of neoclassical rhetoric, medical terminology, and familiar terms like *attifer* to create the tone Baudelaire was seeking: "l'ironie criarde des anciennes *Danses macabres* et des images allégoriques du moyen âge" (Letter to Calonne, 1 janvier 1859). It is about this poem that Baudelaire wrote what is perhaps his most detailed analysis of a particular word. He was writing to Calonne about the proofs (the poem was to be published in *La Revue contemporaine*), and he expressed his dismay that the editor had chosen a variant that eliminated the word *gouge* in the line "Bayadère sans nez, irrésistible gouge":

> *Gouge* est un excellent mot, mot unique, mot de vieille langue, applicable à une *danse macabre*, mot contemporain des *danses macabres*. UNITE DE STYLE, primitivement, *une belle gouge* n'est qu'une belle femme; postérieurement, la gouge, c'est la courtisane qui suit l'armée

> . . . Or, la Mort n'est-elle pas la Gouge qui suit en tous lieux la *Grande Armée universelle*, et n'est-elle pas une courtisane dont les embrassements sont *positivement irrésistibles*? Couleur, antithèse, métaphore, tout est exact (11 February 1859, 1:546-47, italics Baudelaire's).

This letter reveals how precise Baudelaire was in his choice of words. He expected them to have resonances at many levels of signification: in this case "color," because it was an obsolete term; metaphor (death as the courtesan whose charms are irresistible); and antithesis. His insistence on "unité de style" was presumably intended to forestall Calonne's objection to the word as out-of-place: Littré and other lexicographers classify it as not only "vieilli" but also "très-familier" or "trivial." But Baudelaire seems to protest too much: "unité de style" is a curious defense for a text whose basic structuring device is the contrast between its traditional theme and modern references and language (which alone justify its inclusion among the *Tableaux parisiens*). The unity of style to which the word *gouge* contributes is one of disharmony. The antithesis this term creates, then, is one of diction as well as rhetorical figure.

"A une mendiante rousse" is another poem that makes use of obsolete terms; they function in its contrast between the present and earlier times. In this poem Baudelaire also plays on the tension between the two kinds of "prosaism" I have described above (the conventionally poetic and the commonplace) in the same way as in "La Muse vénale." Here again, upon closer examination simple oppositions break down in the context of the text's thematic and figural structures. Familiar discourse stands out conspicuously, and it seems simple at first glance, taking its place as one aspect of the contrast, central to the poem, between the coexistent beauty and poverty of the character described. This paradox is indicated in several related ways: semantic, syntactic, rhythmic, and prosodic. In the first line, for instance ("Blanche fille aux cheveux roux"), the placing of the adjective before the noun is an indicator of poetic syntax and therefore has the effect of underlining the contrast set up between a valued characteristic—white skin—and the devalued, supposedly lower-class trait of red hair.[12] This inverted syntax is in counterpoint to the natural syntax that predominates in the poem. Such a play of contrasts could be traced throughout the text, put into relief by parallelisms in alliteration and internal rhyme. *Haillon trop court/ habit de cour* is a prime example. Other devices include the use of sharply contrasting rhyming words: the central *beauté/ pauvreté*, plus *velours/lourds, rousseur/douceur*, and the like. The central contrast is pointed out further in the discrepancy between the lowly subject, as announced by the title, and the verse form that recalls the prosody of Ronsard's songs to his mistress.

On a thematic level, the opposition of the beggar to ladies and heroines of past times is related to that between what is and what might have been (marked by the subjunctive and conditional moods), extended to that between the past and the present. Thus, the time of the Valois court and the poets of the Pléiade is set against modern Paris and the "poète chétif." *Vieux débris* used to designate the beggar's mark, then, not only forms a contrast with the young pages and valets who would formerly have sought the woman's favors, but also indicates the leavings of an earlier age.

The role of familiar diction in such a text is obvious: in the last three stanzas, it performs an immediately perceptible shift from the poem's archaic or archpoetic diction that is parallel to the opposition between the beggar girl and beauties of former times. The earlier variants of this poem contained even more obsolete expressions (*blanchette, une pipeuse d'amants*, and *tétins*), but in this version we still find *lois* in the sense of a woman's power over her lover, *gueusant, gisant*, and *maints*. Words with only literary uses contribute as well: *déduit*, which Littré places in the "langage des poètes érotiques," and *cothurne*, whose associations with the theater, on the level of the signified, are underlined by its status as a term used exclusively in literature. In the context of such conventional language as well as the traditional verse form, familiar language stands out sharply, as the beggar girl does in her poverty. The expression *vieux débris* is in sharp contrast with its counterparts, the young lovers, not only in its reference to age and decrepitude, but also because it is a popular expression. Similar fallings-off from the norms of poetic diction include the familiar *guettant* (in the sense of trying to catch someone on his/her way); the colloquial "Oh, pardon," its spelling changed form "ô" in the earlier version; and the notation *vingt-neuf sous.* This last expression is unconventional both because of the exact number and because it is an intrusion of everyday life; and it is especially remarkable in its oxymoronic juxtaposition with *bijoux.* "Quelque Véfour/De carrefour" presents another such juxtaposition; Adam points out the irony in the mention of this very expensive restaurant (380).

It might be considered that such diction could be naturalized as realistic, in two senses: as appropriate to the milieu described and in its opposition to the imaginary worlds of literature and legendary history to which the text alludes. But it is important to note that the contrast here is not so much between women of former times and those of the present, but rather between women subjects of former poetry and those of modern verse. The poem makes frequent references to earlier texts, on several levels, including direct allusions to Ronsard and Belleau and the words *roman* and *cothurnes.* Somewhat less direct are the mentions of clothing typically worn by heroines of earlier works (trains, *noeuds mal attachés,* jewels); and typical novelistic or poetic situations and elements: a golden dagger, young men writing love poetry, the coy mistress. Other, indirect allusions include the Ronsardian prosodic form and the use of vocabulary like *déduits* and so on whose serious use is found only in verse. Adam has pointed out that "la belle mendiante" was a favorite subject for Baroque poets (380): the text seems to be calling for a comparison between itself and earlier verse.

As can be seen from the foregoing description, the system of oppositions in this text could easily be charted in semiotic fashion as a system of positive and negative values on scales like old/new, rich/poor, and so on. In such a chart, the element opposing earlier poetry—that of Ronsard and Belleau as well as the young "rhymers," would be this text itself. But here, the system of simple oppositions breaks down, referentially and stylistically, since the term includes its opposing term: it turns upon itself, taking on the structure of a *mise en abyme* typical of figural language in general. Rather than being "about" a beggar girl, the text is about poetry and about itself. Taking this idea further, it can be said that the stripping away of ornament alluded-to in the last stanza describes the process of undercutting traditional poetics that the poem itself accomplishes, largely through its use of familiar discourse. When Baudelaire eliminated many of the obsolete expressions from the first version of the poem he lessened its parodic force, but the many ultraconventional devices and allusions that remain serve to destabilize its tone. As in all parody, devices are simultaneously used and undercut; and the metaliterary nature of such discourse leads to questions about the nature of poetic language itself. It is not just that the detritus of the modern world is a fitting subject for the contemporary poet, although the "poète chétif" is linked explicitly to the beggar girl in the rhyming symmetry of *poète chétif / ton corps maladif.* The description of her body incorporated in the text becomes also an example of self-referential discourse: her stripped-down body (divested of both clothing and flesh) is like the poem, which has been stripped of its neoclassical trappings. There seems to be an implicit play on the traditional notion of rhetoric as the clothing of thought. But when "rhetoric" is stripped away in order to get to the "real" world, what is revealed is itself highly rhetorical.

"Le Jeu," describing a seedy gambling parlor, might seem like a more "realistic" poem than "A une mendiante rousse." The familiar discourse it incorporates contributes to its depiction of physical and moral decay. Like "A une mendiante rousse," it is constructed around an interrelated series of antitheses: between illusion and reality, light and darkness, fullness and emptiness. The language of the text traces a continual degeneration, both as signifier and as signified. Imagery of sickness and death predominates; and in the second stanza, the metonymies isolate parts of the gambler's bodies, reducing them to their parts and at the same time taking away even these characteristics: "des visages sans lèvre, / Des lèvres sans couleur, des mâchoires sans dent." No verb comes to set in motion the living dead players in this "noir tableau"; and though it is said to move ("se dérouler"), it gives the impression of a static image. In a decentering play of mirrors, the speaker sees himself seeing, and then comments on his point of view: "je me vis . . . enviant" and later, "Et mon coeur s'effraya d'envier." This structure is of course highly relevant to a text built on a structure of absences: the chairs have lost their color, the courtisans their youth, the faces their features; fingers grope in empty pockets. The speaker is himself in a recess; and his reaction, one of envy (a sensation of lack), is fitting in a text treating gambling, itself a seeking to fill a gap, to remedy a loss. All these images have the structure of desire, as the line "fouillant la poche vide ou le sein palpitant" makes clear. Moreover, what the speaker wants *is* desire; and still further, that desire is for yet another lack: the speaker envies the poor man (something missing here again), "courant avec ferveur à l'abîme béant."[13] The piling up of figures here has a vertiginous effect: we seem to be approaching a figural abyss. The choice offered the gambler or the speaker/poet is that between pain and death, between hell and nothingness; and whereas the gambler is presented as preferring the former elements of these pairs, he has paradoxically been presented as seeking the abyss; and the imagery of death used to describe the gamblers in life makes it seem as though they have already chosen death.

We are witnessing here the process of degradation that Derrida, in "La Mythologie blanche," sees as constituting the primary characteristic of metaphor; and the economic ramifications he notes as well are present here, too. The play of figures is linked to *le jeu* in the sense of gambling. Out of the *usure* of metaphor, its continual using-up, come further lacks, leading to more metaphor that ends in the words "le néant" and then, necessarily, silence. It is as though the poem has run out of steam, or rather, out of money to play with. From the very first, the speaker had portrayed himself as cold and *muet*. The figural structure of the text, then, parallels the structure of gambling: a continual paying out and loss and redoubled efforts to win more linguistic capital, ending merely in increased emptiness. The exchange is explicitly noted in the lines "trafiquant . . . l'un de son vieil honneur, l'autre de sa beauté": in the game of life, abstract qualities have turned into merchandisable quantities.

The description of the gamblers and their settings, though

emphasizing their ugliness and decrepitude, is on a perfectly acceptable linguistic plane until the speaker's outburst beginning at the end of the fourth stanza:

> Je me vis accoudé, froid, muet, enviant,

> Enviant de ces gens la passion tenace,
> De ces vieilles putains la funèbre gaieté,
> Et tous gaillardement trafiquant à ma face,
> L'un de son vieil honneur, l'autre de sa beauté!

Here, the violence and bitterness of his reaction, as seen in the repetition of *enviant*, the indignant *à ma face*, and the exclamation point, call forth a parallel linguistic violence. He uses the words *vieilles putains* to insult the old women, a term Littré does not even classify as vulgar, calling it a "mot grossier et malhonnête." This degraded/degrading language serves to separate the speaker from them and simultaneously to reduce him to their level in a *va-et-vient* of absence and presence like the pattern of envy and lack. In the last stanza, the expression *en somme* (with its resonances of both plenitude and money) and the familiar expression "*soûl* de son sang" continue this level of language. This latter term can mean not only "drunk with the rushing of his blood" but also "drunk on his blood" (as the earlier line "qui viennent gaspiller leur sanglante sueur" makes clear): the gamblers are bleeding themselves dry, a link with the imagery of sickness and death as well as the structure of continual loss. Familiar discourse in this text, then, serves to convey or translate the disgust expressed in these lines. As a translation, like a metaphor, it is itself figurative; it figures the mingled repugnance and longing envinced by the speaker. Both of the vulgar terms, *putain* and *soûl*, on the level of the signifier represent objects of desire normally forbidden. Both call forth images of hollows and abysses. That they are examples of "low" language as signifiers as well contributes to the downward thematic thrust of the text.

It is hard to see in what sense we should call a poem like "Le Jeu" realistic, even if the term itself were an unproblematic one. On one level we might be able to tie its imagery of exchange and loss to the materialism of capitalist society. Benjamin sees the image of the gambler as "the characteristically modern complement to the archaic image of the fencer" (178). But what has become of the impartial observer that is one of the staples of realist fiction? As in "Les Petites Vieilles," dispassionate observation has become obsession; here, the passionate desire for passion. The foregoing analysis of certain of the *Tableaux parisiens* has shown that Baudelaire's use of references to contemporary life (a use that is, in the last analysis, a very restrained one—see Joxe, 157-58) and his introduction of familiar language do not effectuate a turn to the *propre*, the literal. Such discourse represents more than the mimetic reproduction of the language of Paris or contemporary life or decadence; in its intrusion into the unfamiliar world of verse, it also becomes a figure representing those worlds and their opposition to the standard subjects and language of poetry.

As we have seen, Baudelaire's language has been characterized in several, interrelated ways. It has been called "prosaic" and "realistic," it has been criticized for its "trivialités" and "défaillances de style." These critical terms have all proved to be both difficult to define and difficult to apply to Baudelaire's texts, which undercut such definitions by playing on the tensions established by shifts in style. Indeed, a reading of *Les Fleurs du mal* shows that familiar language itself can become a kind of figure, in Genette's sense—a figurative sense—of the gap between the expression used and that which would be felt to be "normal" in its context. In the next chapter, on Verlaine, I will examine more systematically the ways in which the reader accommodates such language and the names we give the different levels on which it is integrated.

FIVE

Verlaine: Wringing the Neck of Eloquence

Verlaine's work is particularly useful in showing how familiar diction, rather than lessening the importance of figure, allows for even greater (or at least different) possibilities for figurative language. If conventionally "poetic" words and their opposite are marked vocabulary in poetic texts, it is because their existence permits a kind of movement that can be called tropological: the use of familiar diction calls attention to the surface of the work, preventing its language from being "down-to-earth" in the sense of being stabilized or giving the reader a more direct link to the outside world. Rather, it plays on the estrangement implied by its identification as an element of a specific register. As metaphor has been considered the breaking of the semantic rules of a language, register-shifts constitute a breaching of its pragmatic rules. And this breach is one aspect of the figural dimension of language.

When familiar terms are used instead of their conventional counterparts, the reader must attempt to integrate them into some kind of structure. By examining the role of informal or colloquial diction in the figural structure of Verlaine's poems, we can see the different ways in which they exploit its possible stylistic motivations. Incorporating such language into coherent interpretations of the texts does not prove to be simple, however, and such an analysis reveals the complexity of a poet whose works have often been seen as direct, univocal, and even simplistic. Among the questions they raise are the role of diction in intertextual reference and the problem of "vulgarity."

Given the entrenchement of neoclassical diction, it is not surprising that Verlaine's use of familiar language has had a varied critical response, ranging from hailing him as a revolutionary to condemning his later works (in which such language is more prevalent) as vulgar or "prosaic." Bruneau tries to excuse his use of low language by referring to his low life:

> Avec Verlaine, nous avons affaire à un pauvre brave type, qui sort du bistrot ou de l'hôpital, traînant la patte, et qui nous raconte des choses très simples, ou très délicates, ou très élevées, dans la langue de tous les jours. Alors que les Parnassiens, en redingote et haut de forme, sont juchés tout en haut d'un trépied, Verlaine est sur l'asphalte du trottoir parisien. (*Verlaine*, 24)

But in his study of Verlaine's style, Cuénot is much less indulgent: "Une étude complète du vocabulaire argotique de Verlaine aurait une importance lexicographique, mais ne comporterait guère d'intérêt esthétique, puisque la poésie est absente" (137). "Unpoetic" words, then, cannot constitute a poem. Verlaine himself seems to support this view when he writes:

> Tu n'es plus bon à rien de propre, ta parole
> Est morte de l'argot et du ricanement,
> Et d'avoir rabâché les bourdes du moment.
> Ta mémoire, de tant d'obscénités bondée,
> Ne saurait accueillir la plus petite idée . . .
>
> *Sagesse*, 1, iv

Verlaine said that he wrote these lines about Rimbaud, but added, "Après coup je me suis aperçu que cela pourrait s'appliquer à 'poor myself' " (Garnier ed., 600). He had introduced language of varying degrees of familiarity during the whole of his poetic career, and especially so after *Sagesse*, where these lines appear. And indeed, he does so in this very passage: *tu n'es plus bon à . . .* , *la plus petite idée*, and *rabâché* are certainly casual, familiar expressions. His word, then, rather than being destroyed by slang, receives a new impulse forward.

In order to make sense of such discourse, in order to make poetry of it rather than rejecting it out of hand, the reader must try to "naturalize" it, that is, to justify its use within the context of the poem. This naturalization can operate in various ways, on various levels. First, familiar language can be integrated by assigning the text to a "low" genre such as song or satire, where such diction would be the norm rather than an intrusion. Or it can be analyzed in relation to an intertext; Verlaine's poems often exploit this dimension of literary language. On another level it can be naturalized as appropriate to the poem's subject-matter: the signified might be "low" life (i.e., a popular subject) or "modern life," calling forth signifiers that mirror the level of the signified. Many examples of such motivation can be found in Verlaine. In texts that escape such categorizations, familiar diction must be incorporated at another level. Critics often link it with general characteristics of Verlaine's style, like "fadeur," imprecision of vocabulary, "simplicity," or the affectation of a decadent manner. "Art poétique" on the other hand provides an example of a text whose self-referentiality leads to taking its unconventional language as signifying a rejection of conventional poetry. Other texts seem unmotivated even at this metapoetic level and present a challenge to readability itself. In all these texts, we must examine to what extent Verlaine's work justifies the naturalizations imposed on it by the urge to legibility and to what extent it defies any such analysis.

I. Genre

Perhaps the simplest way to analyze "low" language is to read it with reference to a genre characterized by the low style, such as song, satire, or parody. We have seen that it was in his poetry of invective and in his *Chansons* that Hugo usually incorporated such language. A good deal of Verlaine's poetry can come under the heading of "light verse" or "songs." "L'Ami de la nature," for example, is a poem evidently designed to be humorous, and its humor consists in the play of its language, its use of slang discourse. Written in 1868, eight years before Richepin's *Chanson des gueux* introduced the contemporary *argot* of the Paris streets into published verse, it supposedly created a sensation at the literary salon of Nina de Villard. Though it was

not published until 1890, it still preceded the works of Jehan
Rictus and Aristide Bruant in what became a whole subgenre.
The last two stanzas go as follows:

> Nous arrivons, vrai, c'est très batt'!
> Des écaill's d'huîtr's comm' chez Baratt'
> Et des cocott's qui vont à patt's,
> Car on est tout comme chez soi
>   A la camp—quoi!

> Mais j'vois qu'ma machin' vous em . . . terre,
> Fait's-moi signe et j'vous obtempère,
> D'autant qu'j'demand' pas mieux qu' de m'taire . . .
> Faut pas se gêner plus qu'au bagne,
>   A la campagne.

In this poem the elimination of mute *e*'s, *campègne*, and its
shortened form *camp*' mimic lower-class Parisian pronunciation. None of the familiar or slang expressions have gone entirely out of use: *rien*, used as an affirmative in an earlier line,
and *batt*' (usually spelled *bath*) are not very common, perhaps,
but words like *chouette* or *boîte* (used in previous lines) are
very much alive today. The poem's popular syntactic constructions are also still common, including the dropping of *ne* in the
negative and the contraction "Faut pas se gêner." The poem
steers just clear of terms classified as vulgar, however, as the
correction of *em-merder* to *em-terrer* shows. The use of this
language is of course motivated by the presentation of an obviously lower-class speaker. The comedy of the situation, the
city man's amazement at the country ("des cocott's qui vont à
patt's"), is heightened by this reproduction of popular speech,
so incongruous for a poem at this time. Verlaine has been criticized for his self-conscious use of slang expressions, but their
very excess contributes to the humor of this poem. Thus, one
would not want to say that its diction is effaced by its correspondence with its context or that naturalizing it with reference to the speaker binds too closely the levels of signifier and
signified. In order to have its comic effect, the popular speech
must remain highly perceptible.

This text, though interesting to the literary historian, represents neither a typical nor an important poem for Verlaine,

but much of his verse has been considered—and sometimes dismissed—as light verse. "En patinant" (*Les Fêtes galantes*), for example, is a poem whose familiar speech can be seen as motivated by the poem's light tone and its intimate situation: a lover is speaking to his mistress. Familiar expression is uncommon in *Les Fêtes galantes*, however, and Cuénot points out that those used in "La Lettre," for instance, are themselves archaisms, "ce qui sauve l'unité de ton" (135). But what we find in "En patinant" is a series of contradictions in diction, a mixture of archaisms, latinisms, and colloquialisms. Phrases like "si ma mémoire est bonne" or "En somme," exclamations, and colloquial expressions like *filons* and *vertigo* are characteristic of spoken language (the entire poem is in direct quotation); *aphrodisiaque* was a technical term at the time; and, beginning with the title, the text is full of archaisms.[1] These expressions are intermingled: no pattern is established in which they would serve to contrast some parts of the next with others the way the archaic/colloquial distinction did in Baudelaire's "A une mendiante rousse." The very first lines, "Nous fûmes dupes, vous et moi, / De manigances mutuelles, / Madame . . .", juxtapose the familiar term *manigances* with the literary past and the formal address and title. Such shifts in tone are parallel to the reversal the text operates between the serious and the frivolous, a reversal articulated in the lines:

Ce fut le temps . . .
Des baisers superficiels
Et des sentiments à fleur d'âme.

The play on the expression "sensibilité à fleur de peau" leads to a doubt about the level on which the text itself should be taken. In his edition Robichez points out the possible double entendre of the words "nous jouissions" (560); and Cuénot finds that the "vulgarité" of the epithet *poivrée* "détonne singulièrement" (135) because he takes "haleine poivrée" to refer to an aphrodisiac. What in the poem authorizes us to take it in this sense? Not only the earlier use of the word *aphrodisiaque*: because of its familiar discourse, it is more likely that the poem will be interpreted as "obscene." In a way, when the boundaries of polite language have been passed, anything becomes possible. This text has been read in a serious way as a commentary on the stages of love affairs, coming and going like the seasons. On the other hand, it has also been seen as a mere divertissement. But, in either case, its light tone does not suffice to incorporate its heterogeneous diction. Rather, it is the unconventionality of its diction that makes possible such divergent interpretations.

"Monsieur Prudhomme" is an example of a poem whose satirical quality helps to motivate the use of "low" language, satire being another genre characterized by the low style. It appears in the section of the *Poèmes saturniens* called "Caprices." The title already makes its status clear: Joseph Prudhomme, the main character in Henri Monnier's novels, was the archetypical bourgeois. The lampoon begins with the very first line, with the words "Il est grave" and the stock expression "père de famille" heightened by the homonym *maire/mère*. M. Prudhomme is deaf, his ears "engulfed" in his collar (the word *faux* is also relevant here), as well as blind to the beauties of nature—spring is reduced to the level of his slippers. The rest of the poem confirms this description of his antiaesthetic, antipoetic sentiments. Even the insults he addresses to poets are consummately bourgeois in the attitude they reveal (poets are unshaven, unkempt, and lazy), and in diction—*maroufles* or *vauriens* are perfectly acceptable terms. Indeed, Cuénot points out that *maroufle* is an archaism, from the language of seventeenth century comedy: "Il [M. Prudhomme] se ridiculise en laissant voir combien il est archaïque dans son langage" (129). It is curious to note, however, that in order to form a contrast with his insensitivity, a conventionally poetic diction is used: not only is the subject nature and flowers, but the periphrase "l'astre d'or" for the sun is eminently neoclassical. It seems that when Verlaine wants to signal "poetry," he needs the easily recognizable "poetic" expression to do so.

Features of other registers conflict with this diction, like *coryza* and *cossu. Machin* is "très trivial" (Littré) and doubly comical here, recalling the word *machine* and indicating that the prospective fiancé is so conventionally bourgeois as to have lost all identity. The succession of adjectives in the tenth line

("Il est juste-milieu, botaniste et pansu") is funny, too, the physical epithet *pansu* following two nouns used as adjectives. *Botaniste* in this series indicates the only interest nature might have for him.

If the use of a conventionally poetic signifier is itself a sign, whose message is "I am poetry"; then slang expressions like those used here to ridicule the dehumanized characters should be a sign of opposition to this language. Often they do have this role. But in this text, where poets are referred-to explicitly, and a traditionally "poetic" subject, the flowering spring, appears twice and ends the poem, where M. Prudhomme's *rêve sans fin* turns out to be his thoughts of a profitable marriage for his daughter, the traditional diction is valorized and paradoxically opposed to the characters who would be likely to approve only such language, who would surely say of this text: that isn't poetry. As in Hugo, the use of familiar diction cannot be directly correlated with "low" genres. Not only did these genres traditionally maintain a higher level of language than that to be found here, but also the way Verlaine puts such diction to use makes it difficult to assign his poems to conventional genres at all.

II. Intertextuality

When "M. Prudhomme" is called satirical, however, it is not because it is a parody of another piece of literature, but rather because it represents a criticism of the character depicted.[2] On the other hand, there are many instances in which familiar diction plays a role in the relation between a poem and an intertext, what Genette or Riffaterre could call its "hypotext." Verlaine's poems present examples of various kinds of intertextual references and various kinds of hypotexts. "Un Pouacre" (*Jadis et naguère*) is an example of the transformations operated by what Genette calls "travestissement," "la transformation stylistique à fonction dégradante" (*Palimpsestes*, 33). This kind of intertextuality gave rise to a common genre in the baroque period, the "travestissement burlesque," which involved treating traditionally noble subjects (like Virgil and the *Henriade*) in a trivial style. Genette outlines three main characteristics of the travesty: a change in prosody from the alexandrine to the octosyllable; the use of a familiar style; and the introduction of vulgar or modern (anachronistic) details.

"Un Pouacre" incorporates most of these elements. It is based on the cliché of seeing the spectre of one's past, and Baudelaire is often mentioned as a possible source. In this poem familiar language is at odds with rather than justified by its context: whereas the figure of remorse is usually not a subject to be taken lightly, here the spectre of the past is gay enough, with its singing and dancing and casual language. The alternance of ten- and eight-syllable lines gives the poem a sing-song rhythm, likewise at odds with its subject. A comic devaluation operates at the thematic level as well. There are features in the poem typical of horror stories (an intertext common to poems of this sort): the death's head, eerie moonlight, the already-green corpse. But these details contrast with other, more comic features, like the exchanged insults (*turlupin*, and so on) and the annoyed guitar—presumably crying out in irritation. And finally, the text's familiar expressions also contribute to the disparity between the subject and its treatment. From *le drôle*, *ricaner*, *fredonner*, and *tralala*, which are more or less acceptable, to the more properly colloquial *disons*, *pouacre* (as a noun, an ugly, filthy old man), *farce* (as an adjective), and *morveux*, to the only somewhat euphemistic ending, "tu peux t'aller faire lanlaire," for a poem about remorse its language does not make it sound very remorseful.[3] Indeed, the ending is not euphemistic enough to prevent the Classiques Larousse edition from censoring the last two stanzas.

What are we to make of this incongruity? Critics have often read the poem as an expression of Verlaine's emotional anguish. Reading only the stock situation and not its treatment, they have not taken into account its role as parodic commentary.[4] In spite of the ominous beginning, the speaker, instead of being shocked into an awareness of his sins, insults the ghost of his past. When the spectre warns, "C'est moins farce que tu ne penses," we would expect a grim reminder calling the protagonist to order. But instead, the spectre is as flippant as he and as casual in his language:

"Et quant au soin frivole, ô doux morveux,
  De te plaire ou de te déplaire,
Je m'en soucie au point que, si tu veux,
  Tu peux t'aller faire lanlaire!"

Genette outlines the role of familiar or "trivial" language in this kind of intertextuality:

> le travestissement ne fonctionne pas seulement comme n'importe quel divertissement trans-stylistique fondé sur ce que Charles Perrault appelait la "disconvenance" entre style et sujet, mais aussi comme un exercice de traduction . . . il s'agit de transcrire un texte de sa lointaine langue d'origine dans une langue plus proche, plus familière, dans tous les sens de ce mot. (*Palimpsestes*, 69)

But at the same time, "Un Pouacre" plays on the unfamiliarity of colloquial and slang language in this context: it is this unfamiliarity that brings about the poem's humor and satirical force. The apostrophe *ô doux morveux* is an encapsulated version of the poem's conflicting registers and the way the slang expressions puncture the expectations set up by the more noble terms. But enough of the hypotext remains to come into play with the text's language. The shocks in language serve as a parallel for the thematic content of the poem: the speaker's ambivalent attitude towards the past. This attitude is figured in the chiasmus in the first stanza: "Tout mon passé, disons tout mon remord, / . . . Tout mon remords, disons tout mon passé": rather than assimilating the two terms, this figure marks a divergence between them that would not have been noticed had only the first line been used. The ghost of this past, however, is a degraded figure ("Avec les yeux d'une tête de mort / que la lune encore décharne," "un vieillard très cassé"). The ghost, then, is a travesty of the speaker's past. Furthermore, through its irreverent language, the poem mocks both this travesty of the past and the speaker himself. So, although it meets the specifications of the "travestissement" as Genette defines it, its familiar language makes "Un Pouacre" the travesty of a travesty.

"Paysage," another poem from the section of *Jadis et naguère* called "A la manière de plusieurs," is an example of the kind of intertextuality Genette would classify as a "charge" (see *Palimpsestes*, 96-105). "Charges" imitate the style of a work with a satiric intent, and Genette's paradigm case is the "A la manière de" genre. "Paysage" is one of the "Vieux Coppées" that Verlaine wrote—as did many others—in the *Album zutique* and elsewhere. Coppée had written a series of dixains called *Promenades et intérieurs*, in which he presented the little homely details of the life of "les humbles," as he called them. In their banality and sentimentality, they were easy marks for parodies, which usually involved either the introduction of still "humbler" elements, usually quite vulgar ones, or a pseudo-picturesque description of a simple object. Rimbaud has one to a broom. One of Verlaine's contains the passage:

> . . . dixains chastes
> Comme les ronds égaux d'un même saucisson
> (Pléiade edition, 298)

which is a good description and illustration of the genre. "Paysage" pushes the "humble" elements to the extreme, with its unpleasant day and ugly countryside. The lines "un plat soleil d'été tartinait ses rayons . . . ainsi qu'une rôtie" compare the sun to food (as we have seen, a banned topic in poetry) and to very ordinary food at that. *Plat* seems to allude to Coppée's work (and this text itself) as well as to the sun. Furthermore, the word *tartiner* is itself a familiar term. In the sense of spreading butter and jam on bread, it is not listed in the dictionaries of the time, and the *Petit Robert* dates it from 1884 ("Paysage" was written in 1874).[5]

But this poem does not in fact have the characteristics of the *charge* that Genette outlines. This is partly because of Verlaine's stylistic innovations and partly because of the interference of another intertext. Verlaine does not push to an extreme the language of Coppée's poetry: no matter how humble the subject, Coppée rarely makes use of low language as Verlaine does here in familiar expressions and constructions like *tartiner*, "c'est bête, la campagne" and "c'était *pas trop* après le siège." Genette detects behind the exaggerated diction used to parody a hypotext the idea of a stylistic norm "qui serait cette idée (simple) que le bon style est le style simple" (*Palimpsestes*,

104). But though Coppée's style is a simple one, Verlaine's is not. There seem to be two kinds of intertextuality at play here, the "charge" based on Coppée and at the same time a "travestissement burlesque" of romantic verse. The familiar romatic topos of a day in the country spent with a loved one is turned around: with its ugly landscape and quarrels, the day is hardly a chance to commune with nature: it is a disaster like the siege. The words *maisons de campagne* are in quotes to show that what remains is only the wrecks of former villas; the only thing intact seems to be the artillery shells, "tout neufs." But in this context, the familiar terms have an important function: it is through the lowering of the style of a subject that the satiric transformation takes place. In this way, paradoxically, such language is very much in harmony with the rest of the poem: "flat" language equals "flat" countryside; and the romantic metaphorical relationship between nature and man is preserved. Familiar diction, then, seems to serve several ends in this poem, escaping classifications that might explain its use in a univocal way.

Several texts in the collection *Parallèlement* are Verlaine's own critiques of his earlier work: in "A la manière de Paul Verlaine" each stanza parodies an early volume; in "La Dernière Fête galante," the Cythera of the earlier collection becomes Sodom and Gomorrah.[6] "Poème saturnien," by taking its title from Verlaine's first published volume, invites a reading that takes it as a reading itself, a critique of those early poems. It is dated 1885 and was not published until 1889; it is typical of the late poems of *Parallèlement*, where coarse language is used to describe various kinds of debauchery. Verlaine called this volume "le deversoir, le dépotoir de tous les 'mauvais' sentiments que je suis susceptible d'exprimer" (Garnier ed., 422). In this poem the characteristics of his earlier collections are pushed to extremes: "saturnien" means sad or melancholy, and the section "Melancholia" of the *Poèmes saturniens* had developed this theme. Here, melancholy ("black bile"), has become *bile enflammée*, a medical term. The oil lamps call to mind the gas jets in "Croquis parisien"; and we move inside the cabarets mentioned in the earlier poems. Zimmermann has pointed out other echoes from earlier collections and the way they parody and "destroy" these intertexts: "Ce piano dans trop de fumée" recalls "le piano que baise une main frêle" ("Ariettes oubliées," 4); "refrains de cafés-concerts / Faussés par le plus plâtré des masques" deforms the "masques et bergamasques / Jouant du luth . . . " of "Clair de lune." The light, conversational tone of the earlier collections has been changed by the use of many slang and vulgar expressions: *débagoulé, galopins, voyous, engueulai, troquets*, and so on. These serve to effectuate the devaluation of the subjects of earlier poems through a lowering of language level. The subject of the poem—a drunken orgy—and the unpleasant experiences described (inflamed bile, false notes in the cabarets, an attack by *voyous*) point to a possible way of naturalizing this extremely low diction. But this subject itself is unlike that of the *Poèmes saturniens* or the other early collections. As in "Paysage," although the language of this text has the aggressivity associated with the "charge," it does not parody the style of the earlier verse: it opposes it. In doing so it has metatextual rather than intertextual implications: the older way of writing is devalued, and we can infer that Verlaine is proposing a new poetics in its stead.

There are several other instances in Verlaine's poetry of a kind of intertextuality that poses problems in interpretation because of the conflicts between multiple intertexts, conflicts that are echoed by discordances in the poem's diction. In "Images d'un sou" from *Jadis et Naguère*, the speaker is like a barker at a carnival, inviting the reader into his tent to see his collection of rare and picturesque marvels:

> Accourez à mes magies!
> C'est très beau. Venez, d'aucunes
> Et d'aucuns. Entrez, bagasse!

In this poem Genevieve de Brabant brushes elbows with Pyramus, the forest of Arden with Spain; there are allusions to literature, comic opera, and folk songs. The language, too, is heteroclite: it ranges from the archaism *d'aucunes et d'aucuns* to *Allons vite qu'on se presse*, from spoken discourse. The word *image* designates both popular prints, in which one might find such subjects and such a mixture, and poetic images, where different elements are juxtaposed, like the metaphors and zeugmas characteristic of Verlaine's style. The language, then, parodies the incongruity that is the subject of the poem:

> De toutes les douleurs douces
> Je compose mes magies!

The many allusions to other hypotexts are secondary to this poem's self-referentiality, a topic to which we will return in discussing "Art poétique."

The sixth "Ariette oubliée" from *Romances sans paroles* ("Jean de Nivelle") on the other hand, presents a more subtle form of self-reference. An ariette is a musical form especially popular in the eighteenth century, particularly in the comic operas whose freely rhythmed forms interested Verlaine in the early 1870s. This text recalls that genre and is remarkable in general for its intertextuality. There are references to literary works: François-les-bas-bleus was a character in Nodier's story of that name; Médor and Angélique are characters from Ariosto. La Ramée is the hired killer in Molière's *Dom Juan* and the soldier in many a folk tale; and a line from *Les Femmes savantes* is echoed in the verse:

> Tant d'or s'y relève en bosse

The most prominent hypotexts are folk songs; some critics have taken the poem as simply a pastiche of them. *La boulangère* recalls the song "La Boulangère a des écus que ne lui coûtent guère," and the poem's epigraph in the manuscript was "Au clair de la lune, mon ami Pierrot." La mère Michel and Lustucru are characters from the song "La Mère Michel."[7] Jean de Nivelle was the son of the Duc de Montmorency who refused to come to his father's aid when called upon, giving rise to the proverb: "C'est le chien de Jean de Nivelle qui s'enfuit quand on l'appelle." He is also the subject of a folk song, one of whose stanzas goes:

> Jean de Nivelle a trois beaux chiens
> Il y en a deux vaut-riens,
> L'autre fuit quand on l'appelle.

Thus, the poem keeps some of the characters' traits but mixes together elements from different sources.

There are plays on words, too: *Loss* mimics the French pronunciation of Law, the financier under Louis XV who defrauded the public treasury; and this spelling creates a bilingual pun. The lines "Petit poète jamais las / De la rime non attrapée" is very much applicable to this text, where feminine and masculine rhymes mix and where we find false rhymes like *homme/cum* and *arrive/naïf*.

In such a context it is not surprising that the diction, too, should seem a hodgepodge of different registers. Archaisms (*Oui dam*, [a contraction for *oui dame*] and *palsembleu*), church Latin, insults (*robin crotté, petit courtaud*), and colloquial expressions (*sacrant, grigou, son vieil homme*) are intermingled. The use of familiar expressions, then, can be explained partly as another characteristic of folk songs, almost another allusion. Critics have called the text a "fantaisie" and a "joyeux potpourri de chansons populaires"; we would not expect to find the strictures of more serious verse observed in such a context. Its diction is also motivated thematically: Jean-François "s'en égaie"; and in a poem where the scribe is naive and inattentive, we should not be surprised to find inscribed false rhymes, broken syntax, and a mixture of rhetorical figures like "lumière obscure," allusions to various genres and characters, and unaffected language. But not only is the diction unacceptable in terms of conventional poetry, so are the popular songs that are the poem's intertexts. In this respect Verlaine's effort distances him from Banville's use of folk songs whose diction is archaic rather than vulgar, like "Nous n'irons plus au bois" (*Stalagtites*). Besides, these are not the only intertexts in "Jean de Nivelle": the various sources are incompatible with each other, and it is not possible to integrate them in a coherent structure. In addition to the play between the hypertext and the hypotext that Genette points out, there is a play among different, conflicting hypotexts. Like Laforgue, Verlaine uses just these conflicts in constructing his text. As in the other poems we have examined, "Jean de Nivelle"'s intertextuality does not provide a means to naturalize the use of its familiar diction. Rather, it presents an expansion of interpretive possibilities.

III. Expression and Content

As we have already seen but not yet examined, the link between the signified and the "low" register level of the signifier can be naturalized in ways that relate to the text's thematics. In such instances it can serve a variety of functions, marking relations between characters, milieux, emotional states, and so on, and playing an important role in structuring these texts. For example, in "Parisien, mon frère" (*Sagesse*), it establishes a contrast between Paris and the countryside, the former described in familiar, the latter in noble or neutral discourse. In "Nocturne parisien" (*Poèmes saturniens*), familiar diction sets modern Paris apart from the conventional subjects of romantic and Parnassian poetry, as well as from the diction characteristic of such verse. It is this opposition of subjects and styles that Jules de Goncourt noted in a letter to Verlaine: "Votre pièce sur la *Seine* est un beau poème sinistre, mêlant comme une Morgue à Notre-Dame. Vous sentez et vous souffrez Paris et votre temps (*sic.*)" (Pléiade, 1084). In this poem a description of the Seine follows a catalogue of ancient or exotic rivers, alluded-to in varied but acceptable diction, as in:

> Le gai Guadalquivir rit aux blonds orangers
> Et reflète, les soirs, des boléros légers

The Seine, on the other hand, is characterized as unhealthy, as the depository of Paris's victims; and there is a marked shift in diction, beginning with the first line of this section:

> Toi, Seine, tu n'as rien. Deux quais, et voilà tout.

The familiar tone of this line, with its short sentences, suppression of the verb, and the expression *voilà tout*, is typical of this part of the poem, containing words like *crasseux*, *bouquin*, and *tapoter*. Towards the end of the poem there is a mixture of classical allusions (to Venus, Orestes, and so on) and modern elements (*becs de gaz*, *vieux sou*) as in "Croquis parisien." So familiar diction is used to set modern Paris apart from the conventional subjects of romantic and Parnassian poetry, (represented by the Nile, the Mississippi, the Ganges, and so on), by means of its contrast with the romantic and Parnassian diction used to describe these rivers. In this way it approaches the kind of metapoetic statement that will be explored further in "Art poétique."

Another poem in which familiar diction is used to form a contrast is "Voix de l'orgueil," from *Sagesse*, where the speaker describes the different voices (of Pride, Hatred, Flesh, and so on) using varied and often low diction. He then tries to throw off such

> Sentences, mots en vain, métaphores mal faites,
> Toute la rhétorique en fuite des péchés,

in favor of the "voix terrible de l'Amour." Paradoxically, the difference in tone is marked by a shift to conventionally noble (though comparatively direct) language after the line:

> Nous ne sommes plus ceux que vous auriez cherchés.

Here the text explicitly calls attention to itself as poetic discourse, thereby investing its choice of words with thematic significance.

In the sixteenth poem of *La Bonne Chanson*, there is a sharp contrast between the description of the city scene (incorporating "prosaic" elements and colloquial diction), and the final words "avec le paradis au bout." Familiar language in "Qu'en dis-tu voyageur" (*Sagesse*) marks a difference between characters. The poem is written as a dialogue between a bad, cynical speaker and a Christian interlocutor, who responds in the last four stanzas. A conversational tone, pejorative details, and elements from contemporary life like cigars and train depots combine with familiar language to create the impression of a base, petty person. When the second speaker replies, beginning, "Sagesse humaine, ah, j'ai les yeux sur d'autres choses," the level he attempts to reach is signaled by the change in diction: there are no familiar expressions in the last four stanzas. It is in a different sense that the language of "Le Ciel est, par-dessus le toit" can be considered appropriate to its subject: the words "simple et tranquille" could be used to refer to the poem itself. The bits of spoken language ("Mon Dieu, mon Dieu" and the last stanza) fit in well with the text's thematized and stylized simplicity.

In all these works (and many others could be cited), stylistic uses of register-levels imply a correspondence between diction and content: the signifier is taken to mirror the signified in ways that have significance for the poem's thematic structure. Verlaine also has texts where one might consider "low" diction to be motivated by the "low" subject of the poem as a whole. An example of such a poem is "L'Auberge" (*Jadis et Naguère*), which bears closer examination to see to what extent this expression/content parallel can be maintained. Cuénot compares this poem to a genre painting, and explains Verlaine's interest in this kind of work by the contemporary rise of the realist novel (136). The popular milieu calls forth many elements usually excluded from poetry: *vin bleu* (cheap wine), cabbage soup, and so on. The pictures of the wise men and Malec Adel (the hero of a popular novel) would be typical in such an inn. In its homely and banal elements, the text resembles the poetry of Coppée or the Parnassian poets who treated rural subjects or even the descriptive poetry of Delille; and in this respect it does have analogies with the realist / naturalist novel and its portrayal of lower-class life.

But what differs in Verlaine's treatment of the subject is, in fact, the intrusion of familiar diction. He goes much further than Hugo does in his poetry of domestic life. The language of the poem contains discourse one might expect to hear in a country inn, and not just in reported speech: shortened forms like the elliptical first and fourth lines, including "pas besoin de passe-port" and familiar expressions—*n'a pas tort, entendez-vous, marmots* ("kids"), and *teigne* ("scabby"). They are not used in a denigrating way as in *La Bonne Chanson* XVI or "Qu'en dis-tu voyageur." Everything about this milieu is presented in a positive light and opposed to the dusty, painful road. Unlike those in Baudelaire's portrayal of contemporary Parisian life, the familiar words are neither pejorative nor startling: the casual tone they create is in harmony with the place described, where one can obviously be at ease.

These expressions play a role in the figural structure of the text as well, which is built on a correspondence between inside and outside. It is a poem concerned with signs, or language. "Ici l'on fume" and so forth, of course, imitate the messages on signs in shop windows; i.e., they are linked with the life inside the inn. Thus they recall the sign in the first stanza: "Happiness" is, or should be, the inn's name, since that is what is to be found within. And of what does this happiness consist? Of *talking* about happiness and comfort and love: "l'hôtesse . . . / Parle d'amour, de joie et d'aise, et n'a pas tort!" So it is removed to yet another level, as the designatum of the inhabitants' conversation. The images or prints on the other hand are metaphors for the life outside; and they are called violent to underline the contrast. Thus, in the last line,

Et la fenêtre s'ouvre au loin sur la campagne

the opening window is yet another "image" of the exterior world, framed by the window sill. The language of the poem functions as an imitation (another metaphor) or as another sign of the language of the environment.

In such a context, the speaker is placed in an ambivalent position: he is allowed, even invited within, but an inn is only a temporary lodging, a contingency of his travels. His link with it is an arbitrary one, as the phrase "pas besoin de passe-port" shows; he is just an observer. The poem is indeed like a genre painting, like a print hung on the wall of city person's apartment with a title like "The Pleasures of the Simple Life." But the "simple life" has turned out to be another signifier, or another metaphor; and the language of the text, rather than grounding it in a correspondence between subject and register-level, serves to destabilize the depiction of a world that seemed attractive in its stability.

Another thematic significance that can be assigned to familiar diction, one related to the problem of realism, is its association with the contemporary. In a letter to Delahaye, Verlaine himself writes of "ma poétique de plus en plus moderniste" (12 Octobre 1872). There is an element of "modernism" in much of his poetry, from the *Poèmes saturniens* onward, in the sense of portraying nineteenth-century life as Baudelaire did. Much of Verlaine's verse, and particularly "Croquis parisien," which echoes Baudelaire's title, recalls the *Tableaux parisiens* section of *Les Fleurs du mal*. Dedicated to Coppée, whose sentimental verse usually has Parisian settings, it thematizes the opposition between the contemporary and the past. It is usually printed without the third stanza, omitted in *Les Poèmes saturniens*:

La lune plaquait ses teintes de zinc
　　　Par angles obtus.
Des bouts de fumée en forme de cinq
Sortaient drus et noirs des hauts toits pointus.

Le ciel était gris. La bise pleurait
　　　Ainsi qu'un basson.
Au loin, un matou frileux et discret
Miaulait d'étrange et grêle façon.

Le long des maisons, escarpe et putain
　　　Se coulaient sans bruit,
Guettant le joueur au pas argentin
Et l'adolescent qui mord à tout fruit.

Moi, j'allais, rêvant du divin Platon
　　　Et de Phidias,
Et de Salamine et de Marathon,
Sous l'oeil clignotant des bleus becs de gaz.

Even without its third stanza this poem was the target of several critical attacks. It was said to be "impressionistic," cacophonous, its images supposedly impossible to understand. Bornecque quotes Jules Lemaître in this regard, "Il y a dans tout cela bien des mots mis au hasard. —Justement. Ils ont le sens qu'a voulu le poète, et ils ne l'ont que pour lui" (166). Lemaître criticized especially the first stanza, which contains elements like *zinc* and *par angles obtus*.[8] Indeed, the use of artistic terminology, unusual images, elements from modern life, and familiar expressions, in their novelty, constitute a metaphor for modern life itself. In other words, as in *Nocturne parisien* (though more strikingly), new forms of expression are to traditional poetry as the new age is to the old.

Like the artist's vocabulary, *angles obtus* is an unexpected lexical item, an intrusion from mathematical terminology. Elements normally considered low are included in the poem—gas jets, the meowing tomcat. Colloquial expressions like *bouts de fumée* and *moi, j'allais* also stand out in this manner while giving the impression of a casual, conversational style. In the eliminated stanza, *escarpe*, a slang word for thief, and *putain*, which Littré calls a "terme grossier et malhonnête," are even stronger and are surely at least part of the reason for the stanza's suppression. The poem's rhythm contributes to its conversational tone: the five-syllable second line of each stanza throws off its regularity. And the short, declarative sentences, without the inverted syntax characteristic of traditional poetry, tend to negate their division into verses. The rhymes are all masculine, another unusual procedure; and the false rhymes—*zinc/cinq* and *Phidias/gaz*—reinforce their unconformity. These devices heighten the contrast set up between nineteenth-century Paris and ancient Greece. The sculptor Phidias is opposed to the aquafortists and sketchers of modern times; the battles of Salamis and Marathon to those between the prostitute and her clients, the thief and his victims, and by implication, Plato's city state to the modern city of Paris. The winking gas jets are the guiding lights of a new age, and their mention in the last line of the poem brings us back to the everyday world.

The familiar expressions in such a poem, then, can be naturalized as appropriate to their subject, Parisian street-life, a subject or field that is itself unusual. But also, the thematization of the modern, explicitly in opposition to the classical world, is paralleled in its language: the "divine" Plato is no more as the word *divin* is no longer in everyday use. And the poem's protagonist does not ponder Plato's philosophy; he is dreaming as he travels through the city. A conversational language and tone, then, is doubly appropriate to the text.

It is interesting to note that the artistic vocabulary employed here refers primarily to etching, as the title of the section in which it appears ("Eaux-fortes") would lead one to expect. *Plaquer, teintes, angles,* and *en forme de* refer to art work in general, whereas *zinc* and even *argentin* recall the metal engraving plate, and *mordre* is the expression used for the corrosive action of the acid's inscription in the metal. The line "Des bouts de fumée en forme de cinq" makes explicit the link between such inscription and writing: written figures are analogous to engraved figures (or shapes); and this analogy is itself a figure, in yet another sense of the word. It is not the city that the poem describes (or that is inscribed in the poem), but rather, a sketch, an etching of the city. The text, then, is the representation of a representation. The scene is similarly presented as a series of unrelated impressions; and the line beginning "Moi, j'allais . . . " underlines the speakers detachment from what he sees. In his preoccupation with ancient Greece, he makes no attempt to comprehend what he sees and hears around him. But the final line makes clear the specular relation between him and his surroundings: he is himself observed by the gas jets: he is part of the picture. This integration by means of the eye incorporates the world of Greece as well, as the analogies between it and modern Paris show. And yet, the final line does not accomplish altogether a metaphoric totalization of the disparate images in the text. Plato and the famous Greek battles are known to the speaker and to us only through books, or, as here, through his dreams. The scene is that of a sketch; and even the rain is likened to music, rather than being a natural sound. So this written text cannot be said to describe the real world, but only another text; it is the metaphor of a metaphor, opening on to the possibility of the limitless play of relations characteristic of figurative language.

IV. Metapoetics

As poems like "Monsieur Prudhomme," "L'Auberge," and "Croquis parisien" show, even texts whose familiar diction would seem to be motivated by genre or subject matter can be seen to resist the totalization imposed upon them by the process of naturalization. Such resistance can be seen even more clearly in "Art poétique," which calls for analysis at another level: as a metalinguistic text, it has often been taken as a description of Verlaine's poetics. It exhibits a characteristic trait of the *ars poetica* genre: the tending toward the limit of performative, toward what Austin in *How to Do Things with Words* called the coincidence of action and utterance. Of course, there is no explicit performative "I hereby poeticize correctly," but the poem itself comes to represent such an utterance, and its theory/illustration model can bring into play a certain amount of self-referential discourse.

> De la musique avant toute chose,
> Et pour cela préfère l'Impair
> Plus vague et plus soluble dans l'air,
> Sans rien en lui qui pèse ou qui pose.

Il faut aussi que tu n'ailles point
Choisir tes mots sans quelque méprise:
Rien de plus cher que la chanson grise
Où l'Indécis au Précis se joint.

C'est des beaux yeux derrière des voiles,
C'est le grand jour tremblant de midi,
C'est, par un ciel d'automne attiédi,
Le bleu fouillis des claires étoiles!

Car nous voulons la Nuance encor,
Pas la Couleur, rien que la nuance !
Oh ! la nuance seule fiance
Le rêve au rêve et la flûte au cor !

Fuis du plus loin la Pointe assassine,
L'Esprit cruel et le Rire impur,
Qui font pleurer les yeux de l'Azur,
Et tout cet ail de basse cuisine !

Prends l'éloquence et tords-lui son cou !
Tu feras bien, en train d'énergie,
De rendre un peu la Rime assagie.
Si l'on n'y veille, elle ira jusqu'où ?

O qui dira les torts de la Rime ?
Quel enfant sourd ou quel nègre fou
Nous a forgé ce bijou d'un sou
Qui sonne creux et faux sous la lime?

De la musique encore et toujours !
Que ton vers soit la chose envolée
Qu'on sent qui fuit d'une âme en allée
Vers d'autres cieux à d'autres amours.

Que ton vers soit la bonne aventure
Eparse au vent crispé du matin
Qui va fleurant la menthe et le thym . . .
Et tout le reste est littérature.

In this text there are moments of theoretical statement simply followed by illustration. The second stanza, for instance, can be taken as a reading of the third, where the juxtaposition of the 'indécis" and the precise is demonstrated. The reference to beautiful eyes, presumably clear and bright (on the level of the signified), is followed by "derrière des voiles" which blurs the effect of the first part of the line as veils might do eyes. The word *tremblant* annuls the effect of "grand jour" (broad daylight) in the same way as does *attiédi* for "ciels d'automne." Similarly, the last line incorporates the contrast between *fouillis* and *clair*, whereas *bleu* gives the impression of their fusion, since it contradicts the whiteness of *claires étoiles*.

There are several examples of what could be called "méprises" in the text as well. *Soluble en l'air* contradicts the meaning of *soluble*, which refers to a liquid; *assassine* is used as an adjective; and not only is the jewel said to be forged, but it conflicts with "d'un sou." *Vent crispé* is another example: *crispé* means "dont la surface est un peu crispée par le souffle de quelque vent" (Littré); and there is an added resonance of the English "crisp air." But there are always instances of "méprises" in the choice of words; for the confusion of words, the taking of one for the other, is just another way of designating tropes. *Bijou d'un sou*, for example, can be called an oxymoron, *vent crispé* a kind of hypallage.

The last two stanzas present themselves as a summa of the precepts set forth in the poem. It incorporates vague expressions like *la chose*, *d'autres*, and plural nouns. There is a "méprise" in *la bonne aventure*, which here has the sense of "adventure" as well as its usual meaning of "fortune" (telling); it can also be taken as a metonymy for "fortune teller" or gypsy. That its epithet is *éparse* is another instance of a turning away from normal usage. Only *aventure/littérature* is a rich rhyme. But there are moments where precept and illustration coincide more directly. First, with reference to the rhythm: "préfère l'Impair" is part of a nine-syllable line. Second, there is an instance of onomotopoeia in which the coincidence of sound and sense parallels the precept enunciated: "sans rien en *lui qui pèse* ou *qui pose*." The stanza on rhyme, a critique of Parnassian verse and its extremely rich and rare rhymes and the funny, tricky rhyme of Banville, incorporates a mixture of internal rhyme and alliteration in *f* and *s* to a degree that has been called cacophonous. The two interior lines—where *ou* is repeated six times and echos the rhyme in the preceding stanza—are difficult to read aloud, and their exaggerated rhyme has a comic effect. And the phrase "sans *quelque* méprise" itself illustrates imprecision.

But perhaps the clearest example of self-referentiality is the line "Prends l'éloquence et tords-lui son cou!": the expression is itself the antithesis of eloquence, both as signified and as signifier, since the use of *tords-lui* and *son* rather than *le* are markers of a more casual style.[9] This "neck-wringing" takes place throughout the poem in its conversational rhythm and use of familiar expressions. *Fouillis* is a colloquial expression, and its tenor underlines its contrast with *claires étoiles*. *Grise*, though obviously representing the *indécis/précis* distinction, carries with it a resonance of its familiar meaning, "tipsy." Other elements from conversational speech include the *tutoiement*, "*C'est des* beaux yeux," *tu feras bien*, and *elle ira jusqu'où*, where the omission of the interrogative inversion is reinforced by its position as a rhyming word. Elements from situational registers usually avoided in poetry can be found here, too: *assagie* carries a connotation of childishness; and *ail de basse cuisine* is highly unusual in poetry. The use of familiar speech and elements from everyday life serve to create a contrast with the title, which would have led one to expect an elevated style like that of Boileau (and like that Boileau recommended). And in this contrast itself resides the "message" of the *art poétique*. There is a reversal of the hierarchy: "la pointe," or eloquence, which should have been "elevated," is "basse" here. Its epithet, *assassine*, is an archaism: it too is obsolete. And it is music, not poetic language, that is "before everything else," that lets verse fly away and the soul go off to "other skies."

But curiously enough, there are parts in the poem that are self-contradictory rather than self-referential. *Cou/jusqu'où* is an example of the exaggerated rhyme censured. Though impure laughter is to be avoided, "cet ail de basse cuisine" is used to refer to it. And the most curious instance of this procedure occurs in the fourth stanza, where *nuance* is repeated three times, contrasted with color to render it even clearer and creating an internal rhyme like that descried in the seventh stanza.[10]

The harping tone created by all this repetition is reinforced by the demanding "nous voulons"; and *pas, rien que* and *seul* are also pleonastic. All this thwarts the nuance so expressly called-for. This circumventing of the theory/illustration model can be seen again in the relation of the lyrical last two stanzas to the rest of the poem. The didactic tone—though at times a comic one—of the first section is absent here; the imperatives have become much more gentle subjunctives; there are no traces of familiar vocabulary (in fact, *vont fleurant* is an obsolete, literary construction); the garlic has been transmuted into much more delicate seasonings. This poem then, might seem to repeat the pattern of a text like Hugo's *Réponse*: polemical passages using familiar discourse followed by a return to elevated style. In that case the last two stanzas would represent ideal poetry, whereas the preceding explanations could be dismissed as didactic theorizing. But this poem cannot be called a simple statement of Verlaine's poetics—nor a "simple" statement" at all. Verlaine himself said of it: "Puis—car n'allez pas prendre au pied de la lettre *L'Art poétique* de *Jadis et Naguère*, qui n'est qu'une chanson, après tout, JE N'AURAI PAS FAIT DE THEORIE" ("Préface" aux *Poèmes saturniens*).

The last line, "Et tout le reste est littérature," by relapsing into the casual mode forestalls an interpretation that would divide the poem into a theoretical first part followed by a contradictory application. The *Petit Robert* gives as one meaning of the word *littérature*: "ce qui est artificiel, peu sincère," and uses this line as the example. But there was no such meaning of the word at the time: it is this poem itself that turns *littérature* into a pejorative word. The use of familiar discourse in this poem then, because it is a "song" and in its deviation from conventional diction constitutes a sign denoting a rejection of traditional "literature." Verlaine has taken Boileau's title for a poem that, in its shiftings of style and tone, is distinctly anticlassical. The text's awareness of itself as language, as indicated by the title, leads to its disruption as simple assertion. Each time it seems to refer to something outside itself, beautiful eyes, for instance, it refers instead to its own language: here, the words "beaux yeux" and what follows. The signs become the referents; and the poem itself refers to this referring, or deferring. This oscillation between the surface of the text and its referent puts into action the figural movement of the text, a circular motion indicated by the imagery of joining and the figure of the sun. It seems to be a text about poetry in general; but it can only be "about," and turning about, itself.

Other texts likewise play on the reader's recognition of the stylistic incongruity of familiar language and invite interpretations that can take it into account. The title of "Kaléidoscope" as well as its use of the future tense, allusions to dreaming and metempsychosis, and its evocation of a "ville magique" suggests obvious ways of naturalizing its incompatibilities in diction. Poems like "Charleroi" and "Pantoum négligé" combine elements from different milieux and several registers to produce a humorous tone or the disorienting effects prized so greatly later on by the decadents. The title of "Sonnet boiteux" (*Jadis et Naguère*) is self-referential, calling attention to the thirteen-syllable lines, which convey the sensation that everything is in excess. The English words (*Sohos, indeeds, all rights, haôs*) are all in the plural (the last three are italicized), and their intrusion in the poem without any reference makes them into nonsense syllables. Familiar constructions and words take their place in a structure that seems to deny meaning and emphasize unfamiliarity.

V. Toward Unreadability

Sometimes it seems that such contradictions in tone and level are impossible to incorporate at any level whatever. An example of such an instance is "Nouvelles Variations sur le Point du Jour" (*Parallèlement*) where a description of Paris calls up familiar language with no contrasting elevated moments.

> Le Point du Jour, le point blanc de Paris,
> Le seul point blanc, grâce à tant de bâtisse
> Et neuve et laide et que je t'en ratisse,
> Le Point du Jour, aurore des paris!
>
> Le bonneteau fleurit "dessur" la berge,
> La bonne tôt s'y déprave, tans pis

Pour elle et tant mieux pour le birbe gris
Qui lui du moins la croit encore vierge.

Il a raison, le vieux, car voyez donc
Comme est joli toujours le paysage:
Paris au loin, triste et gai, fol et sage,
Et le Trocadéro, ce cas, au fond,

Puis la verdure et le ciel et les types
Et la rivière obscène et molle, avec
Des gens trop beaux, leur cigare à leur bec:
Epatants ces metteurs-au-vent de tripes!

The diction ranges from casual ("Il a raison le vieux" *voyez donc*) to slang (*birbe*, ["old man"], *type*, *bec*, *épatants, je t'en ratisse*) to vulgar expressions like *metteurs-au vent de tripes* (murderers, who disembowel their victims), and especially *ce cas*. This last word has two slang senses: "excrement" and "penis"; and whichever applies in this case is highly improper in poetry.[11] This poem appears in the section of *Parallèlement* called "Lunes," with its "obscene" connotation. Robichez finds such usage an "aveulissement du langage" (697). Since there is no opposition of such language to a different milieu, it cannot be naturalized in the same way as in "Parisien, mon frère" or *La Bonne Chanson*, XVI. It seems that the language of the poem is taking over, responding to the impulses of sound and figure rather than logic. Word play is evident, as in the phrase "Sur le point de" in the title. "Point blanc de Paris" calls forth "aurore des paris"; and it is related to the gambling imagery in the text: *paris, bonneteau*, and *je t'en ratisse*, meaning to "take" someone in a card game. As in a card game, the relations between the words are purely arbitrary or metonymic; they have only their sound in common. Thus *le bonneteau* becomes "la bonne tôt . . . "; *Paris* calls up *paris; tant, t'en*. The name of the neighborhood, "Point du Jour," has no relation to its referent either, since it is situated at the west of Paris. Verlaine had noted this fact earlier in the poem "Aube à l'envers," evidently referred-to indirectly in the title "Nouvelles Variations." The manuscript of the later poem shows an alternative title, "Couchants," which makes this link explicit and which contains another twist because of the sexual meaning of

coucher. Grâce à rather than *par la faute de* is another shift
from what would be expected; and *épatants* seems an unlikely
epithet for "metteurs-au-vent de tripes." *Car* has lost its function of drawing a conclusion from evidence: the countryside
has no obvious connection with the maid's virginity. Besides,
we have already been told she is corrupted and that the old
man is in fact wrong despite the assertion "Il a raison, le vieux."
The poem seems carried along by its words as by the river it
describes: the accumulation of disparate nouns and contradictory adjectives joined by *et*'s, *puis*, and *avec*, the repetitions of
the first stanza, all seem purely gratuitous. There is no consciousness ordering experience, no totalizing power. Attempts
to link the white color of the dawn to the virginity of the maid
or to her apron in a metaphoric process are futile: only metonymic relations of sound and contiguity seem to apply. The
use of vulgar diction contributes to this contravention of the
traditional mode of poetry, indeed of language in general. The
only element joining this fragmented assemblage together is
the poem's rhythmic structure, its rhyme, and its disposition
into stanzas on a printed page. "Variations" could lead one to
expect a theme in which the variations would be grounded.
But the point of "Le Point du Jour" is its pointlessness: that
where there should be a theme there is a hole or rather, a river,
carrying the unordered detritus of the life in the city.

"Nouvelles Variations" is only an extreme example of a process seen in the poems discussed earlier: familiar discourse can
play an important role in the texts where it appears, but it is an
intrusion into conventional poetry, and it does not let itself be
dismissed with easy generalizations. It reminds us of its other-
ness, and as such, improper language becomes *im-propre*, figurative, standing for a message not carried by its surface signification. As it participates in the figural structure of the text, it
escapes our attempts to account for it fully. The texts in which
Verlaine uses familiar discourse, then, are far from lacking
"poetry"; they are not to be excused by referring to his low life:
from *Les Poèmes saturniens* on, they exploit important stylistic resources. It is clear that, rather than representing a rejection of rhetoric, Verlaine's use of such diction exploits to the
full their rhetorical possibilities. Because of the resistance
these texts oppose to the reader's efforts to incorporate them

into seamless, totalizing interpretations, they show Verlaine to be a much more complex, innovative, and interesting poet than the naive versifier he is often taken to be.

Verlaine has been credited with a central role in the nineteenth-century renewal of poetic language.[12] Poems like "Nouvelles Variations" show the disorienting effects he achieves through mixing expressions from diverse sources. In contrast to the Rimbaud, however, he uses few technical or scientific terms. Rather, he follows Baudelaire's lead in introducing references to contemporary life and informality in tenor, though pushing much beyond Baudelaire in the use of popular speech. Critics have often pointed out that Verlaine's use of familiar diction increases in the works written towards the end of his life. To some extent this increase can be associated with the practice of other poets during this period, and especially with the decadents.[13] Nonetheless it should be clear from examples like "Monsieur Prudhomme," "Croquis parisien," and "L'Auberge," all written in the 1860s, that the use of familiar diction was a feature of Verlaine's style from the beginning of his poetic career.[14] To some extent its increasing use by other poets was an effect of the growing reputation of his earlier work, reprinted by Vanier in the 1880s.

Yet despite his affinities with others, Verlaine's poems have called forth critical reactions that differ somewhat from those accorded his predecessors and contemporaries. I quoted some of these at the beginning of this chapter. There seem to be two questions raised about the propriety of the use of low language in his poetry: one relating to its efficacity and the other to its supposed correlation with his "vulgarity" of thought.

A brief look at a poem that pushes Verlaine's tendencies towards vulgarity the farthest in instructive in this regard. The dixain "La sale bête . . . ", dated 1875-76, is among the poems using slang diction to the greatest extent. It describes Rimbaud studying languages in preparation for embarking on business ventures abroad:

> La sale bête! (En général). Et je m'emmerde!
> Malheur! Fait-il qu'un temps si précieux se perde?
> Le russe est sans l'arabe appliqué, j'ai cent mots
> D'Aztec, mais quand viendront ces cent balles! Chameaux.
> Va donc! Et me voici truffard pour un semesse

Et c'est Pipo qu'il faut quoiqu'au fond je m'en fesse
Eclater la sous-ventrière! Merde à chien!
Ingénieur à l'étranger ça fait très bien,
Mais la braise! Faut-il que tout ce temps se perde?
Mon pauvre coeur bave à la quoi! bave à la merde!

This is obviously another of the "Vieux Coppées." Another intertext is Rimbaud's poem "Le Coeur volé," whose first verse, "Mon triste coeur bave à la poupe," is echoed and distorted in the last line of the dixain. This allusion parallels Rimbaud's rejection of his poetic vocation; his present mercenary inclinations are the butt of the poem.

It is often asserted that slang and popular language change rapidly, and Verlaine's poetry shows to what extent this can be true. Words like *pouacre*, for example, have gone out of use. When Cuénot says that "rien ne change plus que la langue populaire," he implies that Verlaine should have avoided it on these grounds (133). But this text reveals how much slang has remained the same and neither passed into standard usage nor disappeared since the last century.[15] Most of the expressions are still current or at least understandable: *cent balles, chameaux, la braise* (for money), and *merde à chien* (*chien* still has the negative connotations expressed in "quel temps de chien!" and other locutions). *S'emmerder*, which was absent even from many slang dictionaries in the nineteenth century, is anything but obsolete today. *Pipo*, a slang term for a student at the Ecole Polytechnique, is dated at 1875 by Robert, so this is a very early use. Other expressions might be considered as familiar rather than as popular or slang, including *la sale bête, va donc!*, and *ça fait très bien*. These, with the exclamations and syntactical constructions *bave à la quoi* and so on, are also typical of the conversational mode still common today. The imitations of contemporary lower-class pronunciation are still comprehensible: *un semesse* is obviously the popular pronunciation of *semestre*; and *je m'en fesse* (used for *je m'en fasse* in a variant of the popular expression "manger à s'en faire péter la sous-ventrière") has the added resonance of *fesser*, to spank. The only expression not to be found in a current layperson's dictionary would be *truffard*, which Delvau's slang dictionary defines as "soldier."

This poem also shows how much of Verlaine's colloquial

language and slang is still striking over a hundred years later. It is significant that not only was this poem not published during Verlaine's lifetime, it was not included in the posthumous editions of his work until 1948, not even in the *Correspondance* with the letter in which it had been inserted. This is perhaps neither an important nor very interesting poem in other respects, but it is a reminder that the use of such diction in poetry still has a good deal of shock-value.

"Vulgar" expressions are by no means fully accepted in print today. In fact, I myself am obliged to use the words *vulgar* and *low* in order to speak of these levels of language. Even *populaire* in French has a decidedly pejorative cast. In a 1954 article, Marouzeau takes pains to distinguish "langue vulgaire" from vulgarity of attitudes or objects, which could be expressed at any level of language.[16] But he goes on to speak of such language in a negative manner: it arises from a "défaut de culture," he tells us, caused by "d'une part l'ignorance de la discipline grammaticale et des formes littéraires, d'autre part par l'absence de la coércion qu'exerce ce qu'on appelle l'éducation" (245). Here again, it is clear that low language is opposed to literature. Furthermore, the words *défaut*, *ignorance*, and *absence* reveal his belief that the people are missing something: they lack discipline; they are out of control. The same attitude can be seen as he goes on: 'D'autres caractéristiques de la langue populaire sont fonction de la mentalité propre aux couches inférieures de la population: en premier lieu, défaut de ce qu'on est convenu d'appeler éducation, c'est-à-dire absence de cette contrainte sociale qui refoule les instincts élémentaires et en tous cas leur refuse la libre expression" (248).

This kind of criticism has been addressed to Verlaine as well, largely, I think, because of what is known about the debauchery of his last years. As it was for Baudelaire, a correspondence is posited between Verlaine's life and his works in comments like the following by Cuénot on "Amoureuse du diable" (*Jadis et Naguère*):

> "Ah! si je bois, c'est pour me soûler, non pour boire", est déparé par un grossier vulgarisme. "C'est une espèce d'autre vie en raccourci,/Un espoir actuel, un regret qui *rapplique*". Toute la poésie est abolie par ce mot où se révèle

la grossièreté de celui qui parle. Il semble que le vin, comme la débauche, transforme Verlaine en une sorte de voyou. Le vice, sauf quelques trouvailles littéraires, le dégrade aussi bien dans sa poésie que dans sa moralité. (134)

Part of what makes some Verlaine texts unreadable or what has led to their rejection is the loss of control that is perceived when popular language comes into play. It is not easy to get a grasp on what it stands for, what its referent can be. One solution (Cuénot's and Bruneau's for instance) is to find a motivation between signifier and signified in the relation between Verlaine's poems and his life. Such an association means that the entire practice of the use of familiar diction is naturalized in its correspondence to the world. Language is reduced to reference. The problems such an equation raises will be the subject of the next chapter, on Rimbaud.

SIX

Rimbaud: Poetics and Politics

"Rimbaud bourre ses vers de mots triviaux, écrit dans une langue très voisine de la langue parlée," writes François Ruchon. These "mots roturiers . . . sont la traduction de l'état de révolte, d'ironie, de haine où il vit, dans la contrainte de Charleville et dans l'âpre ennui qui succède à ses escapades" (175). This quotation epitomizes the critical commentary on Rimbaud's linguistic innovations in verse: "revolutionary" poetic discourse equals revolt against society. This equation has been formulated in various ways and has been applied in different ways to various texts, but the underlying implication is the same. Several of the main features of this approach can be seen in the preceding quotation: first, that the use of familiar discourse reflects a kind of loss of self-restraint ("Rimbaud bourre ses vers"); second, that it is aspects of Rimbaud's life and character (Rimbaud the great rebel against convention, rejecting the "contrainte de Charleville") that provoke such usage; and third, and most important, that there is a one-to-one correspondence, here expressed as a "translation," between diction and thought, between the signifier and the signified. The word *traduction* is especially apt in its link to the root meaning of metaphor, for this concept represents in essence a metaphoric linking between the text and the world. Of course, such a concept is not particular to studies on Rimbaud, nor is it anything new. It is the basis both of theoretical positions like Bonald's 1806 statement supporting the distinction between noble and "roturier" vocabularies, "distinction aussi fondamentale en littérature qu'en politique" (988) and of the poetic text that best epitomizes the romantics' opposition to traditional poetic diction, Hugo's "Réponse." As we have seen, it was the line "je mis un bonnet rouge au vieux dictionnaire" that became the catchword for the metaphorical equivalence between revolt in poetics and in politics.

Rimbaud's use of technical or scientific terminology, familiar discourse, slang, and childish expressions, and his attention to subject matter (and the corresponding vocabulary) of contemporary life and aspects of lower-class life are still easily perceptible today. He used such language from some of his earliest poems until the end of his work in verse, though it appears less frequently in the *Derniers Vers*. As throughout, I will be treating verse texts only. Effects of disruption and disjunction are typical of Rimbaud's work as a whole, but the introduction of such language into verse brings about a conflict in codes that points up one of the problems I will discuss in particular, the question of the "prosaic."

Rimbaud's innovations exploit the possibilities raised by Hugo's rejection of neoclassical periphrasis in favor of the *mot propre*. And it is these devices that lead to his characterization as a "revolutionizer" of poetic discourse as he was a rebel against society. This poetic/political parallelism becomes particularly clear when we turn to poetic texts whose subject matter is itself overtly political. I will study two such texts in detail, "A la musique" and "L'Orgie parisienne," to see how this equivalence holds up. In other poems the use of familiar discourse contributes to establishing a kind of middle style in which the "prosaic" signified is neither romanticized nor devalued in its treatment. "Ma Bohème" is a good example of such a text. Still other poems, like "Ce qu'on dit au poète," which presents itself as a kind of poetic manifesto, pose very different questions regarding resistance to poetic tradition and the relationship between the signifier and the signified. But before examining these poems, it is important to look at Rimbaud's diction in general and the problems it raises in distinguishing between the levels of content and expression, for it is here that the question of the poem's referentiality arises.

I. Innovation and Signification

Rimbaud is well-known for widening the scope of poetic vocabulary. Although the directions he developed had all been explored by Hugo, Baudelaire, Verlaine, or all three, there are in his work both a high incidence of unconventional vocabulary and striking use of clashes between conflicting registers. On the level of the signified, he introduced a large number of contemporary references as well as features of everyday or lower-class life, that is, semantic fields formerly considered beneath the notice of poets. Examples would be the hair ointment and *caoutchoucs* of "Mes petites amoureuses" or the photographers, telegraph poles, and references to public figures in "Ce qu'on dit au poète." These would seem to belong in newspapers or advertisements rather than in poetry. A similar device is the presence of the banal and the commonplace: potatoes and fried eggs in "Ce qu'on dit au poète," cheap wine in the "Bateau ivre," shoe elastics in "Ma Bohème," rustic or vulgar elements in "Les Reparties de Nina" (*fumiers, une vache fientera*, the description of the farmhouse and the peasant people). Such elements attract notice because they are features of everyday or lower-class life, linguistic fields formerly considered beneath the notice of poets.

Innovations in mode include the reproduction of speech associated with the lower classes, a stylistic marker of this field. *"C'est une bonne farce"* ("Soleil et chair"), *"tra la la," "tu sais bien"* ("Le Forgeron"), *"Ah va, c'est bon pour vous"* ("Les Premiers Communions"), and *"Veux-tu finir! . . . Oh! C'est encore mieux"* ("Première Soirée") are among many examples of directly or indirectly quoted speech that lend a realistic air as well as an everyday tone to the texts in which they appear. Hugo had made a similar use of reported speech, in "Les Pauvres Gens," for example. Like Hugo, Rimbaud is especially noted for his use of familiar or popular expressions, a violation of the standards of "formality."

Again on the level of the signifier, sequences of short, simple words (as in "Les Effarés"), terms from particular linguistic domains, like commercial or scientific vocabularies (the *"déficits* assez mal ravaudés" in "Vénus anadyomène" for instance), and prosaic rhythms have similar effects. In "Au Cabaret-

Vert," for example, there is a tension between the regularity of the sonnet-form (rhyme, alexandrines) and the rhythm of the poem, which tends to break free from the restrictions imposed by the division into verses. From the beginning of the poem,

> Depuis huit jours, j'avais déchiré mes bottines
> Aux cailloux des chemins. J'entrais à Charleroi.
> —*Au Cabaret-Vert*: je demandai des tartines
> De beurre et du jambon qui fût à moitié froid.
>
> Bienheureux, j'allongeai les jambes sous la table
> Verte: je contemplai les sujets très naïfs
> De la tapisserie. . . .

the punctuation and the use of enjambements pull the lines into the rhythm of spoken language. In a poem like "Le Dormeur du val," also written in October 1870, the *rejets D'argent, Luit, Dort,* and *Tranquille* serve to accentuate important elements in the poem. But in "Au Cabaret-Vert" the words thus set off (*De beurre, Verte, D'ail,* and *De la tapisserie*) hardly merit such emphasis. They have no special interest; they neither form a combined effect nor a contrast with other elements in the poem. Rimbaud seems to contradict the reader's impulse to assign value to the *rejets* or to stop at the end of each line: *tartines* and *gousse* have to be carried over to the next line for completion; *verte* and *de la tapisserie* require the preceding line in order to make sense. Such prose rhythms combine with the simple past tense typical of narrative, the natural syntax, the colloquial expressions and provincial terms, and banal, lower-class elements (bread and butter, ham, garlic, *la chope*) to establish a tone that might be called "realistic" in the sense that it incorporates elements more likely to be found in realist novels of the time. But the expectations set up by these devices are themselves undercut by the more conventionally lyrical last lines of the text:

> . . . la chope immense, avec sa mousse
> Que dorait un rayon de soleil arriéré.

And the tone is again unsettled by the pejorative connotations of the last word of the text, *arriéré*.

As we have seen in studying other poets, familiar, vulgar,

and technical poetic discourse can be used to a variety of stylistic effect. It can be considered as motivated by evocation of,
say, the milieux of peasants or the working classes. But Rimbaud also extends its use to more conventionally "aesthetic"
contexts, where such terms are often in sharp relief against
religious allusions (e.g., "Les Pauvres à l'église"), characters
with heroic qualities (like the military heroes invoked in "Les
Douaniers"), or conventionally lyrical subjects (as in "Mes petites amoureuses" or "Michel et Christine"). In such texts their
shock value is especially great. "L'Eclatante Victoire de Sarrebruck" is an excellent example of this process: grandiloquent
terms (*éclatante*, *apothéose*, *Empereur*) are played off against
the slang terms and infantile expressions (*dada*, *Pioupious*,
etc.), and the result is a picture of the Emperor as thoroughly
ridiculous. Familiar and vulgar expressions used in conventionally lyrical contexts can be directed against the people described, as in "Vénus anadyomène," "Les Assis," and "Accroupissements," where they appear to be a form of attack, a series
of insults. In such contexts they are in conflict with the text's
own subject matter. "Les Premières Communions" is a particularly good example of such a use.

In applying the concept of register to poetic texts it is important to distinguish as carefully as possible among the levels of
discourse and in particular between the signifier and the signified. It has been a useful step for critics dealing with Rimbaud's style to make distinctions between the subject represented and the language levels used in their representation.
Thus, Riffaterre has noted that in "Vénus anadyomène" Rimbaud writes a kind of "contreblason," using pejorative and
vulgar discourse to treat a conventionally "poetic" subject
(*Production*, 93-97; see also Scarfe, 173-74). At the opposite extreme, a text like "Accroupissements" derives its humor from
the elevated diction used to describe bodily functions, a semantic field avoided in the poetry of the time. "Rayons de
lune," for instance, loses its lyrical quality in the next line,
where we find that the moon's rays make "aux contours du cul
des bavures de lumière." But often when critics turn to specific
examples, the distinctions they establish break down. Thus,
Scarfe does not distinguish between the signifier and the signified, grouping together as "pejorative" or "unaesthetic" such

disparate language levels as those exemplified by "mouches éc-
latantes," "pioupiesques," "c'est une bonne farce," and "coeurs
de saleté." Similarly, he finds that the "Stupra" sonnets have a
"scabrous vocabulary" (171), whereas they are lexically perfectly tame. The title of the third piece, "Sonnet du trou du
cul" (beginning "Obscure et froncé . . . "), includes the only
phrase that belongs to a level of vocabulary lower than that
usually found in poetry, and this title was perhaps given by
Verlaine, who wrote the quatrains. Whereas in earlier texts
Rimbaud had used expressions like *Je pisse vers les cieux, ulcère à l'anus*, and so on, there are no other examples of such
daring vocabulary in these supposedly obscene texts. And no
one seems to have objected to the use of *leurs culs en rond* in
the more "esthetic" text, "Les Effarés." The "obscenity" of this
sonnet arises from its subject and the reader's deciphering of
the text with reference to parts of the body—*oeillet* as the
opening; *mousse* as the pubic and anal hair; *larmes de lait* as
semen, etc. In fact, the very lack of more vulgar terms, the fact
that the poems are couched in such genteel language, gives
them a humorous note. The third sonnet appeared in *L'Album
zutique* as a parody of Mérat's "Idole," a series of sonnets cele-
brating various parts of the female anatomy. And, with respect
to their language, incorporating such eminently lyrical words
as *ardeurs, charmante, fleurit, anges*, and *glorieuse*, Rimbaud's sonnets would not be out-of-place in such a series. This
aspect of the sonnets makes them into kinds of *éloges para-
doxaux* of the parts of the body (the penis, the buttocks, and
the anus) not included in such verses as Mérat's. Though, as
Kerbrat points out, the stylistic function of a term and its pejorative or meliorative function are often related in practice
(101-2), these poems play on the divergence between their referents and the positive connotations of their language.

A certain imprecision in critical terminology arising from
the failure to distinguish between the signifier and the signified can be seen even in Baudry's brilliant analysis of Rimbaud's discourse. He contrasts two kinds of "subversion" operating within the literary code in Rimbaud's verse, "l'interdit,"
or "ce qui ne doit pas être dit" and "le prosaïque," "qui devrait
par définition être exclu de la poésie" (51-52). It is a measure of
the difficulty of this task that once he turns to examples, his

distinction starts to break down: the examples he gives of each
class of expression could be used to illustrate the other. *Ulcère
à l'anus* (from "Vénus anadyomène"), an example of "l'interdit," is a term that would be more appropriate to a medical
context and so could be considered "prosaic"; whereas the language of "Mes petites amoureuses," a text he classifies as "prosaic," includes vulgarisms (*dégueulé*), scientific terms like *hydrolat*, neologisms, provincialisms, and more. These terms
would certainly fall under the heading of "l'interdit," that
which should not be uttered in poetry. Furthermore, as Houston has pointed out (*French Symbolism*, 99), the term "prosaic" itself tends to be misused: familiar or slang diction is not
necessarily characteristic of prose. The "prosaism" Baudry
finds in "Et mon bureau?" from "Les Réparties de Nina" seems
to refer to Nina's unromantic attitude rather than to the qualities of her speech. It is interesting that critics of all schools call
Nina "prosaic": the speaker in the poem is seen as the poet;
what is opposed to him must be not-poetry, the "prosaic."[1]
This meshing of expression and content is as capable of leading
us astray as it is compelling; and it shows how easy it is to posit a
union between the text and the world.

Because of the particularly restricted poetic vocabulary of
neoclassical French poetry, the nineteenth-century texts that
introduced elements from registers hitherto considered unacceptable tend to be described by critics in terms of "revolutionary" acts. But despite its usefulness in particular instances,
the equivalence so posited is theoretically untenable: works
from Lamartine to the socialist poets of the nineteenth century to Soviet socialist realists show that opposition to bourgeois society is not necessarily expressed through opposition to
its linguistic standards or its literary conventions. And vice
versa, stylistic innovation cannot always be associated with so-
ciopolitical rebellion. Wordsworth, Eliot, and the Decadents
(Rimbaud's successors in the introduction of vulgarisms into
poetry) would be among the many possible counterexamples.

Why is it so tempting to call Rimbaud's verse "revolutionary" and to slide back and forth between referring to poetic
devices and to political attitudes (with side-slippings to Rimbaud's "anti-social" behavior at the time he was writing)? One
reason is the attention that has always been given to his biog-

raphy. His alleged participation in the Commune, his rebellion against provincial life, his outrageous behavior in Paris and London even by the standards of bohemian poets and artists, his subsequent rejection of poetry, his gun-running, all these elements that Etiemble has examined in *Le Mythe de Rimbaud* contribute to his image as the great "révolté." Events in his life are deduced from reading the poems and the poems are interpreted with reference to his life.[2] Another reason is that many of his texts do deal with social injustice, the constraints of bourgeois society, and so on. Other poems represent opposition to poetic tradition in their choice of subject matter: "unpoetic", "unaesthetic" objects and situations are described. Examples of such texts will be examined below.

But further, our conception of poetic language leads us to seek analogies among the various stylistic levels of a text: phonetic, semantic, syntactic, thematic, and so on. "Motivation," "overdetermination," "coupling," "projecting the principle of equivalence from the axis of selection into the axis of combination," such catchwords represent what Genette has called a "poetic cratylism," i.e., the concept of poetic language as the "rémotivation de la langue courante" ("Formalisme," 237; "Valéry"). Whereas the principle of the arbitrary sign is generally accepted for ordinary speech, in poetry the critic finds a "mimelogical" relation between signifier and signified. This relation is most often posited between sound and sense but it is also used in the study of diction. In speaking about remotivating standard language in the context of nineteenth-century French poetry, however, it is important to remember that when it is incorporated within a poem, everyday language, far from being neutral, is marked diction set against the standard poetic lexicon. It is in fact in its supposed correlation with the thematics of revolt that it becomes motivated. Genette sees this phenomenon in our critical methods as a typically romantic-symbolist one (he examines Mallarmé and Valéry in particular).[3] We can go farther and point out that it has affinites with the valorization, beginning with the romantics, of metaphor and more precisely, with the romantic tradition of metaphorizing the relation between the text and history: the specular relationship between the poet and nature is transferred to that between the poem and the exterior world. A representative quote from a contemporary theorist shows to what extent our critical discourse is still imbued with this conception of poetry: "Ce qui doit intéresser le poéticien, ce n'est pas d'isoler les éléments d'un vocabulaire dont la spécificité ne serait qu'évocatrice mais de montrer que l'effort poétique cherche à intégrer des structurations hétérogènes à celles de la langue dans une totalité dont il lui revient de souligner le fonctionnement globilisant" (Delas, 96).

The words *intégrer, totalité, globalisant* show clearly the metaphoric process at work. Of course, poets since the nineteenth century have themselves worked in this tradition, structuring such parallelisms into their works: the onomatopoeias of Poe or the concrete poetry of the twentieth century are especially clear examples, but the principle is the same with less obvious devices. Although the word "revolutionary" may be a homology rather than an analogy, Rimbaud does use unconventional language in texts expressing a reaction against his society. His work is part of the reason we are likely to draw such a parallel between poetics and politics when we read modern poetry.

II. The Poetics of Revolt

One reason it is easy to make the leap from poetics to politics is that our critical vocabulary tends to come already weighted with the poetics/politics analogy: we speak of poetic "convention" and "norms"; innovation is "opposition to poetic tradition," it is called "deviation," "violation of the rules." Finding neutral critical terms in order to avoid confusion is virtually impossible. When the subject matter of the text is opposition to bourgeois society or to the political regime, it is most tempting to analyze such discourse as itself "revolutionary," and to analyze it, the way Baudry does, as resistance to the code of the contemporary cultural text or as opposition to the political regime. There are many examples of such texts in Rimbaud's *Poésies*, referring to specific political events, like "Chant de guerre parisien" or "L'Eclatante victoire de Sarrebruck"; opposing religion ("Les Pauvres à l'église," "Les Premières Communions," "L'Homme juste"); or commenting on social injustice or insensitive bureaucrats ("Les Effarés," "Les Douaniers"). A study of two such poems, "A la musique" and "L'Orgie parisienne," serves to show the ways we can analyze the special parallelism between "revolutionary" thought and unconventional expression.

"A la musique" is an example of the use of familiar discourse in a piece of social criticism. An early poem, it is an interesting piece on several levels, especially in the attitude it manifests towards language in general. It seems to point to a rejection of language itself, as the contrast between the speaker and the people described in the text becomes that between speech and silence. The society presented in the poem is obviously antipathetic. The people are as chopped-off and mean as their surroundings: they have so deformed nature that even the trees and flowers are "correct"; and they have destroyed any semblance of life in themselves. Thus, instead of charms hanging from the watch chain, it is the notary himself who hangs. These charms are inscribed with the owner's initials and have become symbols of possessiveness. Even the women are commercialized: they have "des airs de réclames." Imagery of sickness and death predominates; and the people seem to be strangled by their own weight and their restricting clothes: wheezy townsfolk, choked by the heat; bloated clerks; the fat burgher with his overflowing pipe. The uselessness and vacuity of their lives is suggested by retired men who stir the sand, as though one could get fire out of it. It seems to be their own appetites and acquisitions that destroy them. Their interest in things is translated by a predominance of concrete objects and therefore concrete nouns in the poem: almost all of the people are described as wearing or carrying something: schakos, charms, lorgnons, walking sticks, and so on. As the first stanza points out, the bourgeois "*Portent* . . . leurs bêtises." Similarly, *bureaux* is used in its third sense, referring to the workers in an office; they are reduced to the objects to which they sacrifice their humanity, like the women portrayed earlier who have become advertisements.

The young man who speaks in the last three stanzas is opposed to these people from his first words, as the line beginning *Moi, je suis* indicates. He is *débraillé*: literally "undressed," figuratively, "unrestrained" or "indecent." Likewise, as he undresses the young girls in his mind, he is removing all the trappings of stifling, restricting bourgeois society. Unlike their elders, the girls are alert, not complacent; their embroidery, too, is really their hair, in *mèches folles* at that. And more important, both they and the young man are set against the bourgeois through their silence: he says, "Je ne dis pas un mot"; and they speak only "tout bas," and the indiscreet things they have to say are expressed with their eyes alone.

This is in marked contrast to the speech of the bourgeois, which is mimicked earlier in the poem in a good example of Rimbaud's use of reported speech. *Prisent en argent*, for instance, is a contraction for taking snuff from silver snuffboxes. This ellipsis leaves what is essential to them, *argent*. The quotation, "En somme . . . " (another allusion to money, besides) is evidently ironic from the mouths of retired men, especially after the sarcastic *fort sérieusement*: the ridiculousness of their armchair politics is heightened by the pretentiousness of their language. The next instance of reported speech indicts itself in a similar way: "Vous savez, c'est de la contrebande." First, the speaker is a called a bourgeois: he need not fear judicial reprisals. Also, he is described as complacently satisfied with his situation: *épatant . . . les rondeurs de ses reins, bedaine, savour, déborde*; he seems to live for his appetites. The joy he takes in his little "contraband," the fact that the word is used for small amount of illicit snuff, all these are measures of the placidity and monotony of the lives of these people, to whom this seems exciting. The last line of the poem, "Et mes désirs brutaux s'accrochent à leurs lèvres," is in sharp contrast to such coyness.[4] In the context of such a description, the word *onnaing* is of special interest. It is a provincialism referring to a type of pipe, a kind that "faisait plus riche" (Bruneau, "Patois," 5). It is itself overflowing as are the people, and the word indicates the social situation of the man described; but also it calls attention to itself as a word used by provincial people, in both the literal and figurative senses of the term. Even sounds other than words are denigrated in this text: the band music is filled with mistakes; the sound of the trombones is said to cause amorous feelings; and a "waltz for fifes"—which critics have actually tried to find—would be a very silly piece indeed. The title, in its sense "To Music," can only be ironic when applied to such a concert.

Not only is the language of the bourgeois pompous and inappropriate; it is also commercialized: the inanimate objects that have become language, the dresses and the charms, carry messages similar to those of the people's speech, concerned with treaties and contraband. Indeed, all the objects they wear and carry signify their social standing and political beliefs. The soldier's caressing of babies in order to wheedle the maids' favors is only the most obvious instance of the exchanges that are going on. As Saussure showed, language itself can be seen as exchange, both in the sense of interpersonal communication and in the sense of the continual substitution of figure that constitutes it. In "La Mythologie blanche," Derrida points out that "l'inscription du numéraire est le plus souvent le lieu de croisement, la scène de l'échange entre le linguistique et l'économique" (257). I have indicated the ways in which Rimbaud's text explicitly presents language as a system of barter. The watch charms inscribed with their owners' initials are perhaps the best example of the link Derrida shows between writing, the *propre* (the literal), and property.

In consequence, language, as it both incarnates and constitutes society, seems to be opposed to nature in this text. It could be considered, as it often has been, as a kind of clothing, disguising both desire and thought. Like the bourgeois' clothing, like their fat, like their tobacco, it is in excess, it should be stripped away. In Marxist terms it would be analogous to the surplus-value generated by capitalism. Thus, the last line can be seen not only as a return to the natural (*brutaux*), but also as a way of silencing the young girls, of sealing their lips.

But it is of course impossible to counteract bourgeois society without words. "Je ne dis pas un mot" is necessarily untrue: it is the opposite of a self-referential statement. Not only does the existence of the poem contradict it, but the particular language to be found in it has important connotative value. It is important that the text should include expressions marked as popular or slang, words like *couac, pioupiou, bedaine, voyou*. Such words are in opposition to those of the bourgeois quoted and echoed in the text. The poem's familiar, commonplace language is unfamiliar, alien, in its context, playing against the poem's regular alexandrines and regular rhyme scheme. It is not silence that is set against bourgeois life and speech, but language of another sort. When the speaker says "Je reconstruis les corps," then, we should take it not merely as an opposition to clothing or restrictions: it is only through language that one can construct bodies or nature or any perception of the world. The meaning of *corps* ("corpus") is relevant here: through the language of this poem and in the conflicts between its different registers, the social body is constructed into a text.

It is useful to study familiar language in this poem in the context of opposition to bourgeois discourse, but we must be careful not to push too far the analogy between "subversive" vocabulary and subversive politics. A poem that reveals the problems raised by confusions between poetics and history, between text and world, is "L'Orgie parisienne ou Paris se repeuple." It is generally taken to be an account of the return of the "Versaillais" bourgeois to Paris after the repression of the Commune.[5] Its polemical tone is established from the outset. Its use of a slogan of the Versaillais: "Société, tout est rétabli" recalls the chapter headings of that other vituperative poetic work, Hugo's *Les Châtiments*. The first stanza is largely representative of what is to follow:

> O lâches, la voilà! Dégorgez dans les gares!
> Le soleil essuya de ses poumons ardents
> Les boulevards qu'un soir comblèrent les Barbares.
> Voilà la Cité sainte, assise à l'occident!

"O lâches" immediately sets the speaker in opposition to those he is addressing and prepares for the series of insults that will be hurled at them during the course of the poem. *Dégorgez* not only refers to the debarking of passengers but also, in its sense of vomiting, announces the network of both illness- and orgy-imagery that will predominate in the text. The *Barbares* (capitalized), an ironic reference to the Communards, and "la Cité sainte" (Paris described as Jerusalem) set a sarcastic, bitter tone that is likewise to be continued. That the city should be "assise à l'occident" rather than "à l'orient" and that it is decked out as a prostitute rather than "prepared as a bride for her husband" as was Jerusalem in the biblical source give a measure of the acerbity of the polemical attack. The political stance adopted by the poet could not be clearer.

The semantic fields utilized in the text, similarly, have clear thematic implications. The poem is saturated with imagery of sickness and death, words like *hagards, convulsions,* lines like "Trempez de poisons forts les cordes de vos cous," "Asphyxiant votre nichée infâme / Sur sa poitrine, en une horrible pression"), and death (*râle, flancs morts, cité quasi morte, tu gis,* and so on). This imagery points to the corruption and degradation of the bourgeois and of the society they are in the process of reestablishing. The orgy imagery makes this point even more explicit, especially since its effect is one of revulsion rather than titillation: "le troupeau roux des tordeuses de hanches" or "Tas de chiennes en rut mangeant des cataplasmes," for example, are hardly alluring. Such images seek to offend the reader's sensibilities, and they mark the ugliness and degeneracy of the bourgeois described. Indeed, these returning Parisians are reduced by the text to the level of machines without intelligence or sensibility, as shown by the accent on physical needs, the repetition of the word *pantins,* and the line "Fonctionnez plus fort, bouches de puanteurs."

On the level of the signifier, the language of the text reinforces such imagery, both syntactically and in its levels of discourse. Repeated and insistent imperatives, action verbs, and exclamation points create an impression of frenetic and undirected motion. Also, the levels of discourse employed represent a departure from the norms of poetic language of the time. The vulgarism *putain* is only the extreme point of a markedly familiar diction, including expressions like *tas de* and "Qu'est-ce que ça peut faire," and comprising as well a remarkable series of insults addressed to the bourgeois: *fous, syphilitiques, hargneux pourris* and so on. Rimbaud draws on another lexicon also usually excluded from contemporary verse: medical and scientific terms (*cataplasme, spasme, ulcère, asphyxiant,* etc.) Such terms are all the more striking in their juxtaposition with more conventionally "poetic" expressions: "Superbes/nausées," "azurs/blafards," "quoiqu'on n'ait fait jamais d'une cité/Ulcère plus puant à la Nature verte,/Le Poëte te dit: 'Splendide est ta Beauté!'" Further, the neologism *râleux* goes beyond the bounds of the French language itself.

The use of such discourse seems to provide clear parallels with the poem's thematics. The repulsive imagery translates the speaker's revulsion against the disgusting bourgeois; the rhythm of the text parallels his agitation; and most important, the poem's diction is itself revolting against the poetic norms of the day, just as the speaker revolts against bourgeois society. There is an analogy between the poem's style and its rejection of the conventions, attitudes, and actions of that society: in a word, poetic practice equals political stance. Moreover, poetic practice leads to a kind of praxis: the shock effects provided by the poem will create a corresponding feeling of revulsion in the reader as well; for who could sympathize with the bourgeois so described?

Yet such an assumption regarding the practical effects of the text is highly problematic: it is very doubtful that the "lâches" and "fous" to whom the poem is ostensibly addressed would read the text at all, let alone with any sympathy; and effects on more sympathetic, left-leaning readers either at that time or now would be difficult, not to say impossible, to measure. Besides, there are elements in the text itself that contradict the neat analogy I have drawn up between style and content. Clearly, the poem has many traditional aspects, too. First, there is a network of positive imagery in counterpoint to the distasteful imagery noted earlier, like the sun washing the boulevards, the luxurious light, the "bonté du fauve renouveau." Second, there are levels of discourse counteracting the use of familiar diction, slang, technical terms, and so on. These include classical allusions, religious vocabulary and allusions, and neoclassical diction, expressions like "pleurs d'or astral" or "le clairon" or "Le Poëte" (capitalized, with a dieresis). Third, the form of the poem is perfectly conventional: regular alexandrines, grouped in quatrains, inverted syntax, the use of the simple past, and so on. As for rhetorical figures, the allegorizing capitalizations of words like "la Cité," "L'Avenir," and "Progrès" are used seriously toward the end of the poem, in counterpoint to the ironic use of the device earlier, for words like "Barbares" and "Vainqueurs." Other devices, like the frequent use of apostrophe ("Ô cité douloureuse, ô cité quasi morte"), enumerations, anaphora, and exclamations, place the text solidly within the tradition of romantic heroic verse. This "revolutionary" poem turns out to be quite conventional after all.

How can we fit such contradictions into an interpretive strategy for analyzing this text? It is not the case that when "Le Poëte" speaks about the beauty of the city and his hope for its progress there is a shift in language levels from the low to the elevated (the way diction changed at the end of Hugo's "Réponse"); and even if there were, the supposed "revolutionary" nature of the text would be impaired: there would be a backsliding into a conventional mode of expression for a conventional subject. We could try to integrate the innovation/convention contrast on another level, positing that this juxtaposition itself parallels the situation of Paris—destroyed and brought to her knees, yet turned to the future, a symbol of defeat, a prostitute, yet a symbol of the possibility of concerted action and revolution. The poem, then, would itself represent the "supreme poetry" the poet finds in the city: it would be a hymn to the future and to Paris, but expressed in terms that would otherwise inspire disgust. Yet such ingenious interpretive strategies belie the ambiguous tone of the text in its mixture of rhetorical bombast and puncturing irony. The last lines illustrate the vacillations of tone that counteract efforts to arrive at a logically-satisfying, all-encompassing interpretation of the text:

> —*Société, tout est rétabli*: (a bourgeois slogan)—*les orgies*
> *Pleurent leur ancien râle aux anciens lupanars*:
>   (neoclassical personification, repetition, use of a literary euphemism, *lupanars* for a house of prostitution)
> *Et les gaz en délire, aux murailles rougies*, (the gas lights, an element of modern life, are contrasted in semantic field with *en délire*)
> *Flambent sinistrement vers les azurs blafards!* (a double juxtaposition: *flambent* is devalued by its epithet and *azurs*, an ultra-"poetic" term, by the pejorative and banal *blafards*).

Thus we can see that even such an overtly political text, referring to a particular historical moment, resists the one-to-one correspondences we attempt to ascribe to its relation to history. The signifier (in terms of language levels and stylistic devices) does not simply reproduce the signified (the subject matter of the text); nor can we say, in consequence, that the text as a whole is a signifier that faithfully reproduces the historical moment it signifies. In "L'Orgie parisienne" the poet admires the beauty he finds in the very repulsiveness of Paris, saying, "L'orage t'a sacrée suprême poésie." According to this text, then, poetry is not history; rather, history is poetry. As it is fashionable to say: history is itself a text. As in any concerted analysis of textual strategies, a close reading of "L'Orgie parisienne" shows that our critical tendency to metaphorize, to totalize, is resisted by the text: unmotivated, arbitrary elements give the poem a life of its own and thwart the categorizations we attempt to impose on it. Such a conclusion, in turn, puts into question the mimetic relationship of a literary work to history, not only as implied by what Hayden White calls the "reflection" theory of literature as the mirror of society, but also in the concept of the stylistic level of a text as reflecting its ideological content.[6]

III. The Unpoetic Poet

Looking at the question from another perspective, we see that the use of familiar and slang expressions in Rimbaud's verse does not always have the effect of shocking the reader. In the *Derniers Vers* and in poems like "Soleil et chair," we must find other ways of reading its presence. "Ma Bohème" is another such text. Like "Ce qu'on dit au poète," it can be taken as an *ars poetica*, but the view of the poet and poetry it presents is a very different one. An analysis of this poem shows how the everyday character of the vocabulary contrasts with more conventionally aesthetic words in a way that creates a split in the discourse at many different levels. This in turn establishes the ironic mode of the text and, ultimately, puts into question the terms "poetic" and "prosaic" themselves. We have seen that Baudelaire, too, grappled with this issue, but Rimbaud's solution leads to a very different kind of poem.

In his essay "The Rhetoric of Temporality," Paul de Man examines Baudelairean irony, noting:

> The ironic subject at once has to ironize its own predicament and observe in turn, with the detachment and disinterestedness that Baudelaire demands of this kind of

> spectator, the temptation to which it is about to succumb.
> It does so precisely by avoiding the return to the world
> . . . by reasserting the purely fictional nature of its own
> universe and by carefully maintaining the radical differ-
> ence that separates fiction from the world of empirical
> reality. (199)

Such an ironic mode is present in "Ma Bohème," where a totalization of the self and the world is undermined by the speaker's attitude towards his experience, an attitude articulated by
his diction.

The poem sets up a metaphorical relationship between the
young wanderer presented and the universe around him: metaphorical in the sense that it is effectuated through the use of
tropes and also because a system of identities and analogies is
established between the self and the world. In the line, "Mon
auberge était à la Grande-Ourse," for example, *Grande-Ourse*,
sounding like a plausible name for an inn, is more than a metaphor describing his sleeping under the stars ("à la belle
étoile"): the line makes of him a wanderer among the stars. He
says "*mon* auberge," and "*mes* étoiles." He seems even to be one
of the stars: "ma course" can be taken in its sense of the
movement of the heavens. Not only is he capable of hearing the
stars (the traditional image of the music of the spheres) but in
the line "mes étoiles au ciel avaient un doux frou-frou," it becomes the sound of women companions, the expression *frou-
frou* referring to the sound of silk or taffeta gowns. The physical world and the speaker seem to exchange attributes, as in
the metalepsis "mes souliers blessés" and the metaphor linking the sweat of his brow to the dew. The word *égrenais*, linking his verses with grain, presents another example of his
union with the world about him.[7]

On the other hand, this idealized totalization of the universe and the poet is undercut in several ways, among them the
poeticization of the banal. A certain oscillation is exemplified
by the line:

> Mon paletot aussi devenait idéal.

The ideal is of course contrasted with matter; as the coat disin-
tegrates, it loses its material aspects and becomes ideal. It also

exists for the speaker as an idea, because he still feels he is wearing a coat, even when its outward appearance would be that of rags. But *idéal* also means that which is perfect: the coat suits him perfectly well. *Unique culotte* functions in the same way.

There is a certain indeterminacy in the sense in which the reader is to understand many of the expressions used in the poem, and because of it, the stylistic level is uncertain. "Fantaisie" can be a caprice or an imaginative work, an artistic creation; or on the other hand, according to Littré, an "irrégularité dans la conduite." All these senses are appropriate: the wanderer's life is certainly an unconventional existence, and his attitude towards his clothing reveals a rejection of the materialistic values of society. Yet another ambiguous term is *Bohème*, which has connotations of a sordid, tawdry, but also, an exciting and romantic existence. Rimbaud plays on both associations, and through the language of the poem evokes both conceptions, intertwining them by mingling the vocabularies proper to both, and giving us an example of a lyrical poem built on the reconciliation of two incompatible worlds.

Throughout the poem, as in "Oraison du soir" and "Mes petites amoureuses," prose syntax and the everyday character of the vocabulary contrast with more conventionally aesthetic words. On the one hand, there are terms from the vocabulary of neoclassicism, like *idéal, Muse, lyres,* and *amours* in the feminine. But these are rendered familiar by their juxtaposition with familiar terms or by their association with the vagabond. Thus, *idéal* refers to *paletot,* and to a shabby one at that; the effect of *amours splendides* is immediately contradicted by the familiar interjection "Oh! là là!"; the strings of the lyres are nothing but shoe elastics. The details regarding his clothing belong to an ordinary, prosaic milieu; and words like *crevées* and *frou-frou* are familiar terms.

This almost simultaneous valorization and puncturing of the protagonist's attributes establishes the ironic mode of the text. There is a split between the protagonist and the persona who narrates the poem: the slightly condescending character of the line, "Oh! là là! que d'amours splendides j'ai rêvées!" shows the narrator to be older, more mature, and amused by the thought of his earlier life. *Rêver,* used as a transitive verb, has the connotation of "dreamed-up," another deprecatory expression. Calling the wanderer "Petit-Poucet" also reveals this attitude, since this fairy-tale character evokes both admiration and amusement. The parallels between him and the protagonist are many: like the young poet, "Il écoutait beaucoup"; as the poet is isolated from society, Petit-Poucet was "le souffre-douleurs de la maison et on lui donnait toujours le tort" (Perrault, 191). Whereas Petit-Poucet dropped pebbles and pieces of grain to show him the way home, the poet drops his verses. The use of this name puts us in the context of children's stories. We would not expect to take such a character seriously, and other elements in the protagonist's description bear out this impression. He is not really a poet: "rimant au milieu des ombres," he writes only "rimes," like verses for children.

But it is not simply the case that the narrator is denigrating his younger self: this might provoke laughter, but it would remove the essential contradiction necessary to an ironic stance. The narrator would simply be older and wiser; the present would be stable; and "Ma Bohème" would refer to a reckless, bohemian existence, now long gone. But this would negate the positive, attractive side of the life described: Petit-Poucet is qualified by the epithet, "rêveur." Such a view would also undermine the identification of poetry with walking that Jacques Plessen has pointed out in Rimbaud's work and that applies so well to this poem, especially to its last two lines (170-71). The passé composé in the line "Que d'amours splendides j'ai rêvées" has the ambiguity characteristic of this tense: on the one hand, it can be taken as assuring us that this stage is now passed (its "aspect accompli"); while on the other, it retains its link to the present.

Another aspect of this ambiguity is the narrator's stance with respect to himself as narrator. It must not be forgotten that it is poetry itself that is the subject here. The reader of this poem is presented with a "rhyme" written out of the protagonist's experience, like those alluded to along with muses and lyres. The oscillation between valorization and denigration and the conflicting registers, from the very familiar to the traditionally "poetic," are signs of a doubling of the self. Poulet sees a dialectic of *dédoublement* in Rimbaud's creation, "[qui] suppose un créateur qui soit la même personne que sa créature . . . le créateur réveille un autre que lui, qui est pourtant lui" (117; see also 110 and 118-22). But Poulet attributes an "activité magique" to the creator and passivity to the creature; whereas in "Ma Bohème" the creature is himself a creator. This split is not that between the narrator and the protagonist, for this would interfere with the texture of the poem, but within the narrator himself. That he can take himself no more seriously than he can the protagonist is made clear by the poem's subtitle, "Fantaisie": his attitude cannot be simply one of superiority. This split, then, makes us unsure what to think not only of the character and his life but also of the poem's own status. If this amused, seemingly detached treatment of the young poet is itself a fantasy, then where does fantasy end and reality begin? The union of the poet with nature or the universe, then, far from effectuating a metaphoric totalization, is itself as unsettled as the constant motion of the wanderer, Petit-Poucet, and the stars, as unsubstantial as the *ombres fantastiques.*

In examining this poem from the standpoint of linguistic register, we can see that the field is at first sight perfectly acceptable: it is about a wandering poet, certainly a traditional subject for poetry. But other signifieds in the poem come from a field usually excluded: everyday clothing (including *culotte*, *poches crevées*, and shoe-elastics). Furthermore, on the level of the signifier, there are intrusions from the spoken mode, "Oh! là là!", and an informal tenor (*frou-frou*). The contrast between these linguistic intrusions and the terms conventionally associated with this subject, like *lyres* and *Muse*, cannot be analyzed in terms of rebellion (political or social), as in "L'Orgie parisienne" or "A la musique." Nor can it be seen as denigration of the characters described, as in "Les Assis" or "Mes petites amoureuses." Rather, its very undecidability makes possible the distancing necessary for the ironic stance the narrator takes with respect to himself, and it creates a new, intermediate style, neither "lyrical" nor "prosaic."

IV. "Trouver une langue"

Expanding the correspondence between the signifier and signified the poetics/politics connection presupposes, Rimbaud's work shows how poetic effects can be elicited by discordances both between the signified and the signifier and on the level of the signifier itself. These interrelations can be seen in a pair of texts that exemplify the poeticizing of the trivial ("Oraison du soir") and the trivializing of the poetic ("Mes petites amoureuses") and in the metapoetic text, "Ce qu'on dit au poète."

The juxtapositions of lyrical language with unacceptable signifieds in "Oraison du soir" have frequently been noted. The best example is perhaps the contrast between lines 12 and 13:

> Doux comme le Seigneur du cèdre et des hysopes,
> Je pisse vers les cieux bruns, très haut et très loin,

but similar juxtapositions take place at the level of both the signified and the signifier. The first line of the poem opposes two figures from distinctly different real and textual milieux: "tel qu'un ange aux mains d'un barbier." Contradictory elements are brought together, creating striking images: the burns are "douces"; *Acre* is conjoined with *doux*; gold is both young and somber, and it can *ensanglante*: (is it red or gold, then?) Guisto points out the contraditions on the level of expression, seeing the poem as exemplifying Rimbaud's poetic enterprise in 1871, "subvertir la poésie traditionnelle" (118). Of course, Rimbaud needs the reader's familiarity with traditional poetry to make this poem work, because it contrasts conventional poetic vocabulary and religious terms with medical terms (*hypogastre*), botanical vocabulary (including senses of *cannelures* and *ravaler*), and familiar expressions. The romantic *mon coeur triste* is immediately degraded by its paradoxial association with sapwood and with the *coulures*. The heavens are depreciated by the adjective *bruns*. The heliotropes "approve" because they too turn to the sky. Indeed, these contrasts lead to a rereading of the poem in which the elements referred to in elevated diction are reinterpreted in terms of physical functions. Thus, *voilures* become clouds of smoke from the speaker's pipe, the "rêves" his feeling of nausea or vomit (*ravalé* taken in the sense of "regurgitated"); *coulures* the spilled or driveled beer, *me recueille* not meditation, as the religious vocabulary and title would lead us to expect, but the speaker's retiring to relieve himself. This rereading, in which this language itself is "ravalé," is triggered by the cues the lexical contrasts have alerted us to find. The confrontations between and on these various levels creates the humor of this poem. And the contrast between these contrasts and the conventional sonnet form creates another level of contradiction. The poem's effect depends on all these oppositions.

"Mes petites amoureuses" has the same contrasts, though its structure is just the reverse of that in "Oraison du soir": the conventionally poetic subject is treated in language that is violent and vulgar in the extreme. The language is also extremely difficult to understand. But interpretations of this poem differ from those of "Oraison du soir": The violence of the language used has elicited commentaries on the violence of Rimbaud's feelings towards women (or towards himself), provoking speculations regarding young women by whom he may have been rejected, thoughts on his homosexuality, and so on. The language is itself often called "aggressive." The subject matter, then, seems to determine the seriousness with which the poem is regarded. But as Schaeffer has shown, Rimbaud is writing not against particular young girls or against women in general, but rather, against a certain kind of poetry, the kind the title of the poem would lead us to expect (125; see also Giustio, 133). Whereas in "Oraison du soir" "poetic" expressions were devalued by their conjunction with a "low" subject," here, as in "Vénus anadyomène," the standard subject matter of lyrical poetry is brought down through the use of unconventional vocabulary.

But what kind of unconventional vocabulary is used tells us a great deal about Rimbaud's poetic methods as well as about his reception by critics. Schaeffer tells us that the lexicon of the poem "est emprunté au dégoût, au visqueux, au technique, au prosaïque" (116), thus making no distinction between, respectively, reader reaction (or, if he means words *referring* to disgust, semantic field), semantic field, a particular register (scientific language), and literary genre conventions. In conflating these categories, he is presupposing that remotivation of the relationship between signifier and referent Genette points out as "poetic cratylism." A look at the first stanza of the poem shows both how these connections are made and how they unmake themselves:

Un hydrolat lacrymal lave
    Les cieux vert-chou:
Sous l'arbre tendronnier qui bave,
    Vos caoutchoucs

———

Blancs de lunes particulières
    Aux pialats ronds,
Entrechoquez vos genouillères,
    Mes laiderons!

We can make sense of *Un hydrolat lacrymal* in several ways, on different levels. Schaeffer points out the kind of "bégaiement" produced by the concatination of *la/al* sounds. The phrase also takes its place in an interlocking network of imagery relating to liquids, tears, and pain. And finally, the nouns are part of the sequence of scientific/medical terms in the poem. But when we try to see correspondences among the phonetic structure, the imagery, and the register levels of the language used, we find rupture rather than correlation. We do not associate scientific language with tears or with stammering. The various levels confront rather than reinforce each other, stymying our urge to organize the elements of the text into a comprehensible whole.

The text presents many obstacles to interpreters, and critics have been puzzling for the past hundred years about such collocations as cabbage-green skies, a blue-haired *laideron*, or the *arbre tendronnier*. Some terms present problems beyond those posed by unusual images, however. It is worth taking the time to look in detail at some of these difficulties and the ways critics have tried to deal with them. *Laideron* is masculine in the poem, though it was a feminine noun at the time; *étoile* is masculine in the ninth stanza, feminine in the eleventh. What can we make of these "errors": inadvertence? obscure allusion? further denigration of the conventionally "poetic"? *Fouffes* is defined as a provincialism meaning (depending on the commentator) either "un gifle" or "un chiffon."[8] Adam finds that "gifles" would not make sense in this context and proposes the latter definition, though *fouffes* is modified by "douleureuses," and references to pain and cruelty occur throughout the text. *Eclanches* has been given as a provincialism, too, though it exists in Littré and in present-day dictionaries. But Chambon seems surprised that "les commentateurs pensent qu'il s'agit du terme français *éclanches*" (97-98), since the word applies to sheep's shoulders and in particular to a butchered cut of meat. He finds such a meaning unacceptable, though the text incorporates terms like *mouron, bâtées*, and *oeufs à la coque*. He proposes instead a provincial term, *éclinches*, meaning "shoulder." Never mind the other culinary terms and the prevalence of pejorative terms relating to the girls: for Chambon, "shoulders" is more pertinent than the word Rimbaud in fact uses, the "terme français" *éclanches*. The spelling difference and the fact that the term comes from Picardy rather than the Ardennes region are not evidence enough to counteract the urge to readability and regularity. *Pialat* is even more difficult to work into a coherent reading because so far its sense has eluded Rimbaud scholars. Antoine Adam avers that it derives from *se pialer*, "peler de froid" (though he does not list a source); but other commentators, unable to make sense of such a meaning in the stanza, have rejected this definition. Ruff proposes an origin in a slang verb "pialer," meaning "chialer." Ruff can then propose a reading, "les traces . . . des larmes de la pluie" (113). But it doesn't get around the fact that Rimbaud twice wrote "*pialat*" not *chialat* (and the latter does not exist either) in a clearly copied text included in the "Lettre du voyant" to Paul Demeny. Schaeffer, too, refutes Adam's suggestion, proposing instead a reading that can be inserted into the network of sexual allusions and images in the text, that of a breast, un "pis-à-lait." Here again, one would have to discount the spelling Rimbaud used. I have found the word *pialàt* in the *Dictionnaire du Béarnais et du Gascon modernes*, meaning "gros tas, rassemblement, groupe nombreux, foule, masse, amas de choses en tas." But it is difficult to imagine how Rimbaud could have encountered the term, and it does not work well with the word *caoutchoucs* in its first appearance, though it makes more sense in conjunction with the "amas d'étoiles" at the end of the poem. What is clear is that, by means of what is literally agrammatical, Rimbaud is working here not only at the limits of conventional poetic language, but of language itself. The kind of opacity presented by such terms makes it impossible to treat this text as a simple instance of referential discourse. It refuses reference, it makes denotation impossible: *pialat* denotes the null set. It should be clear to what extent readings attempting to correlate the text with events in Rimbaud's life are wide of the mark.

It is possible—and useful—to give a reading of this text analogous to Riffaterre's of "Vénus anadyomène" as a simple reversal of the structure of a typical love poem. Thus, as Guisto has pointed out, the traditional love nest gives us "oeufs à la coque"; stolen kisses have become "salives desséchées"; the graceful ballerina is now an "éclanche" (134). But such a reading can account only in part for the language of the text. The obscure terms prevent a reading that can assign positive or negative values to terms in any simple way, and the collisions on the level of vocabulary between culinary terms, medical expressions, colloquialisms, lyrical expressions, and so on, function in a similar fashion. *Hydrolat lacrymal* combines a pharmaceutical term (meaning a liquid obtained by distilling water over aromatic plants) with a medical expression, and it throws off simple reference in two ways: it makes us ask both what it denotes and how we can conciliate the two referential systems. For Adam "c'est tout bonnement la pluie" (883). But just as we seek to understand what the use of a rhetorical figure adds to a text instead of a simpler equivalent, we expect to be able to determine the stylistic consequences of the use of such a phrase. Here, they are not so easy to establish. *Lunes particulières* is an analogous case: *lunes* can put us into the traditional setting of love poetry, or it can mean "ass" in slang parlance. But what can "lunes *particulières*" refer to in either case? "Special," "peculiar," "private"? Perhaps we should not take as ironic the line "Tu me sacras poète" and Rimbaud's characterization of the poem as "un psaume d'actualité": this poem takes its place in his theory that his age must create a new poetry, for which it must "trouver une langue." He enunciates his poetic program both in the "Lettre du Voyant" (in which "Mes petites amoureuses" appears) and in his other poetic manifesto, "Ce qu'on dit au poète à propos de fleurs."

This latter text incorporates the kinds of language we have found in "Mes petites amoureuses" and adds more besides. Its language shows the full range of Rimbaud's innovations in the poetic lexicon. He illustrates the possibilities open to poetic discourse, both for himself and for others. But because it is a kind of *ars poetica*, its self-referential character permits a certain recuperation of this new diction. At the same time, it is not altogether clear what his prescriptions are.

In this text Rimbaud introduces references to fields uncommon in poetry, to contemporary life and to banal, everyday elements in particular. There are allusions to well-known figures of the time—Banville, Renan, Hachette, Grandville (who had published a collection of drawings called *Les Fleurs animées*), Figuier, author of scientific works, M. de Kerdrel, a famous royalist. Many of the objects mentioned are recent discoveries: rubber, telegraph poles, spoons made by the Alfénide process. Not only do they reveal his interest in the technological advances of the time, but they represent the introduction of unusual subjects into poetry. Rimbaud seems to be calling for a modern poetry for modern times. The same effect is elicited by the scientific terminology so frequently used in this poem (*rayon de sodium, dioptriques, glucose*), the many references to plants and animals, and the medical lexicon: one would expect them to be used in a scientific treatise rather than in a poem. Using this register also allows plays on the sounds of its typically hard-to-pronounce terms, as in the line "L'Ode Açoka cadre avec la"; as Rimbaud says, they permit "A l'Eucalyptus étonnant / Des contrictors d'un hexamètre." This kind of effect is common in Rimbaud's satirical verse (the almost unpronounceable *grappes d'amygdales* of "Les Assis" is one of many possible examples). Industrial and commercial terminology have similar effects. There are references to textile manufacturing (*cotonnier, filer, noeuds*), mining (*filons, gemmeuses*), pharmacology, and leather manufacturing. The "Poète" seems to be proving his acquaintance with such subjects, a knowledge superior to those poets ridiculed in the poem because of their futile and ignorant search for local color ("Tu ferais succéder, je crains / Aux Grillons roux les Cantharides").

A similarly unusual semantic field represented in the text is that of the everyday and the commonplace, including basset hounds, potatoes, ragoûts (in the literal sense), fried eggs, and so on. The impression of what commentators have called the "unaesthetic" is reinforced by the intrusions of the mode of spoken language and the informality of expression, including terms like *pochant l'oeil* and *torcher*. The lyrical status of typically poetic terms is often devalued by their association with vulgar or pejorative terms, creating the kind of oxymoronic diction we have seen in Baudelaire: "O blanc Chasseur, qui cours sans bas," "calices pleins d'oeufs," "ô Farceur," "magnifiques omoplates," etc. These clashes in tone provoke laughter, but at the same time, they represent an implicit refusal to accept conventional poetic language.

The use of neologisms also shows the poem's antitraditionalist stance. True coined words like *gemmeuses* (from *gemme*) and *pectoraires* (a variant on *pectoral*) combine with terms like *pubescences* (a latinism) and *incageur* (an italianism) and irregular usages like *végétaux* as an epithet for *français*, *panique* applied to *Pâtis*, and "*un* pleur." Rimbaud is proposing a new language for a new poetry. Neologisms serve a variety of purposes in Rimbaud's work, creating a dream-like atmosphere, evoking a new world, expressing a rejection of the poetic norm; but in all these cases the effect depends on the way in which neologisms attract the attention of the reader to the coined word itself. The automatic link between signifier and signified is broken, and the reader must supply her own signified according to the context in which the word is found. Thus, refusing the transparency of referential language, the neologism is a particularly effective instrument in focusing on the surface of a text. But in a sense, all the scientific, technical, slang, and vulgar expressions in the poem function like neologisms or foreign words: they belong to levels of language inappropriate to "serious" literature. Rimbaud emphasizes the "revolutionary" nature of his enterprise in dating the poem, "14 juillet 1871," echoing the politics/poetics parallelism studied above. As Houston (*Design*, 56) and Baudry (52) have pointed out, the lilies whose overuse in poetry is criticized in this text are emblematic of both literature and royalism (the latter also alluded to in the reference to M. de Kerdrel).

What kind of poetry is Rimbaud asking for and simultaneously illustrating in this poem? The answer to this question is not so easy to determine as we might expect in a text that presents a poetic program. Though it seems clear that the new poetry will be set against the facile exoticism of Parnassian verse, commentators are divided as to whether the poem represents an attack on Banville or whether addressing the poem to him in respectful terms, echoing passages from the *Odes funambulesques*, and the mere fact of sending the poem to him do not indicate a more positive attitude to the poet Rimbaud included among the "très *voyants*" second romantics in his "Lettre du Voyant" to Paul Demeny. Is the "Poète" addressed in the text Banville? Parnassian poets? The poet of the future? Rimbaud himself? Even more important, is the speaker Rimbaud himself or a "vil bourgeois" who does not understand poetry, as Adam claimed (906 ff.)? And what kind of statement is Rimbaud making about the society of his time? Is he touting the values of an industrial, technological age, as some critics have thought, citing the "Lettre du Voyant": "Cet avenir sera matérialiste, vous le voyez"? Or does he rather criticize the "Siècle d'enfer," "voué" as Adam says "au culte de l'Utile et de l'argent"? (906). Or is it that he marks his opposition to the economic system of bourgeois society by parodying its cultural text, as Baudry claims (52-53)? The differences in interpretation following from the answers to these questions are by no means trivial ones. When giving their own answers, critics seem to need to bolster their arguments with rhetorical force, using "il est clair que" or "il est évident que" with a frequency that would make one think there was critical unanimity on these points. The point here is not to claim that because critics have disagreed about the meaning of the poem this meaning is therefore impossible to determine, that the text is "undecidable." On the other hand, the shifts in register I have pointed out lead to ruptures in tone that make agreement difficult to come by. Irony is an invisible trope, actualized by the reader, and the "cocasse" language and polemical stance indicated by the insulting characterizations of earlier poets make it hard to say whether Rimbaud is recommending utility as the object of the true poet's efforts or whether it is the object of the poem's ridicule.

I think a reading that looks at the text as a self-referential work can shed some light on the question. The text is proposing a properly poetic notion of utility rather than poetry that would be useful. The emphasis on work seen in the repeated use of the verbs *fonctionner, servir,* and *travailler* and in the use of the imperative mood can be understood as indicating what poetry should accomplish. To "trouve[r] au coeur des noirs filons / Des fleurs presque pierres" is to find a new poetic vision. The usefulness of this search is reflected in the poem's industrial and commercial vocabulary; but it is important that such language has itself proved useful *in poetry.* "Ta Rime sourdra, rose ou blanche, / Comme un rayon de sodium, / Comme un caoutchouc qui s'épanche!": poetry is not to associate these colors with flowers (white as a lily, pink as a rose) but to find its references in the technological and scientific world. What is proposed, then, is not a work ethic but an aesthetic of language. The text underlines the importance not of plants, but of plant *names.*

The mixed-up geography of these poets in their search for local color is mocked by throwing together names of unrelated places—*Rios, Rhin, Norwèges, Florides, Habana, Guyanes,* and in contrast, *Oises.* The plural form of many of these names has the effect of denying the reference of each to a specific place, denying its very function as a proper noun. Whereas one would expect that the *ars poetica* genre would call forth a correspondence of expression and content, this kind of usage calls reference itself into question. Proper nouns, the epitome of denotation, are no longer allowed to denote: they have become common nouns again. Poets are to read the works of M. Figuier not only because of the "usefulness" of his works, but also because his name is itself that of a useful tree. In the same way, they are told to go to M. Hachette, whose name is that of a tool, one that might be useful in cutting short traditional poets' lyrical effusions. And so, proper nouns have become useful, useful *words,* words that can be "common," that can refer in a polyvalent way. On the other hand, there is an overabundance of capitalization in the poem—not only for all the flower names and words traditionally allegorized (*la Flore, l'Art*), but also *Plantes, Chasseur, Grillons, des Buffles, Oeufs de feu,* and *Salons.* It represents not only a mocking of the process of personification so common in neoclassical verse but also a reversal of the signification of capitalization. Proper nouns have lost their specificity, whereas common nouns have become proper. In the same way as aesthetic terms are devalued by their epithets ("Les Lys, ces clystères d'extases!") and vice versa, the improper and proper have changed properties, putting into question the notion of property/propriety.

In this poem about how to write poetry, Rimbaud has accomplished what he recommends: he has opened poetic vocabulary to new possibilities and thereby to new poetic effects. That readers are still puzzling over how to deal with his accomplishment is a measure of its effectiveness. On the other hand, it is less clear to what extent the poem can be taken as a statement opposing a political and social structure. The use of such diction can be better analyzed as a sign of resistance to the conventionally "poetic." Genette (in *Figures*, 219-20) has analyzed conventional poetic tropes in a way that can be schematized as follows:

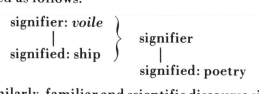

Similarly, familiar and scientific discourse signifies a rejection of neoclassical diction. Because it must call attention to itself as language, it implicitly comments on poetic language in general. The signified of such collocations as *précieuses glucoses*, then, is a reaction against traditional poetic diction. In modern literature, of course, thanks to the work of poets like Rimbaud, what it signifies is again "poetry."

These discordances are analogous to the rhetorical figures that predominate in Rimbaud's work as a whole: oxymoron, zeugma, hypallage, as well as metaphor.[9] The hypallage in "panthères à peaux d'hommes" (instead of men in panther skins) ("Le Bateau ivre") is typical of the startling effects elicited by Rimbaud's use of rhetoric. Perhaps the most striking example of such language is another line from the "Bateau ivre": "dévorant les azurs verts." The color-noun *azur* means blue: *azurs verts* is not merely impossible in fact, it is logically impossible, a contradiction in terms. We can try to understand the expression in the context of the poem, imagining the water as now green, now blue or as indistinguishably blue and green. Or we can assimilate them into blue-green, a distinct color composed of both, mentally inserting a hyphen and an "s" to make *azurs-verts*. But since Rimbaud did not make this insertion, as they stand, the words *azurs verts* bring us to a point of virtual incomprehensibility: Rimbaud has violated a semantic rule. He has violated the standards of propriety in his diction, too, not just in introducing vulgar terms into his texts, but in conjoining terms from disparate registers, forming stylistic oxymorons like *morves d'azur*.

Todorov links the impossibility of representation in the *Illuminations* with those texts' oxymorons and contradictory sentences. He sees Rimbaud's language as essentially "présentatif" rather than representational (129-30).[10] It is possible to read much of Rimbaud's verse not as representations of the world, but as statements about contemporary poetry or about his own poetry. Their use of unconventional diction serves to foreground these intertextual and self-referential dimensions.

The preceding examination of the language of Rimbaud's poetry has repeatedly encountered the question of reference. This is a question raised often with respect to the *Illuminations*, but it is central also to interpretations of Rimbaud's verse works dating almost from the beginning of his writing career. As we have seen, the kinds of terms he introduced into verse—scientific terms, neologisms, and familiar discourse in particular—create discordances in tone, agrammaticalities that call for critical interpretation. When pushed to the extreme, as at certain moments in "Mes petites amoureuses," these anomalies in diction can push a text to the point of unreadability, the way they did in Verlaine's "Nouvelles Variations." When familiar language refuses assimilation by its context in this way, its shock value—even today—is especially great; and it can thereby gain great destructive or constructive force. In doing so it can serve to disrupt referentiality at the same time as it adds another level of reference, reference that functions by means of the figurative dimension of diction.

In his sonnet on Rimbaud, Auden wrote: "But in that child the rhetorician's lie / Burst like a pipe." The phrase "burst like a pipe" echoes Rimbaud's own use of unconventional discourse in poetry. But Auden is presenting the traditional view of rhetoric as artificial, as what is opposed to the real, the genuine, the down-to-earth. Rimbaud's accomplishment is to have used such discourse to its greatest rhetorical advantage, not just in the way it can engage the reader, startling her, perhaps even shocking her, but also in the way it functions like rhetorical figure. And at its strongest, in texts like "Ce qu'on dit au poète" or "Le Bateau ivre," where "le Poème de la mer" transfers the aesthetics of liberation to the poetic lexicon and imagery, it figures the poetic enterprise itself.

SEVEN
Conclusion

The poetics of the unconventional that we find articulated in Rimbaud's work is important for all of the poets I have treated, who were experimenting with new poetic materials. In his preface to *Les Yeux d'Elsa*, Aragon summarizes the poetic theory he inherited from them: "L'art des vers est l'alchimie qui transforme en beautés les faiblesses. Où la syntaxe est violée, où le mot déçoit le mouvement lyrique, où la phrase de travers se construit, là combien de fois le lecteur frémit" (7). These poets, then, participate in the aesthetic and cultural attitudes we associate with modernism. Each contributed in his own way to the development of these attitudes as he and other poets of the time attempted to create a new poetic discourse.

I. Different Voices

The preceding chapters have served to show how the use of familiar language functions in the work of each of the poets treated. They belong to three different generations; each has a very particular poetic vision and poetic project: although they share characteristics that lead us to situate them in the modern tradition, it is not to be expected that devices common to two or more of them should have similar poetic consequences in works that are often very dissimilar in other respects. Looking at the use of a single term from outside the traditional poetic lexicon can help to give us a measure of some of these differences. *Tapage*, though classified by Littré as a familiar term, is not particularly strong language and may not bring about the striking effects we have seen generated elsewhere. But it ap-

pears in poems that represent some of the important characteristics of each poet's style, and it can help us to see how each
makes use of familiar discourse.

Banville uses the word in the "Occidentales" section of the
Odes funambulesques, in a poem entitled "Marchands de
crayons" where a young woman is describing her lost love, her
"prince," Arthur. A sympathetic young man has accompanied
her to the Opera ball to look for him among the crowd of
famous artists, publishers, and literati, but to no avail. Yet
Arthur is an artist too, she tells the young man, a musician: "Il
fait souvent de la musique / Avec son cornet à piston!":

> "Son bonnet brille comme un phare
> Sur son costume officiel,
> Lorsque, aux éclats de sa fanfare,
> Le moineau franc tremble et s'effare
> Et s'enfuit vers l'azur du ciel!
>
> "Il aimait à faire tapage
> Par les beaux jours pleins de rayons,
> Assis en vêtement de page
> Sur le sommet d'un équipage.
> Derrière un marchand de crayons!

In these lines we can see many of Banville's comic devices and
in particular his use of contrasts in diction. The trappings and
the language of neoclassical poetry (*les beaux jours pleins de
rayons*, *l'azur du ciel*, and so on) are in sharp contrast with the
subject and with contemporary and prosaic elements like Arthur's uniform and the pencil seller. The lines "Son bonnet
brille comme un phare" and "Sur le sommet d'un équipage"
are condensed versions of this contrast. *Tapage* is doubly comical, as a familiar term opposed to the traditional diction, and
as characterizing the music dear Arthur produces. Underlying
the poem are familiar themes in Banville, too, the poor taste of
his age, the lack of comprehension accorded to true artists, the
commercialization of bourgeois society.[1]

Striking contrasts are also characteristic of Baudelaire's
style, though in a very different vein from Banville's. A good
example is a poem in which *tapage* appears, "Sisina." Describ-

ing a woman who is a "douce guerrière / A l'âme charitable autant que meurtrière," it is based, like so many of Baudelaire's
poems, on paradox and antithesis. Oxymorons like *douce
guerrière* and "Son courage, affolé de poudre et de tambours"
echo the stylistic conflicts in the first stanza:

> Imaginez Diane en galant équipage,
> Parcourant les forêts ou battant les halliers,
> Cheveux et gorge au vent, s'enivrant de tapage,
> Superbe et défiant les meilleurs cavaliers!

S'enivrant de tapage doubles an oxymoron with the stylistic
incongruity of combining a noble verb with a familiar complement. *Tapage* is especially striking in its context, both because of the mythological allusions in the stanza and because it
is followed by the word *superbe*. Such clashes translate the
conflicting emotions the poem portrays. The simultaneous attraction and repulsion Baudelaire often expresses towards
women is attributed in this text to the woman's own feelings
toward love, itself presented as a kind of combat.

In "Voix de l'orgueil" (*Sagesse*), Verlaine also makes use of
unlikely combinations of words, like "l'endroit fait semblant":

> Voix de la Chair: un gros tapage fatigué.
> Des gens ont bu. L'endroit fait semblant d'être gai.
> Des yeux, des noms, et l'air plein de parfums atroces
> Où vient mourir le gros tapage fatigué.

"Un gros tapage fatigué" is a contradiction in terms like those
in Baudelaire, though *tapage* is in harmony rather than disharmony with its stylistic milieu. There is no mythological allusion or neoclassical diction here. The stanza uses a spoken
rhythm and incomplete or very brief sentences to create the
impressions of colloquial speech. In the very negative scene
created by this stanza, the familiar status of *tapage* underlines
its pejorative connotations. In tension with this tone, however,
are the subject, "la Chair," with its theological resonances, and
the phrase "Où vient mourir." The overall effect is that of simultaneous "imprecision" and strong impression, an effect
that Verlaine achieves in so much of his verse.

Hugo uses *tapage* in "Quelques mots à un autre," from *Les*

Contemplations, addressed to an older man who has criticized Hugo's innovations in poetic language. The speaker is imagining that the man's age should counsel him as follows:

> "Ces gens-ci vont leur train; qu'est-ce que ça vous fait?
> Ils ne trouvent que cendre au feu qui vous chauffait.
> Pourquoi déclarez-vous la guerre à leur tapage?"

As in "Voix de l'orgueil," *tapage* is used in a disparaging way in these lines. Ironically, what is denigrated is Hugo's own work. The text also calls on the connotations of *tapage* as a term referring to the noisy sounds of children's play, contrasting the old man's maturity (at least the maturity the speaker says he should have) to the youthful efforts of poets like Hugo. Because of this connotation, the contrast between *guerre* and *tapage* underlines the disproportion of the old man's actual reaction. The use of this level of language is highly relevant to the text as a whole, because, as in "Réponse à un acte d'accusation," its major theme is Hugo's stylistic innovations and the violent objections they have encountered. The older generation, according to the speaker, has rejected them out of hand: "Vos yeux par la clarté du mot propre brûlés;/Vous exécrez nos vers francs et vrais; vous hurlez/De fureur en voyant nos strophes toutes nues." As in "Réponse," Hugo links together freeing up the alexandrine, introducing familiar language, and rejecting rhetoric in favor of the literal term. His lexicon incorporates on the one hand neoclassical diction, mythological terms, and didactic expressions, and on the other, popular and familiar expressions.[2] As I have noted in chapter 2, such usage is typical of Hugo's polemical verse, especially in *Les Contemplations* and *Les Châtiments*. Despite his dismissal of traditional eloquence, however, these poems retain their oratorical tone, rather than creating the more properly colloquial tone we find in Verlaine, for instance.

Rimbaud uses *tapage* in the second stanza of "Le Bateau ivre":

> J'étais insoucieux de tous les équipages,
> Porteur de blés flamands ou de cotons anglais.
> Quand avec mes haleurs ont fini ces tapages,
> Les Fleuves m'ont laissé descendre où je voulais.

Like Hugo and Verlaine, Rimbaud uses *tapage* in a deprecating way. But here, such a use is paradoxical, because it refers to the massacre of the boatmen by the Indians in the first stanza: "Des Peaux-Rouges criards les avaient pris pour cibles,/Les ayant cloués nus aux poteaux de couleurs." The violence of this image both indicates the rejection of civilization expressed in these stanzas and prepares the reader for further shocks on the drunken boat's voyage. Incongruous in its reference, then, *tapage* is highly appropriate in its connotation: it underlines the childishness of the "redskins" story and prepares the way for the images of children to appear later in the text, especially at the very end, where "un enfant accroupi plein de tristesses, lâche / Un bateau frêle comme un papillon de mai." As a familiar term, it is a comparatively mild element in this poem, whose vocabulary includes neologisms, latinisms, biblical allusions, scientific words, culinary terms, provincialisms, and more. With the other familiar expressions, however, it provides a counterpoint to the exotic words and places, forming a contrast that is central to one of the poem's major themes, the conflicting desire for and fear of the unknown. It takes its place in the rich lexicon that Rimbaud uses to such striking effect throughout his verse.

Familiar language, then, has many different stylistic and rhetorical possibilities, exploited differently by each of these poets. When Hugo mixes levels and periods in lines like "Cours, saute, emmène Alphésibée / Souper au Café de Paris" ("Genio libri"), he is bringing them together in the overarching union of multiplicity that is his vision of the universe. We have seen how Baudelaire, on the other hand, leaves such contradictions unresolved. They take their place in a poetry informed by philosophic dualism and a sense of the disorientation and fragmentation of modern life. Banville is able to draw comic effects from his incongruous allusions and language levels: "Patron des fabricans d'ombrelles, qui protèges / Chryse, et qui ceins de feux la divine Cilla, / Regardez ce que font ces imbéciles-là!" ("Réalisme"). In "A la manière de Paul Verlaine," (*Parallèlement*) Verlaine pastiches his own style, showing the extent to which he relies on conflicting registers:

Je pardonne à ce mensonge-là

En faveur en somme du plaisir
Très banal drôlement qu'un loisir
Douloureux un peu m'inocula.

Many of his poems are based on such stylistic irresolution.
Rimbaud uses contrasts like these throughout his verse, and
particularly in his social and political satire. A rather surprising characteristic of such poetry is its use of familiar alongside
with scientific or medical expressions. We find examples of
this usage in Baudelaire, Verlaine (as in the lines quoted
above), Rimbaud, Corbière, and even Banville (see "La Tristesse d'Oscar," for instance). Contrasts in diction lend themselves
easily to effects of irony, exploited most fully by Laforgue, but
present in the others as well. Ultimately, the mixing of elements and levels can lead to a breakdown in logical development that brings us to the edge of unreadability, as we have
seen in both Verlaine and Rimbaud.

The poets I have been studying were not, however, the only
ones to experiment with expanding the poetic lexicon through
the use of familiar language. Nor was this development the
only (or even the most important) direction that poetic language was taking. Of those other poets working in an oral style,
the most important and most adventurous is surely Corbière.
Because of his rich poetic lexicon and the way he pushes these
devices to extremes, Corbière is an important part of the
movement I have been examining, and he made a strong impression on later poets, especially Pound and Eliot.[3] Richepin's work is of lesser importance and certainly lesser influence, though he had his successors in the genre of *poésie argotique* that flourished in the 1890s. We have seen that Hugo introduced *argot* into *Les Châtiments*; Verlaine has several
poems in slang; and he, Rimbaud, and Corbière used popular
language and slang both in direct quotation and in the poet's
own voice. But although Richepin's *La Chanson des gueux*
(1876) represents the first sustained attempt to write in true
argot, we do not see the striking use of low diction in conjunction with more elevated language that we find in the other
poets. In the end, despite the reputation he acquired, Richepin's practice is a good deal tamer than that of Verlaine, Rimbaud, or Corbière.[4]

The little magazines that flourished in the 1870s and 80s were printing many examples of poetry that made use of colloquial language.[5] Many of these poets were members of the circles that were called or who called themselves "Decadents." The use of colloquialisms was an important feature of decadent style, coexisting with its search for rare and esoteric terms.[6] Yet, despite their use of colloquialisms, the Decadents sought to create a language far removed from everyday speech. Their goal was the antithesis of Hugo's democratization of poetic language; the decadent hero, after all, was an aristocrat. Their taste for artificiality and their desire for a new kind of poetry led to the creation of a new preciosity, a special language for the initiated. It is no wonder that such verse was easily and frequently parodied. Writing in 1897 about Symbolist poetry (including that of Verhaeren, Kahn, and Tailhade), Vigié-Lecocq enunciates a distinction between the "langue vulgaire" of common writers, "banale expression d'idées banales," and a "langue de lettrés" characterized by "le souci de l'exactitude, le respect des origines latines, l'emploi judicieux et consciencieux des termes les plus divers, la recherche érudite et patiente d'une écriture personnelle, belle de ses propres beautés" (285). We have come full circle from Hugo's time: this erudite language will include what had been called "vulgar" (popular) language; but there will again be a separate, properly "poetic" language.

Mallarmé and the Symbolists who followed him also sought to create a very special poetic language. Though it was different from the neoclassical one, it, too, had words that were properly "poetic" in that they recurred frequently in verse and acquired special, enriched meanings. Such terms could originate in the traditional poetic lexicon, like *azur* and *ébat*, or they could come from other sources, like *aboli* or *stérilité*. The injunction to "donner un sens plus pur aux mots de la tribu" ("Le Tombeau d'Edgar Poe") applied in either case. Elements from everyday life (cigars, fans) and a few familiar constructions do appear in Mallarmé's poetry, but they are elevated and transformed by their lexical and syntactic context, excluding "le réel parce que vil" ("Toute l'âme résumée").[7] So even within the Decadent and Symbolist movements, the turn towards the common language was not a universal phenomenon.

It should be clear that the relation of poetic to what Aristotle called "foreign" and "commonplace" discourse was by no means established once and for all by the poets I have studied. Laforgue and Verhaeren as well as many other minor fin-de-siècle writers used familiar diction in their own ways; the poets of the twentieth century have so frequently incorporated such language that its use has lost some of its stylistic force; and theorists from the Russian Formalists to more recent critics trying to separate poetic from standard or scientific or neutral language, cognitive from expressive discourse, are still engaged in trying to determine the nature of this relation.[8]

II. Modernism and the Unconventional

The above examples reveal some of the ways the poets I have treated differ in their use of language levels. On the other hand, the foregoing study of their language has met with a number of elements they have in common, among them the very project of reforming the French poetic language. Their attitude to their poetic materials is part of what makes us think of them as "modern." Aragon formulates this position as follows: "il n'y a poésie qu'autant qu'il y a méditation sur le langage, et à chaque pas *réinvention* de ce langage. Ce qui implique de briser les cadres fixes du langage, les règles de la grammaire, les lois du discours" (*Elsa*, 10). The attitude Aragon expresses here is not only a Surrealist one; rather, it encapsulates the modernist view of poetry. It shows to what extent the values implied by the poetic practice of nineteenth-century poets have taken hold, making effects of dissonance, surprise, and confrontation acceptable, even desirable. The anticonventional has become the convention. This does not imply, however, the elimination of a hierarchy of poetic genres and styles. As Molino et Tamine point out, in the modern period, "les grands genres sont les genres d'avant-garde" (100). An aesthetic based in some measure on a capacity to startle has certain limitations, however. As juxtapositions of language levels have become more common, they become less perceptible, and their effects are dulled. The more "poetic" prosaic language becomes, the fewer poetic effects are generated. It is perhaps in recognition of this fact that French poetry has taken many different directions during the course of the twentieth century, only some making use of the familiar vocabulary now a part of the poetic lexicon.

The poets I have been studying, however, were able to put unconventional language to good use in their work. They did so in several related ways, though their applications of these ways vary with their own poetic worlds. Several aspects in the work of some or all of them bear closer examination: a rejection of eloquence, a search for originality, an attempt to depict contemporary life, an implied linking between poetic language and politics, and an aesthetics of rupture and surprise.

One of the themes we have seen repeatedly in the reaction of these poets against the stifling constraints of neoclassical form is a rejection of eloquence (usually taken as synonymous with rhetoric) and a corresponding valorization of the literal term. This is the attitude that Hugo enunciates in "Quelques mots à un autre" and that Pound expresses in discussing Laforgue: "Bad verbalism is rhetoric, or the use of *cliché* unconsciously, or a mere playing with phrases" (283). When Laforgue writes "Faire de l'éloquence me semble si mauvais goût, si jobard," (*Correspondance, O.C.* 4: 163), he is echoing Verlaine's "Prends l'éloquence et tords-lui son cou" and Hugo's "Plante là toute rhétorique." Lines like these, incorporating familiar constructions, show how practice correlates with precept, for one of the major elements in the style informed by such a view is, as we have seen, the use of colloquial expressions and syntax. In "Voix de l'orgueil," Verlaine foresees a time when all the "Sentences, mots en vain, métaphores mal faites, / Toute la rhétorique en fuite des péchés" will die before "la voix terrible de l'Amour!" The dismissal of rhetoric becomes in effect, a rejection of language altogether. But the impossibility of doing without either is obvious. Furthermore, we have also seen to what extent using lower language levels creates new rhetorical possibilites rather eliminating them: there is no zero degree of rhetoric.

When these poets disparage rhetoric, it is in reaction against the abuses they perceive in their predecessors, and it is an aspect of another characteristic associated with modernism, the pursuit of originality. Laforgue put it most bluntly: "J'écris de petits poèmes de fantaisie, n'ayant qu'un but: faire de l'original à tout prix" (*Correspondance*, 5: 20). In his letter to Demeny, Rimbaud announces, "les inventions d'inconnu réclament des formes nouvelles" (Bernard ed., 349). Ironically, though these poets are often seen as breaking with romanticism (and Rimbaud's "Lettre du Voyant" is a major text in this regard), the desire to break with tradition is itself a romantic trait.[9] It is clear that, from Hugo on, one of the most important innovations we can discern is the renewal of poetic language I have been studying: Hugo's "bonnet rouge au vieux dictionnaire," Banville's claim to have found a new comic language, and Rimbaud's call to "trouver une langue" make explicit what is implied in the work of all these poets. It is interesting to note how often a critic writing about one of them will claim the merit of this "revolution" in poetic diction for his or her poet. Often, a device or an expression signaled for its novelty will have appeared earlier in another poet's work; sometimes examples can be found in Boileau or Malherbe. I do not mean to assert that Corbière does not use more slang than Baudelaire, for instance, or that Verlaine's role in this development is less significant than has been claimed, but rather, to point out the extent to which novelty and originality have become valued characteristics in poetry. We have come a long way from when Carpentier's dictionary was praised for helping poets to "fixer leur goût dans l'emploi des expressions, dans le choix des tournures."[10]

Part of being modern is depicting what is modern; and the portrayal of the contemporary scene, theorized by Baudelaire, is another important aspect of the work of all these poets. Hugo was among the first to introduce bourgeois domestic life as a subject for poetry. His portrayal of the lives of the lower classes led to a great deal of verse following his example, by many minor poets like Coppée and Manuel as well as the works we have seen by Verlaine and Rimbaud. Banville naturally drew on contemporary people, scenes, and events in his satirical verse, which carries an indictment of the society it presents. In this respect it is related to Baudelaire's depiction of modern urban life, where the monstrous and the demonic are ever present.

The depiction of contemporary life involves, for all these poets, a reliance on concrete detail and on familiar and slang discourse. The extent to which originality and the modern are associated with unconventional diction can be seen in the poems in which familiar language is used to signal the modern world whereas neoclassical or archaic diction and mythological allusions indicate the contrasting world of the past. Yet, as my examination of Hugo's poetry of domestic life has shown, its point is not the direct representation of the contemporary world. Verlaine's "Croquis parisien" links Paris to a mythological past; the humble settings and characters in Hugo's poems (and those of Rimbaud as well) are the bearers of political or philosophical messages; and, as Baudelaire puts it in his "realistic" poem, "Le Cygne," "tout pour moi devient allégorie."

An important part of what such language and such portrayals signify is their political message, especially the criticism of bourgeois society shared by all of them except Hugo (whose object of attack is, rather, the political regime). We have seen that this is a major theme in Banville's verse. His "Monsieur Coquardeau" is a close relative of Verlaine's "Monsieur Prudhomme" and Corbière's RUMINANT ("Litanie du sommeil"). A similar critique is central to many of Rimbaud's poems. Such texts often seem to fly in the face of the decorum associated with bourgeois life. Thus, these poets concentrate on semantic fields that had usually been passed over in silence, especially those having to do with the body, like food and clothing. Particular items of clothing are often mentioned, both because of this emphasis on the body and because of their link with the fashionable, the contemporary. The range covered by these poems shows again how similar elements can be used to radically different effect. Baudelaire emphasizes the body itself, especially its more repugnant aspects. Verlaine presents the most revolting results of drunkenness and debauch. Rimbaud carries this emphasis even further in his "Stupra" sonnets and in the scatological "Accroupissements" and "Oraison du soir."

Bourgeois decorum is violated in the descent in style to levels of informal tenor as well. The introduction of new diction was part of the attempt to "épater le bourgeois" we associate with avant-garde art. Vigié-Lecocq saw it in this light: "Ce riche lexique déroute le bourgeois, se servant au besoin de quelques centaines de mots ternis par le long usage; effaré, il déclare ne plus comprendre" (270). Such an attitude is part of the attack on its own readership that Sartre views as characterizing French literature between 1848 and 1914 in *Qu'est-ce que la littérature* (148-56). As the chapters on Hugo and Rimbaud have made clear, the link between revolutionary politics and the introduction of colloquial speech has a long history. It is very common to find the latter expressed in terms of the former, by poets and critics alike. In Boileau's "Art poétique," we can see how the opposition between high and low diction takes on political implications:

> Quoyque vous écriviez, évitez la bassesse.
> Le stile le moins noble a pourtant sa noblesse.
> Au mépris du Bon sens, le Burlesque effronté
> Trompa les yeux d'abord, plut par sa nouveauté.
> On ne vit plus en vers que pointes triviales;
> Le Parnasse parla le langage des Hales.
>
> (lines 78-84)

In this passage nobility of language equals nobility of birth; "low" language is that of les Halles, of the lower classes. Neoclassical theorists like La Harpe, Bonald, and Delille also link restrained or free diction to political institutions. At the end of the nineteenth century, Brunetière uses imagery of height and depth similar to Boileau's and Hugo's (in "Réponse") when he takes the romantics to task for having abandoned their national tradition: "En ce qui touche à la langue d'abord, et sous le prétexte assez spécieux de lui restituer son ancienne liberté, le romantisme n'a rien négligé de ce qu'il fallait pour la faire tomber du point de perfection où les classiques l'avaient portée" (*Etudes critiques*, 321).

My examination of Hugo's "Réponse" dealt with the importance to this poem of the politics/poetics parallelism. Just as Hugo does for his own verse, Hazlitt compares Wordsworth's innovations to the French Revolution:

> It partakes of, and is carried along with, the revolutionary movement of our age: the political changes of the day were the model on which he formed and conducted his poetical experiments. His Muse . . . is a levelling one. It proceeds on a principle of equality. . . . His popular, inartificial style gets rid (at a blow) of all the trappings of verse, of all

>the high places of poetry. . . . Kings, queens, priests,
>robes, the altar and the throne . . . are not to be found
>here (quoted in Abrams, 39-40).

(In late nineteenth-century France, of course, it was the bourgeois rather than kings and nobles who were seen as opposing the leveling of class represented by the new poetic language.)

When Eliot discusses the way poetic language changes, he too compares the return to common speech to a revolution: "Every revolution in poetry is apt to be, and sometimes to announce itself to be, a return to common speech. That is the revolution which Wordsworth announced in his prefaces, and he was right: but the same revolution had been carried out a century before . . . and the same revolution was due again something over a century later" (23). Butor expresses the same idea when he writes that the object of poetry is "le salut du langage courant. Lorsqu'elle s'en est complètement isolée, on est à la veille d'une révolution littéraire (Malherbe, Wordsworth, 'J'ai mis le [*sic*] bonnet rouge au vieux dictionnaire' de Hugo)" (43). Butor's point of view reflects again the quest for originality that is such an important legacy of romanticism. Unlike Eliot, who sees the poetic task as varying from one period to another (28-29), Butor clearly valorizes the revolutionary. The poetics/politics analogy seems to be a part of the way we have come to talk about poetry.

But, as we have seen, the shock of conflicting registers has different implications for each poet, implications often related to politics only indirectly, if at all. That these poets put the same devices to varied uses should alert us not to assign them a univocal meaning. Even more, it should make us wary of deducing from them facts about the poets' lives or vice versa. We have seen how the use of vulgar language has been attributed to aspects as different as Hugo's democratic politics, Baudelaire's vices, Verlaine's drunkenness, and Rimbaud's social rebellion.

This language is unsettling not only because of its opposition to the previous standard and the political stance such an opposition may imply, but also in the way it is used in the poems themselves. All the poets studied seek effects of juxtaposition and rupture, the "negative techniques" of modern poetry that Friedrich classifies as fragmentation, incoherence, and dissonance. The clashes in diction I have been studying are an important aspect of this development. Such juxtapositions are often used to counter and deflate what has been elevated by means of neoclassical diction, as in Hugo's "Leur coeur, leur vertu, leur catarrhe" ("Eblouissements"). This is, naturally, a common device in Banville's humorous verse. When Baudelaire uses it, it is with poignancy or a kind of mordant humor, as in "Le Monstre," "Au lecteur," and "Une Charogne." Rimbaud uses the deflating power of the informal tenor for violent attacks on his targets, in "L'Orgie parisienne" and "Mes petites amoureuses," for example. Hugo's reducing of proper names to the status of common nouns finds an echo in Rimbaud, who irreverently turns common nouns into proper ones as well, putting into question their capacity to refer at all.

An especially effective way to create effects of disjuncture is to play language off against a poem's subject. These poets often use informal language for a traditionally poetic subject, creating a kind of "travesty" (in Genette's terms, defined in *Palimpsestes*). Thus, addresses to the muses are no longer in a sustained high style in Hugo's *Chansons*, Banville's "Evohé" poems, or even Baudelaire's "La Muse vénale." The muse as prostitute is in fact a theme common to these poets and to Corbière as well. Love poetry has a mischievous air in Verlaine's "En patinant" and a distinctly unromantic tone in Rimbaud's "Vénus anadyomène" and Corbière's "A une demoiselle." The other side of this procedure is the use of neoclassical diction for a contemporary, "prosaic," or even repugnant subject. Such a practice is related to the "charge" as Genette defines it. Rimbaud's "Oraison du soir," Baudelaire's "Une Charogne," and Banville's "Monsieur Coquardeau" include examples of this latter technique. Both charge and travesty depend on poetic conventions because such discourse functions only when it runs counter to the reader's expectations of harmony between style and subject. But it is not with satiric purpose alone that these poets break down the boundaries between prose and poetry. In doing so they put into question this very distinction, and they open serious verse to new elements and new techniques. Baudelaire's vision of a new poetics is expressed in his essay on Banville: "De le laideur et de la sottise il fera naître un nouveau genre d'enchantements" (2:167). Such an aesthetic underlies the lexical experimentation of all these poets.

Since the lexical innovations I have been studying and the dissonant effects they can create are intrusions in the texture of traditional poetry, they take part in the flouting of artistic conventions we have come to associate with the modernist work. Thus, Breton writes: "Au sens le plus général du mot, nous passons pour des poètes parce qu'avant tout nous nous attaquons au langage qui est la pire convention" (66). In this passage he is speaking of the Dadaists, but the resistance to convention and the emphasis on the material of construction (language in this instance) he expresses characterize the art of the avant-garde in general.

In breaking the rules, unconventional diction attracts the reader's notice to the surface of the works where it appears. Because of this foregrounding, these texts exhibit another of the major traits of modernism: the artwork's gesturing toward the process of its own construction. Each of these poets has written major poems about the writing of poetry and the poet's place in the world: Banville creates his poet-clown; Hugo's "Réponse" is only one of many poems about poetry; Baudelaire begins *Les Fleurs du mal* with his cycle on art; Verlaine gives us his "Art poétique," Corbière, "I Sonnet," and Rimbaud "Ce qu'on dit au poète" and "Ma Bohème." In all these works, there is a coincidence of theory and practice, and the language levels used play an important part in the functioning of the text.

As the surfaces and the process of constructing these poems gain in importance, the referential dimension of their language is diminished. Rather, they become self-referential. Foucault sees this characteristic of modern literature as leading to what he calls counter-discourse. It is opposed to the classical conception of representation by means of naming and by the deferral of the name through rhetoric: "A l'âge moderne, la littérature, c'est ce qui compense (et non ce qui confirme) le fonctionnement significatif du langage" (59). Hugo's vision of a language adequate to represent the world gives way to a prolif-

eration of language beyond control. He was to "nommer le cochon par son nom"; but the pig turns out to have many different names, with different significances and stylistic potential.

Despite their place in the creation of modern literature as
Foucault defines it, it would be a mistake to view these writers
as heroes in a success story of poetic evolution. Theirs was a
swing of the pendulum away from a specialized literary vocabulary, not altogether unlike previous ones, and not a stopping
of the pendulum's movement. But that does not diminish
their significance in the development of that strain of modern
poetry that looks to the resources of the common language in
its attempt to create a new poetic voice. In taking what had
been considered base, unformed lexical material and making
poetry out of it, in unleashing its rhetorical power, these poets
are all practitioners of verbal alchemy.

Notes

ONE. Poetic Language and the Language of Poetry

1 The term *register* is also used as an equivalent to these expressions, but I prefer to use it in a more precise sense, as detailed below.

2 It should be kept in mind, however, that dialectal and archaic expressions can play an important role in poetry, too. In fact, archaism is often a significant component of poetic diction.

3 Ure and Ellis give an overview and a bibliography of the literature on language varieties through 1966. More recent descriptions of these categories, with some variation in terminology and order, are given in Gregory, Turner (165-202); Enkvist (59-62); and chap. 3 ("Stylistic Analysis") of Crystal and Davy. Halliday elaborates on them in "Text as Semantic Choice" and in *Language* (33-35, 62-64, 142-50). Other ways to classify the components of speech situations have been proposed by Hymes, who sets up a sixteen-part schema (51-62); Joos, whose five levels of style (from intimate to frozen) are more or less a description of the dimension of *tenor*; and Jakobson, who analyzes language according to function. I will be discussing various classifications of French language levels later on.

4 For an expanded description of these dimensions, see Halliday, *Language* (142-45).

5 For more examples and further discussion, see Halliday et al. (92-97) and Gregory and Carroll, chap. 6.

6 Kerbrat studies the connotative value of phonetic, morphological, and syntactic aspects of language as well as vocabulary. I will concentrate on lexical elements, but all these aspects are closely interrelated.

7 Delas and Filliolet point out the limitations of the idea that certain terms have an "evocative" effect and emphasize instead the structuring of the text as a whole (96, 98; see also 116). Indeed it is only when it is actualized in discourse that, as Kerbrat shows: "un mot peut se poétiser, se vulgariser, ou perdre au contraire sa marque connotative, et les effets du contexte peuvent neutraliser un terme marqué ou marquer un terme neutre" (97). Enkvist gives an overview of the ways context has been defined in relation to literary texts, including Riffaterre's distinction between *microcontext* and *macrocontext* (54-62).

8 Catford suggests "a 'poetic genre' as a super-variety characterized by potential use of features appropriate to all styles" (85), whereas Ure and

Ellis as well as Halliday et al. (92) see literature as a register in itself. Bally places literary language alongside the language of science, administration, and sports, albeit in a "place d'honneur" (28). Vinay and Darbelnet, discussing "niveaux de langue," put "langue littéraire" and then, "langue poétique" at the top of their hierarchy (34), with technical languages or "jargons" on a horizontal axis equivalent to "langue écrite." Joos likewise associates his most formal category, "frozen style," with literature (27). I will not enter into the debates about the relation of poetic to "standard" language. Fowler presents criticisms of the " 'poetic language' fallacy" (184-86); and he recommends taking language varieties into account (20-21). Iser summarizes the objections to the concept of style as deviation from a norm (86-92); and Kerbrat outlines various theories of the "neutral" term and proposes instead the kind of conventional and contextual norms I am presenting here (96-98).

9   For a critique of such "romantic" theories of poetic discourse, see Todorov (99-104) and Molino and Tamine (86). On the romantics' resistance to convention, see Manley (34-39). Pleynet studies the way the poetry of the last century has attempted to come to terms with the way the literary text "est appelé à dialectiser son rapport à la convention (au code) s'il veut donner un maximum de rendement" (98).

10   Iser discusses such expectations in the constitution of a text's "repertoire" (69-71). See Manley for definitions of different kinds of conventions (33, 47).

11   For example, Zumthor has studied what he calls the "register" of medieval poetry (but what could more properly be called its code), defined as "a pre-existent network of lexical, rhetorical, and even syntactic probabilities . . . [that] constitutes the basis of the poetic expression of the *trouvère*: it provides him with a set of predetermined poetic requirements" (273).

12   Meschonnic takes the position that any word has the potential of becoming "poetic" (*Poétique*, 55-62); whereas Kerbrat points out that there are words "à vocation poétique" (95). Riffaterre distinguishes between the poetic potential of a word in the *langue* from its use in the *parole* of a particular text, where its context may neutralize its poetic connotations (*Essais*, 204). He studies the various ways terms and phrases that are conventionally poetic are used in literary texts (182-202).

13   The poetry Aristotle is discussing here, however, is not lyric poetry. Genette points out that he does not discuss lyric poetry at all in the *Poetics* (*Architexte*, 16).

14   Aristotle indicated a style for three kinds of rhetoric and distinguished between written and spoken styles in his *Rhetoric* (bk. 3, chap. 12); and Cicero also divided oratorical style into three levels, linking subject-matter and formality (bk. 4, §§8-11, 252-69). Although these classifications addressed oratory in particular, many genre systems were based on these distinctions. Some critics of the French neoclassical period like La Harpe and Bonald criticized such systems, however.

15   Mailloux points out that "how a particular author's practices relate to

the tradition, how he uses the conventions according to his purposes, and what literary and extraliterary meaning his use of them produces are always *specific to his unique context of writing*" (403, his italics).

16 Ullmann points out the comic effects that can be elicited by the introduction of vulgarisms and technical terms (162, 167). As we shall see, many other effects are possible.

17 Zola was aware that it was his language that outraged his critics. He wrote in his preface to the novel that "La forme seule a effaré. On s'est fâché contre les mots. Mon crime est d'avoir eu la curiosité littéraire de ramasser et de couler dans un moule très travaillé la langue du peuple. Ah! la forme, là est le grand crime!" (33). He was responding to critics like "Dancourt," who had written: "Il a imprimé dans un feuilleton . . . des mots jusqu'ici confinés dans les dictionnaires et que l'éducation la plus élémentaire interdit de prononcer" (*La Gazette de France*, 20 avril 1876, quoted in Deffoux, 59).

18 It is a historical irony that *langue bourgeoise* (as Guiraud calls it in *Le Français populaire*) should now be the term for the high style: the *bon usage* of the seventeenth century was the language of the court, certainly not that of the bourgeoisie.

19 Other novels using argot include Balzac's *La Dernière Incarnation de Vautrin* (1847) and Hugo's *Le Dernier Jour d'un condamné* (1828) and *Les Misérables* (1862).

20 Brunot finds that it was during the course of the nineteenth century that bourgeois speech "a été envahie par le parler libre et coloré des classes populaires" (Petit de Julleville, 8:829-30); whereas Valdman thinks the "brassages sociaux" of the twentieth century opened the frontiers between the two.

21 Riffaterre rightly points out, however, that poetic effects are not limited to contemporary reactions, even supposing that these could be accurately determined (*Essais*, 205-6).

22 On Littré's methods and categories as well as reactions to them, see Chaurand, 136-38.

23 Other sources for information about levels of formality in the nineteenth century include both lexicons of poetic words and expressions (I will examine in more detail the kinds of language they included and excluded) and dictionaries of slang like those of Larchey, Delvau, and Delasalle. Unfortunately, these slang dictionaries are not altogether reliable; and they tend to disagree on where many terms should be assigned. Cressot criticizes them for including terms accepted by the official dictionaries, omitting others that are not, and tending to classify as *argot* words that are merely familiar (335).

24 Despite wide recognition of the rigidity of neoclassical poetics, theoreticians and historians have analyzed its rules in very different ways. Molino and Tamine point out that there were many kinds of styles, according to the many possible genres (99). Ullmann summarizes systems like these in the seventeenth and eighteenth centuries (158). Often, however, genres have been grouped into either two or three main categories. Bonald, for example, finds the three "species" we usually call genres, (epic,

lyric, and dramatic), at both levels of his two "genres," the public and the domestic (889). Fontanier sees tropes as appropriate according to subject matter as well as the nobility of the genre: "Ainsi, les Tropes conviennent moins sans doute à la tendre et plaintive Elégie, qu'à la Satire maligne ou piquante; moins à la Comédie, dont le ton n'est que celui d'une noble et élégante conversation, qu'à la Tragédie . . . moins à la Tragédie, dont les personnages doivent, par la vérité et le naturel de leur langage, faire oublier le poète, qu'à l'Epopée . . . moins à l'Epopée . . . qu'à l'Ode" (181). In Brunot's *Histoire* Bruneau calls the second of the three usual categories "noble" rather than *médiocre* or *tempéré*; the high style is "langue ornée" (12:57). François divides his genres according to social category represented (heroes [nobles], bourgeois, and people) (2:90). His analysis reflects the confusion between moral qualities and social status Genette notes in Aristotle's formulations (*Architexte*, 16-17). Houston points out that despite such discrepancies, these theories had real influence (*Demonic Imagination*, 21). For my purposes the precise assignment of language levels to genres is less important than the fact that a correlation was perceived. The result was the constitution of a "noble" language.

25   It should not be forgotten that "noble" language was originally that of the court, to be imitated in society conversation and only secondarily in literature. "Precious" language in conversation is another, and a well-known, story, however. On the other hand, the supposedly conversational style in neoclassical poetry did not incorporate familiar language. Genette has pointed out that the "simple" style was really only "un style moins orné, ou plutôt, orné plus simplement" (*Figures*, 208).

26   Historians of French language and literature have examined neoclassical style in much more detail than is necessary here. See especially Bruneau, *Histoire*, 12:21-79; François, especially 2:89-100; and Barat, 5-35. For a summary of contemporary English poetic language, which used many of the same devices as the French, see Sherbo, 1-16.

27   See Molino and Tamine for examples (106-7). The special vocabulary and the ornaments of neoclassical style have become marked terms. Riffaterre has studied the stylistic effects of their use in postclassical poetry in *Essais* (182-202) and *Semiotics* (27-28).

28   On Delille's innovations and their limitations, see Bruneau, *Histoire*, 12:63-64. Houston studies his role in the changing language of late neoclassicism in *The Demonic Imagination*, 3-21. Chaurand discusses Delille's ideas on language and Hugo's opposition to him (129-30).

29   In his "Vie de Joseph Delorme," Sainte-Beuve excuses himself (in the name of his nom de plume) for having introduced into his poetry "quelques mots surannés ou de basse bourgeoisie exclus, on ne sait pas pourquoi, du langage poétique" (*Poésies*, 26). Note that he descends no lower than the "basse bourgeoisie."

30   Genette notes that modern literature has its own rhetoric, which is just the refusal of rhetoric (*Figures*, 221). Meschonnic says that this antirhetoric reveals a consciousness of rhetoric's power (*Poétique*, 123). Molino points out both that nineteenth-century literature is highly rhetor-

ical (in the sense of persuasion) and that it functions as a rhetoric, though a negative one (188-89).

31 Note how, once taken in its figurative sense, *acier* can mean iron. Such tropes do subvert simple reference.

32 The classic statement of this point of view, often attributed to Dumarsais, is the line: "Il se fait plus de figures un jour de marché à la Halle qu'il ne s'en fait en plusieurs jours d'assemblées académiques" (quoted in Genette, *Figures*, 209). Hugo's formulation is similar: "Les métaphores sont des filles de carrefours" (see chap. 2 below).

33 Angelet provides the most complete study of Corbière's "oral" vocabulary and syntax. Dansel studies such style in relation to Corbière's "modernity"; and in *Tristan Corbière* Mitchell frequently touches on questions of language levels in treating individual poems. On Laforgue's diction see King, "Laforgue's Symbolist Language" and Houston, *French Symbolism*, 66-83.

34 Both Cressot (8) and Bruneau, *Histoire*, 12:77, give 1880 as the date by which the romantic linguistic revolution had been completed.

35 On the "code struggle" between verse and prose poems see Johnson, especially 9-10 and chap. 5. Wing's analyses of Rimbaud's *Illuminations* include excellent treatments of the stylistic functions of varied diction in prose poetry.

TWO. Hugo: Responding to "Réponse"

1 Edmond Caro, *Revue contemporaine* (15 juin 1856), quoted in Gély, *Fortune* (51).

2 Ullmann calls the freeing of "banished" words merely a "réforme," but continues, "C'était le triomphe du mot propre, du mot simple et fort, sur la périphrase d'une rhétorique classicisante. . . . [in 1834] Victor Hugo fit le point de la victoire romantique dans sa célèbre *Réponse à un acte d'accusation*" (*Précis*, 178-79). A quotation from the poem follows.

3 According to Vianey in his edition of *Les Contemplations*, it was Veuillot who first pointed out that nowhere does Hugo call the "cochon par son nom" except in this line (1:52).

4 For a stylistic definition of periphrasis as riddle and its conventional character, see Riffaterre, *Essais* (193-94) and *Production* (53-54).

5 Houston sees both of these characteristics as part of romantic verse's movement in the direction of prose (*French Symbolism*, 96-97).

6 It should be noted, too, that in a very few instances, like "Rêverie d'un passant à propos de son roi" (*Feuilles d'automne*), a more conversational tone is used in a text with a political message. On the other hand, once the scene from contemporary life has been set in this poem, the poet's reflections are on a markedly higher plane in diction as well as subject.

7 In *Intimité* Gély has studied in detail Hugo as a "poète de l'intimité" and his relation in this respect to other poets of the period.

8 Voltaire praised Malherbe for having used *cabane*, a word that was "agréable et du beau style" rather than *taudis*, "expression du peuple" (quoted in François, 2:95).

9 The *Larousse du XIXe siècle* lists the word as familiar in the sense of a "terme d'amitié que l'on adresse à des enfants mignons et éveillés," a sense not mentioned in the other major nineteenth-century dictionaries.

10 Béranger himself was condemned for turning the light genre of songs into agressive satire. The prosecutor of his 1821 trial claimed he had corrupted this genre, "celui dont on excuse le plus volontiers les licences. L'esprit national le protège et la gaîté l'absout." After the Revolution, because of agitators like Béranger, "la muse des chants populaires devint une des furies de nos discordes civiles" (quoted in Zevaès, 20-21).

11 On Musset's practice in this respect, see Bruneau, *Histoire*, 12:253; Gautier, *Histoire* (297); and especially Houston, *Demonic Imagination*, (35-42), who sees Musset's practice as the result of his "indifference to certain niceties of diction" (38).

12 Gaudon calls *Eblouissements* a "poème exemplaire" (*Temps*, 177); and the Pléiade editor calls it "un des poèmes les plus caractéristiques des *Châtiments*" (2:1104).

13 Meschonnic studies this breaking down of the proper name until it becomes a common noun, thereby losing its stability (*Hugo*, 280-85).

14 See Nash on the allegorical structure of Hugo's universe and especially 33, n. 21; and Meschonnic, *Hugo*, 1:187-208. Meschonnic shows how, for Hugo, " . . . l'ordre des mots mime l'ordre des choses. Sa rhétorique est une métaphysique" (1:181).

THREE. Banville the Funambulist

1 "Avertissement de la deuxième édition" des *Odes funambulesques*, *Oeuvres*, 6:2. Quotations from Banville will usually be taken from this edition of his works, published in the 1890s, which includes Banville's 1873 commentary on the *Odes funambulesques*. The first edition of the *Odes* was published in 1857; and the second edition (1859) includes twelve new pieces (see the "Note des éditeurs," 291-94). I will refer to the variants from this edition as "1859."

2 See Badesco on Banville's influence (2:1113-42), and that of the *Odes funambulesques* in particular (2:1116-17). Although Banville's humorous verse appears in several collections, including *Odelettes* and *Trente-six Ballades joyeuses*, I will be concentrating mainly on his most famous work, the *Odes*. In *Les Stalagtites* (1846) Banville uses refrains from popular songs like "Nous n'irons plus au bois"; but rather than incorporating popular language, he uses the archaisms and traditional subjects that characterize such songs.

3 Banville was aware of the dangers of writing satire on contemporary themes. In his 1873 commentary he quotes a note to his poem "Evohé" from the 1857 edition: "*Rien de plus difficile que de faire comprendre après dix ans une plaisanterie parisienne . . .* "; and he goes on, "J'écrivais cette note en 1857; que dirai-je aujourd'hui, en 1873?" (6:303-4). Needless to say, in the 1980s . . .

4 Bruneau mentions these devices in his overview of Banville's language (*Histoire*, 13:55-64); see also Rivaroli (50) and Charpentier (155-56).

5 Harms compares these two poems in discussing Banville's parodies of Hugo (47-49). This section was retitled "Autres guitares" (still an allusion to Hugo) in the 1873 edition, and the title *Les Occidentales* was used for the 1869 collection that continued the *Odes*.

6 For a discussion of eating as the sign of the prosaic, opposed to the lyrical, see Johnson's contrast between Baudelaire's two versions of "Invitation au voyage" (103-7). Ironically in this context, the Baudelaire quotation exemplifying this contrast in codes is taken from his article on Banville, whom he sees as the very paradigm of the lyric poet.

7 Bruneau points out, however, that when Banville uses true *argot* like *balle* for head or *voyou*, he puts the terms in italics (*Histoire*, 13:61).

8 I have given the 1859 version. The last lines of the 1873 edition are:

> Triste comme un bonnet, ou comme ces croûtons
> De pain que nous cache une malle!

9 In his commentary Banville points out that the hatred for the bourgeois associated with the romantic era underlies his whole book: "en langage romantique, *bourgeois* signifiait l'homme qui n'a d'autre culte que celui de la pièce de cent sous, d'autre idéal que la conservation de sa peau, et qui en poésie aime la romance sentimentale, et dans les arts plastiques la lithographie coloriée" (6:294).

10 See King, "Poet as Clown" (240). Bray points out that the first instance of this theme in Banville appears in the poem "A Méry," from the *Odelettes* (267). Starobinski has studied this subject in the arts of the nineteenth and twentieth centuries.

11 In his commentary on this poem, Banville says he was trying to express "ce que je sens le mieux, l'attrait du gouffre d'en haut," a theme that doubtless arose from his admiration for Hugo. Storey discusses this theme but somehow sees no apotheosis in this poem, despite the last lines: "Le clown sauta si haut, si haut,/ Qu'il creva le plafond de toiles/ . . . /Et, le coeur dévoré d'amour,/ Alla rouler dans les étoiles" (4-5). Mallarmé seems to echo this poem in his article "Théodore de Banville" when he writes, "J'attends que, chauve-souris éblouissante et comme l'éventement de la gravité, soudain, du site par une pointe d'aile autochtone, le fol, adamantin, colère, tourbillonnant génie heurte la ruine; s'en délivre, dans la voltige qu'il est, seul" (*O.C.,* 521).

FOUR. Baudelaire: De quelle boue?

1 Gautier's article appeared in *L'Univers illustré* in 1868 and was published as the "Notice" to the 1868 edition of *Les Fleurs du mal*.

2 Royère also sees mysticism as leading to "catachresis" in Baudelaire's language (104). Grava studies the metaphysical implications of these "bipolarities," but unlike Cellier he underlines the importance of maintaining a tension between the opposite poles.

3 See Genovali, 14-19; Jouve, 2-4; and especially Wing, who shows how

"rhetorical devices are associated with a style level consistently deflated by contextual elements" ("Stylistic Function," 451).

4   Genovali, following Royère, uses "catachresis," to refer to stylistic incongruities in general. In its implication of a "forcing" together of disparate words, it is an apt term.

5   Letter of 26 janvier 1866 (*Correspondance*, 2:578). Mendès did not accept the poem, and it appeared in *Les Epaves*.

6   Other critics who have called attention to the contrasts between modern or "prosaic" elements and neoclassical diction and rhetoric in Baudelaire include Riffaterre, *Essais* (182-88); Antoine (5-12); and Houston, *Demonic Imagination* (85-124).

7   Jenny has examined in more detail these transitions and their import.

8   Jauss sees *fosse commune* as a "fall from stylistic heights" (*Toward an Aesthetic*, 155). He notes the incongruousness of the objects thrown together in the boudoir section of the poem, but sees them as "prosaic objects" rather than examining the prosaic *terms* (153-54). Like Auerbach, he takes *cerveau* to be a "technical medical term" (153) and calls it an "explosively prosaic rhyme-word" (163).

9   Jenny points out that "les deux principes métaphorique et métonymique se nourrissent l'un l'autre dans la construction du poème" (447).

10   For a detailed treatment of the stylistic shiftings in these lines (but classifications and interpretations of the terms *grouiller* and *fangeux* that differ from mine), see Genovali, 118-20.

11   See in particular Bersani (105-11) and Joxe (especially 145-48), where she discusses the "transmutation de la ville."

12   Under the heading "roux," Littré quotes Hamilton on a "Mme la marquise de Senantes," who "passait pour blonde . . . elle aimait mieux se conformer au goût du siècle, que respecter celui des anciens."

13   The connotations of "pauvre homme" supply a further link between gambling and sexuality, again implying a lack.

FIVE. Verlaine: Wringing the Neck of Eloquence

1   The obsolete term *patiner* means "to caress."

2   Because of its "prosaism," however, Genette sees in it a possible echo of Coppée (*Palimpsestes*, 138).

3   Cuénot notes that in revising the poem, Verlaine added more familiar terms than in earlier versions (156).

4   In his edition Dansel claims that in his cell, "Verlaine, démoralisé, opère un retour sur lui-même, sans indulgence" (72). Zimmermann sees it as one of the poems that express Verlaine's "sentiment de vide, d'abandon, son désespoir" (125-26).

5   Loos takes the word in its familiar sense (current since 1845, according to Robert) of "padding" a piece of written work, and he remarks, "Es ist vielleicht das erste Mal, dass ein französischer Dichter dieses Verbum in einer solchen Umgebung anwendet" (15-16). But in the context "ainsi qu'une rôtie," the first meaning (to spread on bread) seems most applicable.

6   Genette points out that a true self-imitation is impossible, being in principle indistinguishable from any other work of the author. Its existence depends entirely on its being designated as such (*Palimpsestes*, 138-39).

7   C'est la mère Michel qui a perdu son chat,
        Qui cri' par la fenêtr', qui est-c' qui lui rendra.
        Et l'compèr' Lustucru qui lui a répondu:
        "Allez, la mèr" Michel, vot' chat n'est pas perdu." . . .
        "Si vous rendez mon chat, vous aurez un baiser."
        Le compèr' Lustucru, qui n'en a pas voulu,
        Lui dit: "Pour un lapin votre chat est vendu."

8   In his edition Robichez points out these elements as "inédits" (513).

9   Cf. Hugo's line "Plante là toute rhétorique" (see chap. 2 above).

10   Mitchell also notes this repetition of the word *nuance* ("Mint," 241). He shows "the discrepancy between the advice [this poem] proclaims and the manner in which it advises" (240), pointing out its didacticism, its rhetorical nature, and its humor. Grimaud also points out the devices typical of eloquence in this supposedly antieloquent poem, such as exclamations, capitalizations, and *pointes*. He also shows the ways rhyme is emphasized rather than "assagie." Verlaine was aware of this latter contradiction. In his response to the article "Karl Mohr" had written in *La Nouvelle Rive Gauche* attacking "Art poétique," he writes, "D'abord, vous observerez que le poème en question est *bien* rimé" (quoted in Stephan, 53, Verlaine's italics). Neither Mitchell nor Grimaud, however, discusses the ways in which advice and manner coincide in the poem.

11   Baudelaire had used the term in "Le Monstre" (see chap. 4 above) although he wasn't sure of its use. He asked Poulet-Malassis, "Le mot *Cas* peut-il s'appliquer au *Cul* comme à la pine, ou en est-il l'antipode? *Il s'agit du Diable* (Trouver, s'il est possible, un exemple")(quoted in *O.C.*, 1:1147).

12   Marcel Cressot wrote of him in 1938:

     Verlaine a été l'introducteur dans la langue "sacrée" de la poésie, du mot familier, brutal, bas, de la syntaxe de la langue familière, de l'image qui se réfère à l'objet vulgaire. . . . Que ces mots et ces tours reçussent droit de cité dans la poésie, c'était là un fait sensationnel, que cet emploi s'accompagnât d'effets très délicats, c'était une révélation: la cause était gagnée. (10)

     The works by Bruneau, Cuénot, and Loos I have cited list and classify these innovations.

13   Philip Stephan has studied Verlaine's work in relation to the use of neologism, popular diction, foreign words, latinisms, as well as the subjects typical of decadent verse, especially in chapters 6 and 7.

14   J.-S. Chaussivert points out its use in *La Bonne Chanson* (79-80).

15   Sainéan refutes the idea that *argot* changes "avec une rapidité surprenante" (291). He shows how nineteenth-century *argot* retained much of that of previous centuries (290-94).

16 For the distinction between the ways "vulgar" is used, to refer to the signifier and to the signified, see chap. 1 above.

SIX. *Rimbaud: Poetics and Politics*

1 Lapeyre writes: "Tout le poème est conçu pour mettre en valeur le dernier mot, pour aboutir au bureau prosaïque" (420). See also Guisto (132).
2 Chambers examines the ways critics have tried to find referential "keys" to Rimbaud's poetry, especially his later works; and he shows how such referential readings counter these texts' "symbolisation."
3 Todorov has also examined the role of romantic theories of the symbol and their relation to modern literary criticism (101-4).
4 Rimbaud's mentor, Georges Izambard, "corrected" the line, "Et mes désirs brutaux s'accrochent à leurs lèvres" to "Et je sens les baisers qui me viennent aux lèvres." Ruff and the Pléiade edition use the original line; others, including Bernard's, the Izambard version.
5 In his edition Ruff claims that the returning Parisians described in the poem are those who had fled the city during its bombing by the Prussians in February and March of 1871, a return Rimbaud might have witnessed. Other commentators have not been convinced by his demonstration. It does not matter for the purposes of my argument which event it is, except that the very fact the question is raised should give us pause regarding the poem's relation to historical reality.
6 See also Kerbrat's discussion of the relation of connotation to ideology (215-29).
7 Bachelard has examined the "transaction du petit et du grand" in this text in *La Poétique de l'espace* (155-57). See also Kittang (170-71).
8 Suzanne Bernard gives the first in her edition of Rimbaud's *Oeuvres* as does Marcel Ruff in his edition of the *Poésies* (113). Antoine Adam gives the latter in the Pléiade edition, and Bernard's successor A. Guyaux follows him. None of them give their sources, but Charles Bruneau defines "fouffe" as a "gifle" in his article "Le Patois de Rimbaud" (5).
9 See Lapeyre (405-22) for a discussion of Rimbaud's use of rhetorical figures, especially in the prose works.
10 Baudry's position is similar to Todorov's, while he situates Rimbaud's language in an interrelation with his social text: "Cette langue se distingue radicalement de la langue considérée comme moyen de communication et d'expression. . . . Loin donc d'être l'expression d'une réalité extérieure à elle . . . elle est intérieure au texte général (*qui pour être texte est toujours en quelque sorte déjà théorisé*) et en relation dialectique avec lui" (59, his italics). Paul de Man, however, in criticizing theories that link modern poetry with the loss of representation, shows that "all allegorical poetry must contain a representational element that invites and allows for understanding, only to discover that the understanding it reaches is necessarily in error" (*Blindness*, 185).

SEVEN. *Conclusion*

1 In his commentary Banville calls the pencil-merchant who was followed

by a trumpet-player as he displayed his wares "le symbole vivant de la Réclame moderne" (6:356).

2   The poem includes "ce *tas de* crimes-là," *marmot, cancan,* and *ordures* (referring to people), as well as *tapage.*

3   In this connection see Burch (158-215) and Sonnenfeld (176-97).

4   Richepin was prosecuted and condemned for offending public morals. He was sentenced to a month in prison, a fine of 500 francs, and loss of his civil rights. The first edition of *La Chanson des gueux* was destroyed, and five poems were either cut or eliminated from further editions. Needless to say, the resulting *succès de scandale* made Richepin's career as a poet.

5   Already in the 1870s, *La Renaissance littéraire et artistique* and *La République des lettres* published poems presenting contemporary urban scenes. Alongside its serialization of Zola's *l'Assommoir,* the latter periodical printed some of the *Chansons des gueux* and other poems by Richepin as well as a number of drinking songs like Raoul Ponchon's "Chanson vineuse":/ . . . / Et puis ce post-scriptum / Pour mon nez, gé⁼ranium / Digne d'un muséum. / . . . Je ne distingue plus . . . / Le jour de la nuit, l'une / De l'autre blonde et brune, / Et mon cul de la lune!" In the 1880s *La Basoche, La Nouvelle Rive Gauche* (*Lutèce* after 1883), and *Le Chat noir* were among the journals publishing the work of Verlaine and the younger poets who took him as their model. In their pages "low" language as well as technical expressions appear in frequent representations of urban life, as many of the poems' titles suggest: Ajalbert's "Les Balayeurs" and "Chronolithographie," Vautier's "Crépuscule (Charbon)," and Fernandez' "Nocturnités."

6   Works like Lorrain's *Modernités* play on the parallel between modern life and the decadent periods of antiquity that is the defining characteristic of the Decadent movement. Along with a wish to startle and provoke, it is this simultaneous preoccupation with and rejection of the modern world that often motivates the use of slang in such works. Decadent style has been analyzed at greater length than is necessary here by Carter (123-43); Stephan (throughout, but especially 99-123); and Houston, *French Symbolism* (117-30).

7   The "Tombeau" to Verlaine includes a colloquial construction—"Verlaine? Il est caché parmi l'herbe, Verlaine"—but not only is this the only such instance in a sonnet marked by Mallarmé's usual dislocated syntax, not only is it surrounded by words with particular Mallarméan resonances, like "de maints / Nubpoets' influences on other poets later in the nineteenth and in the twentieth century. Stephan discusses Verlaine's influence on the younger generation (173-200). Houston's *French Symbolism* is a sustained effort to draw comparisons between French poetry of the late nineteenth century and modern poetry.

9   Trézenik, one of the editors of *Lutèce,* defends the decadents by linking their goal of originality to that of the romantics: "Il y a tendance de la jeune littérature à faire *neuf,* et pour cela à faire *autre.* Les étiquettes ne signifient si bien rien que les prétendus décadents ont déjà été affublés de l'épithète de *néo-romantiques,* parce que 'romantisme,' au

fond, au temps de sa gloire et de son audace, ne voulait que dire *change-ment*" (italics Trézenik's, quoted in Stephan 94).

10   This passage, from an 1822 article in *Le Miroir des spectacles, des lettres, des moeurs, et des arts* is quoted in Carpentier (ix).

Bibliography

Abrams, M. H. "The Keenest Critic." Rev. of *Hazlitt: The Mind of a Critic* by David Bromwich. *New York Review of Books* 10 May 1984: 37-40.

Adam, Antoine. *Verlaine*. Paris: Hatier, 1965.

Ajalbert, Jean. "Les Balayeurs," "Chronolithographie." *La Basoche* 1 (1884-85):30-31; 211-12.

Angelet, Christian. *La Poétique de Tristan Corbière*. Brussels: Palais des Académies, 1961.

Antoine, Gérald. "Classicisme et modernité." *Baudelaire: Actes du Colloque de Nice*. Faculté de Nice: Minard, 1968. 5-12.

Aragon, Louis. *Hugo, poète réaliste*. Paris: Editions sociales, 1952.

———. *Les Yeux d'Elsa*. New York: Pantheon, 1944.

Aristotle. *Poetics*. Trans. Gerald F. Else. Ann Arbor: U. of Michigan P., 1973.

———. *Rhetoric*. Bk. 3. Chap. 1-12. In *On Poetry and Style*. Tr. G. M. A. Grube. Indianapolis: Bobbs-Merrill, 1958. 65-99.

Auden, W. H. *Collected Shorter Poems 1927-1957*. N.Y.: Random House, 1966.

Auerbach, Erich. "The Aesthetic Dignity of *Les Fleurs du mal*." *Scenes from the Drama of European Literature: Six Essays.* New York: Meriden, 1959. 199-226. Rpt. in *Baudelaire: A Collection of Critical Essays*. Ed. Henri Peyre. Englewood Cliffs: Prentice Hall, 1962. 149-69.

Austin, J. L. *How to Do Things with Words*. Ed. J. O. Urmson. New York: Oxford U.P., 1965.

Bachelard, Gaston. *La Poétique de l'espace*. 5th ed. Paris: PUF, 1967.

Badesco, Luc. *La Génération poétique de 1860*. 2 vols. Paris: Nizet, 1971.

Bally, Charles. *Le Langage et la vie*. Genève: Droz, 1952.

Banville, Théodore de. *Odes funambulesques*. 2d Ed. 1859. Paris: Editions d'aujourd'hui, 1976.

———. *Oeuvres*. 9 vols. Paris: Lemerre, s.d.

———. *Petit Traité de versification française*. Paris: Bibliothèque de L'Echo de la Sorbonne, s.d.

Barat, Emmanuel. *Le Style poétique et la révolution romantique*. 1904. Genève: Slatkine, 1968.

Barthes, Roland. *Le Degré zéro de la littérature*. 1953. Paris: Seuil, 1972.

Baudelaire, Charles. *Correspondance*. Ed. Claude Pichois and Jean Ziegler. Bibliothèque de la Pléiade. 2 vols. Paris: Gallimard, 1973.

———. *Les Fleurs du mal*. Ed. Antoine Adam. Paris: Garnier, 1961.

————. *Oeuvres complètes.* Ed. Claude Pichois. Bibliothèque de la Pléiade. 2 vols. Paris: Gallimard, 1975.

Baudry, Jean-Louis. "Le Texte de Rimbaud" (première partie). *Tel quel* 35 (1968):46-53.

Benjamin, Walter. "On Some Motifs in Baudelaire." In *Illuminations.* Trans. Harry Zohn. Ed. Hannah Arendt. New York: Schocken, 1969. 155-200.

Bersani, Leo. *Baudelaire and Freud.* Berkeley: U. of California P., 1977.

Boileau-Despréaux, Nicolas. *Oeuvres complètes.* Ed. Françoise Escal. Bibliothèque de la Pléiade. Paris: Gallimard, 1966.

Bonald, Louis. "Du style et de la littérature." In *Oeuvres complètes.* 3 vols. Paris: Migne, 1864. 3:976-1016.

Bornecque, Jacques-Henry. *Les Poèmes saturniens de Paul Verlaine.* Paris: Nizet, 1952.

Bray, René. *La Préciosité et les précieux de Thibaut de Champagne à Jean Giraudoux.* Paris: Albin Michel, 1948.

Breton, André. *Les Pas perdus.* 2d ed. Collection Idées. Paris: Gallimard, 1969.

Brooks, Peter. "Romantic Antipastoral and Urban Allegories." *Yale Review* 64 (1974):11-26.

Bruneau, Charles. *L'Epoque romantique 1815-52* and *L'Epoque réaliste.* Vols. 12 and 13 of Ferdinand Brunot. *Histoire de la langue française.* 13 vols. Paris: Armand Colin, 1948.

————. "Le Patois de Rimbaud." *La Grive* 53 (1947):1-6.

————. *Verlaine: Choix de poésies.* Paris: C.D.U., 1950.

Brunetière, Ferdinand. "De la déformation de la langue par l'argot." *La Revue des deux mondes* 3d period 47 (1881):934-44.

————. *Etudes critiques sur l'histoire de la littérature française.* Paris: Hachette, 1894.

Brunot, Ferdinand. "La Langue littéraire de 1815 à nos jours." Petit de Julleville, 8:704-810.

————. "Les Romantiques et la langue poétique." *La Revue de Paris* 6 (1928): 309-31.

Burch, Francis F. *Tristan Corbière, l'originalité des "Amours jaunes" et leur influence sur T. S. Eliot.* Paris: Nizet, 1970.

Butor, Michel. "Le Roman et la poésie." In *Essais sur le roman.* Collection Idées. Paris: Gallimard, 1964. 21-47.

Carpentier, L. J. M. *Le Gradus français, ou Dictionnaire de la langue poétique* . 2d ed. Paris: Johanneau, 1825.

Carter, A. E. *The Idea of Decadence in French Literature, 1830-1900.* Toronto: U. of Toronto P., 1958.

Catford, J. C. *A Linguistic Theory of Translation.* Oxford: Oxford U.P., 1965.

Cellier, Léon. "D'une rhétorique profonde: Baudelaire et l'oxymoron." *Cahiers internationaux du Symbolisme* 8 (1965):3-14.

Chambers, Ross. "To Read Rimbaud: (a) Mimesis and Symbolisation: A Question in Rimbaud Criticism." *Australian Journal of French Studies* 11 (1974):54-64.

Chambon, Jean-Pierre. "Quelques notes de vocabulaire." *RLM* 594-99 (1980): 95-101.

Chantavoine, Henri. "Les Poètes." *Petit de Julleville* 8:22-81.

Charpentier, J. *Théodore de Banville, l'homme et l'oeuvre.* Paris: Perrin & Cie., 1925.

Chaurand, Jacques. *Introduction à l'histoire du vocabulaire français.* Paris: Bordas, 1977.

Chaussivert, J.-S. *L'Art verlainien dans La Bonne Chanson.* Paris: Nizet, 1973.

Cicero, Marcus Tullius. *Rhetorica ad Herennium.* Trans. Harry Caplan. Cambridge: Harvard U.P.; London: Heinemann, 1954.

Coppée, Francois. *Oeuvres complètes.* 6 vols. Paris: Lemerre, 1888-99.

Corbière, Tristan. *Oeuvres complètes.* Ed. P.-O. Walzer. In Charles Cros and Tristan Corbière, *Oeuvres complètes.* Bibliothèque de la Pléiade. Paris: Gallimard, 1970.

Cressot, Maurice. *La Phrase et le vocabulaire de J.-K. Huysmans: Contribution à l'histoire de la langue française pendant le dernier quart du XIXe siècle.* Paris: Droz, 1938.

Crystal, D., and D. Davy. *Investigating English Style.* Bloomington: Indiana U.P., 1969.

Cuénot, Claude. *Le Style de Verlaine.* Paris: C.D.U., 1963.

Dansel, Michel. *Langage et modernité chez Tristan Corbière.* Paris: Nizet, 1974.

Deffoux, Léon. *La Publication de "L'Assommoir".* Paris: Malfère, 1930.

Delas, Daniel. *Poétique/pratique.* Paris: C.E.D.I.C., 1977.

Delas, Daniel, and Jacques Filliolet. *Linguistique et poétique.* Paris: Larousse: 1973.

Delasalle, Georges. *Dictionnaire Argot-Français et Français-Argot.* Paris: Ollendorff, 1896.

Delvau, Alfred. *Dictionnaire de la langue verte.* 1866. 2d ed. 1883. Genève: Slatkine, 1972.

de Man, Paul. *Blindness and Insight.* New York: Oxford U.P., 1971.

———. "The Rhetoric of Temporality." *Interpretation: Theory and Practice.* Ed. Charles Singleton. Baltimore: Johns Hopkins U.P., 1969. 173-209.

Derrida, Jacques. "La Mythologie blanche." *Marges de la philosophie.* Paris: Editions de Minuit, 1972. 247-324.

Dumarsais, César. *Traité des tropes.* 1730. Paris: Le Nouveau Commerce, 1977.

Eliot, T. S. "The Music of Poetry." *On Poetry and Poets.* New York: Farrar, Straus, and Cudahy, 1957. 17-33.

Enkvist, Nils. *Linguistic Stylistics.* The Hague: Mouton, 1973.

Etiemble. *Le Mythe de Rimbaud. Structure du mythe.* 2d ed. Paris: Gallimard, 1961.

Fernandez, Miguel. "Nocturnités." *Le Décadent* 1.7 (1886):2.

Fontanier, Pierre. *Les Figures du discours.* 1821-30. Paris: Flammarion, 1968.

Foucault, Michel. *Les Mots et les choses.* Paris: Gallimard, 1966.

Fowler, Roger. *Literature as Social Discourse.* Bloomington: Indiana U.P., 1981.

Francois, Alexis. *Histoire de la langue française cultivée.* 2 vols. Genève: Alexandre Jullien, 1959.

Friedrich, Hugo. *The Structure of Modern Poetry.* Tr. Joachim Neugroschel. Evanston: Northwestern U.P., 1974.

Fuchs, Max. *Théodore de Banville.* Paris: Cornély, 1912.

Gaudon, Jean. "Victor Hugo: Mesure et démesure." *RHL* 80 (1980):222-32.

——. *Le Temps de la contemplation.* Paris: Flammarion, 1969.

Gautier, Théophile. *Histoire du romantisme.* 1872. Paris: Champion, 1927.

——. "Charles Baudelaire." *Les Fleurs du mal* by Charles Baudelaire. 2d ed. Paris: Michel Lévy, 1869.

Gély, Claude. *Hugo et sa fortune littéraire.* Paris: Ducros, 1970.

——. *Victor Hugo poète de l'intimité.* Paris: Nizet, 1969.

Genette, Gérard. *Figures.* Paris: Seuil, 1966.

——. "Formalisme et langage poétique." *Comparative Literature* 29 (1977):233-43.

——. *Introduction à l'architexte.* Paris: Seuil, 1979.

——. *Palimpsestes.* Paris: Seuil, 1982.

——. "Valéry et la poétique du langage." *MLN* 87 (1972):600-15.

Genovali, Sandro. *Baudelaire o della dissonanza.* Firenze: La Nuova Italia, 1971.

Giusto, Jean-Pierre. *Rimbaud créateur.* Paris: PUF, 1980.

Grava, Arnolds. "L'Intuition baudelairienne de la réalité bipolaire." *RSH* 127 (1967):397-415.

Gregory, Michael. "Aspects of Varieties Differentiation." *Journal of Linguistics* 3 (1967):177-98.

Gregory, Michael, and Susanne Carroll. *Language and Situation: Language Varieties and their Social Contexts.* London: Routledge and Kegan Paul, 1978.

Grimaud, Michel. " 'Art poétique' de Verlaine, ou de la rhétorique du double jeu." *Romance Notes* 20 (1979):195-201.

Guiraud, Pierre. *L'Argot.* Paris: PUF, 1956.

——. *Le Français populaire.* Paris: PUF, 1965.

Halliday, M. A. K. "Text as Semantic Choice in Social Contexts." *Grammars and Descriptions.* Ed. T. A. Van Dijk and J. B. Petofi. Berlin and New York: De Gruyter, 1977. 176-225.

——. *Language as Social Semiotic.* London: Edward Arnold and Baltimore: University Park Press, 1978.

Halliday, M. A. K., A. McIntosh, and P. Strevens. *The Linguistic Sciences and Language Teaching.* London: Longman's, 1965.

Harms, Alvin. *Théodore de Banville.* Boston: Twayne, 1983.

Houston, John Porter. *The Demonic Imagination.* Baton Rouge: Louisiana State U.P., 1969.

——. *The Design of Rimbaud's Poetry.* New Haven: Yale U.P., 1963.

——. *French Symbolism and the Modernist Movement.* Baton Rouge and London: Louisiana State U.P., 1980.

Hugo, Victor. *Les Contemplations.* Ed. Joseph Vianey. Paris: Hachette, 1922.

——. *La Légende des siècles.* Ed. Jacques Truchet. Bibliothèque de la Pléiade. Paris: Gallimard. 1950.

——. *Oeuvres complètes.* Ed. Jean Massin. 18 vols. Paris: Club français du livre, 1967-70.

——. *Oeuvres poétiques.* Ed. Pierre Albouy. Bibliothèque de la Pléiade. 3 vols. Paris: Gallimard, 1964-74.

Hymes, Dell. *Foundations in Sociolinguistics.* Philadelphia: U. of Pennsylvania P., 1974.

Iser, Wolfgang. *The Act of Reading.* Baltimore and London: Johns Hopkins U.P., 1978.

Jakobson, Roman. "Closing Statement: Linguistics and Poetics." *Style in Language.* Ed. Thomas A. Sebeok. Cambridge: M.I.T. Press, 1960. 350-77.

Jauss, Hans Robert. *Aesthetic Experience and Literary Hermeneutics.* Trans. Michael Shaw. Minneapolis: U. of Minnesota P., 1982.

——. *Toward an Aesthetic of Reception.* Trans. Timothy Bahti. Minneapolis: U. of Minnesota P., 1982.

Jenny, Laurent. "Le Poétique et le narratif." *Poétique* 26 (1978):440-49.

Johnson, Barbara. *Défigurations du langage poétique.* Paris: Flammarion, 1979.

Joos, Martin, *The Five Clocks.* New York: Harcourt, Brace, and World, 1961.

Jouve, Nicole. *A Fire to Conquer Darkness.* New York: St. Martin's, 1980.

Joxe, France. "Ville et modernité dans 'Les Fleurs du mal'." *Europe* Avril-Mai 1967:139-62.

Kerbrat-Oreccione, Catherine. *La Connotation.* Lyon: Presses Universitaires, 1977.

King, Russell S. "Jules Laforgue's Symbolist Language: Stylistic Anarchy and Aesthetic Coherence." *Nottingham French Studies* 15 (1976):1-11.

——. "The Poet as Clown: Variations on a Theme in Nineteenth-Century French Poetry." *Orbis litterarum* 33 (1978):238-52.

Kittang, Atle. *Discours et jeu.* Grenoble: Presses Universitaires, 1975.

Laforgue, Jules. *Oeuvres complètes.* 6 vols. Ed. G. Jean-Aubry. Paris: Mercure de France, 1925.

La Harpe, F. *Lycée.* Paris: H. Agasse, an VII (1798).

Lapeyre, Paule. *Le Vertige poétique.* Neuchâtel: A la Baconnière, 1981.

Larchey, Lorédan. *Dictionnaire historique d'argot.* 1872. 5th ed. Paris: E. Dentu, 1881. *Nouveau supplément.* Paris: E. Dentu, 1889.

Larousse, Pierre. *Grand Dictionnaire universel du XIXe siècle.* 17 vols. Paris: Administration du Grand Dictionnaire Universel, 1866-76.

Littré, Emile. *Dictionnaire de la langue française.* 1863-72. 4 vols. Paris: Hachette, 1878. *Supplément.* Paris: Hachette, 1884.

Loos, Arnolds. *Die Volksprachlichen Elemente in der Dichtung Verlaines.* Munster: Poppinghaus, 1936.

Lorrain, Jean. *Modernités.* Paris: E. Giraud, 1885.

Mailloux, Stephen, "Convention and Context." *NLH* 14 (1983):399-407.

Mallarmé, Stéphane. *Oeuvres complètes.* Ed. Henri Mondor and G. Jean-

Aubry. Bibliothèque de la Pléiade. Paris: Gallimard, 1945.

Manley, Lawrence. "Concepts of Convention and Models of Literary Discourse." *NLH* 13 (1981):31-52.

Marouzeau, Jean. *Précis de stylistique française.* 3d ed. Paris: Massin, 1950.

———. "Quelques observations sur la langue vulgaire." *Le Français moderne* 22 (1954):241-51.

Matoré, Georges. *Le Vocabulaire et la société sous Louis-Philippe,* 1951. Genève: Slatkine, 1967.

Meschonnic, Henri. *Ecrire Hugo.* 3 vols. Paris: Gallimard, 1977. Vol. 1.

———. *Pour la poétique.* Paris: Galimard, 1970.

Mitchell, Robert C. "From Heart to Spleen: the Lyrics of Pathology in Nineteenth-Century French Poetry." *Medicine and Literature.* Ed. Enid R. Peschel. New York: Watson, 1980. 153-59.

———. "Mint, Thyme, Tobacco: New Possibilities of Affinity in the *artes poeticae* of Verlaine and Mallarmé." *French Forum* 2 (1977):238-54.

———. *Tristan Corbière.* Boston: Twayne, 1979.

Mitterand, Henri. *Les Mots français.* 4th ed. Paris: PUF, 1972.

Molino, Jean. "Hypothèses sur la rhétorique au XIXe siècle." *RHL* 80 (1980):181-94.

Molino, Jean, and Joëlle Tamine. *Introduction à l'analyse linguistique de la poésie.* Paris: PUF, 1982.

Morier, Henri. *Dictionnaire de poétique et de rhétorique.* Paris: PUF, 1961.

Naquet, Alfred. "Victor Hugo." *La République des lettres* 1.7 (1876):177-85.

Nash, Suzanne. Les Contemplations *of Victor Hugo: An Allegory of the Creative Process.* Princeton: Princeton U.P., 1976.

Palsy, Simin, and Majorat du Félibrige. *Dictionnaire du béarnais et du gascon modernes.* Paris: C.N.R.S., 1961.

Perrault, Charles. *Contes.* Ed. Jean-Pierre Collinet. Folio. Paris: Gallimard, 1981.

Petit de Julleville, L., ed. *Histoire de la langue et de la littérature française des origines à 1900.* 8 vols. Paris: Armand Colin, 1900.

Peyre, Henri. "Sur le peu d'influence de Baudelaire." *RHL* 67 (1967):424-36.

Plessen, Jacques. *Promenade et poésie.* The Hague: Mouton, 1967.

Pleynet, Marcelin. "La Poésie doit avoir pour but . . . " *Théorie d'ensemble.* Paris: Seuil, 1968. 94-126.

Ponchon, Raoul. "Chanson vineuse." *La République des lettres* 2.10 (1876): 239-40.

Poulet, Georges. *La Poésie éclatée.* Paris: PUF, 1980.

Pound, Ezra. "Irony, Laforgue, and Some Satire." *Literary Essays.* Norfolk, Conn.: New Directions, 1954. 280-84.

Princeton Encyclopedia of Poetry and Poetics. Ed. Alex Preminger. Princeton: Princeton U.P., 1974.

Richepin, Jean. *La Chanson des gueux.* 1876. Paris: Fasquelle, 1953.

Riffaterre, Michael. *Essais de stylistique structurale.* Paris: Flammarion, 1971.

———. *La Production du texte.* Paris: Seuil, 1979.

———. *Semiotics of Poetry.* Bloomington: Indiana U.P., 1978.

Rimbaud, Jean-Arthur. *Oeuvres.* Ed. Suzanne Bernard. Paris: Garnier, 1960.

Réédition, ed. Suzanne Bernard and A. Guyaux. Paris: Garnier, 1980.
————. *Oeuvres complètes.* Ed. Antoine Adam. Bibliothèque de la Pléiade. Paris: Gallimard, 1972.
————. *Poésies.* Ed. Marcel Ruff. Paris: Nizet, 1978.
Rivaroli, E. *La Poétique parnassienne d'après Théodore de Banville.* Paris: A. Maloine et fils, 1915.
Robert, Paul. *Dictionnaire analytique et analogique de la langue française.* 8 vols. Casablanca: Société du Nouveau Littré, 1951-63.
————. *Le Petit Robert.* Ed. Alain Rey et al. Paris: Société du Nouveau Littré, 1968.
Royère, Jean. *Poèmes d'amour de Baudelaire.* Paris: Albin Michel, 1927.
Ruchon, Francois. *Jean-Arthur Rimbaud: sa vie, son oeuvre, son influence.* Paris: Champion, 1929.
Sainéan, L. *L'Argot ancien 1455-1815.* 1907. Genève: Slatkine, 1972.
Sainte-Beuve, Charles. *Poésies complètes.* Paris: Charpentier, 1890.
Sandburg, Carl. *Good Morning, America.* N.Y.: Harcourt Brace, 1928.
Sartre, Jean-Paul. *Qu'est-ce que la littérature?* Collection Idées. Paris: Gallimard, 1948.
Scarfe, Francis. "A Stylistic Analysis of Rimbaud." *Archivum Linguisticum* 3 (1951) :166-92.
Schaeffer, Gérard. "Poèmes de la révolte et de la dérision." *Etudes sur les "Poésies" de Rimbaud.* Ed. Marc Eigeldinger. Neuchâtel: A la Baconnière, 1979. 81-132.
Sherbo, Arthur. *English Poetic Diction.* Michigan State U.P., 1975.
Sonnenfeld, Albert. *L'Oeuvre poétique de Tristan Corbière.* Paris: PUF; Princeton U.P., 1960.
Starobinski, Jean. *Portrait de l'artiste en saltimbanque.* Genève, Skira, 1970.
Stephan, Philip. *Paul Verlaine and the Decadence.* Manchester: Manchester U.P., 1974.
Stierle, Karlheinz. "Baudelaire and the Tradition of the *Tableau de Paris.*" *NLH* 11 (1980):345-61.
Storey, Robert. "Pierrot *Narcisse*: Théodore de Banville and the Pantomime." *Nineteenth-Century French Studies* 13 (1985):1-21.
Thibaudet, Albert. *Histoire de la littérature française.* Paris: Stock, 1936.
————. *Intérieurs.* Paris: Plon, 1924.
Todorov, Tzvetan. *Les Genres du discours.* Paris: Seuil, 1978.
Trahard, Pierre. *Essai critique sur Baudelaire poète.* Paris: Nizet, 1973.
Turner, G. W. *Stylistics.* Middlesex: Penguin, 1973.
Ullmann, Stephen. *Précis de sémantique français.* Berne: A. Francke, 1952.
Ure, Jean N., and Jeffrey Ellis. "Language Varieties." *The Encyclopedia of Linguistics.* Ed. A. R. Meetham and R. S. Hudson. Oxford: Oxford U.P., 1969.
Valdman, Albert. "Français standard et francais populaire." *French Review* 56 (1982):218-27.
Valéry, Paul. "Situation de Baudelaire." *Oeuvres.* Ed. Jean Hytier. Bibliothèque de la Pléiade. 2 vols. Paris: Gallimard, 1957. 1:598-613.
Vautier, Adolphe. "Crépuscule (Charbon)." *Le Chat noir* 27 Fév. 1882:2.
Verlaine, Paul. *Choix de poèmes.* Ed. Michel Dansel. Paris: NCL, 1973.

——. *Oeuvres poétiques.* Ed. Jacques Robichez. Paris: Garnier, 1969.
——. *Oeuvres poétiques complètes.* Ed. Y.-G. le Dantec, revised Jacques Borel. Bibliothèque de la Pléiade. Paris: Gallimard, 1962.
Vigié-Lecocq, E. *La Poésie contemporaine: 1884-1896.* Paris: Mercure de France, 1897.
Vinay, J. P., and J. Darbelnet. *Stylistique comparée du français et de l'anglais.* 1958. Montréal: Beauchemin, 1975.
Voltaire. *Dictionnaire philosophique.* Vols. 17-21 of *Oeuvres complètes.* 52 vols. Paris: Garnier, 1879.
Ward, Patricia. "Hugo's Private and Public Personae in *Les Chansons des rues et des bois.*" *Esprit créateur* 16 (1976):207-19.
White, Hayden. "Literature and Social Action: Reflections on the Reflection Theory of Literary Art." *NLH* 11 (1980):363-80.
Wing, Nathaniel. *Present Appearances: Aspects of Poetic Structure in Rimbaud's* Illuminations. University, Miss.: Romance Monographs, 1974.
——. "The Stylistic Functions of Rhetoric in Baudelaire's 'Au Lecteur'." *Kentucky Romance Quarterly* 19 (1972):447-60.
Zevaès, Alexandre. *Les Procès littéraires au XIXe siècle.* Paris: Perrin, 1924.
Zimmermann, Eléanore M. *Magies de Verlaine.* Paris: Corti, 1967.
Zola, Emile. *L'Assommoir.* Paris: Garnier-Flammarion, 1969.
Zumthor, Paul. "Style and Expressive Register in Medieval Poetry." *Literary Style: A Symposium.* Ed. Seymour Chatman. London and New York: Oxford U.P., 1971. 263-81.

Index

Journey
to the Real

Selected Poems of
Takashi Arima

Translated and edited by
Tadao Hikihara and John Michael Kuzel

NEW YORK · WEATHERHILL · TOKYO

First edition

Some of the poems and prose pieces in this book have previously been published,
in *The Memory of India, North, South, East, and West, Stranger's Songs, Mongolian Horses,
Islands, The Beginning of the End, From the Labyrinth, White Night, Repetition, Forging Money,
Metamorphoses, The Twilight Wall, A Woman from the Sea,* and *O Little Planet.*

Published by Weatherhill, Inc.
420 Madison Avenue, 15th Floor
New York, N.Y. 10017

Printed in Mexico

ISBN 0-8348-0276-7

Library of Congress Cataloging in Publication Data

Arima, Takashi, 1931–
    Journey to the real : selected poems of Takashi Arima (1957–1992) / [trans-
lated and edited by Tadao Hikihara and John Michael Kuzel].
        p.   cm.
    List of the author's works: p. 151.
    ISBN 0-8348-0276-7 : $9.95
    1. Arima, Takashi, 1931–   —Translations into English.
    I. Title.
PL845.R479A24   1993
895.6′15—dc20   92-31599
                                                              CIP

Contents

I

II

III

IV

V

VI

VII

I

Darkness
Strange

Out of thin darkness, the sudden thrust of hands. Hand, hand, hand, hand, hand, hand, hand. Each mouth cries out. A black hand tries to snatch my luggage; dark red, tan, white, persistent hands. Parting those waves of hands, no matter that I shove them away, they tug at the bag I carry from behind my back, attempt to make off with it from the side.

In the whites of their eyes, dark pupils gleam. Beneath a dark mustache, a row of white teeth. After passing through Gandhi Airport's gloomy customs, choked by the musty smell of sweat or body odor, jostled by the suffocating crowds, I am exposed to innumerable eyes. A brief sigh of relief at my escape, then in the sodden darkness, penetrated by the weak electric lights, old people felled by sleep. A woman in a Punjabi dress lying beside her baby. A vagrant. A family. A beggar. To top it off, some weird cargolike herd crouches.

It's not at all like vertigo. Body rocked back and forth, as within my field of vision, something wriggles in the strange darkness, again the sudden thrust of hands. Hand, hand, hand, hand, hand, hand, hand. And then as if escaping from them, into this monochrome maelstrom, feeling as though I'm falling forward as I'm sucked in.

Railroad
Homeless

Unkept hair hanging, or growing a dark beard. Turban wrapped, or wearing vermillion makeup on the forehead. With glasses that glitter, or a gray cloth draped over the shoulders. Faces hidden by veils, or hair close-cropped. Both eyes closed, or showing a row of white teeth. On a platform in Delhi Central Station, these have gathered.

I hardly understand a word of their language. Is it Hindi? Telugu, Bengali, Tamil, Urdu, Marathi? Gujarati, Kannada, Malayalam, Oriya? Punjabi, Sindhi, Assamese, Kashmiri? Any of a number of languages spoken by minority tribes? Tangled in an eddy of the throng of people. Unable to communicate, getting lost, I search for the express train for Calcutta. In English.

Unexpectedly stopping short, or looking back. Crouching, or lying down. Screaming, or sitting cross-legged. In profile, or looking down. Or looking up, whispering, stirring. They radiate a variety of heat.

Cattle
in India

The cattle in this country have level humps on their backs, like pedestals on which Shiva might sit, even though Shiva would not take a ride. They plop their rumps down in the middle of a crossing. They direct traffic side by side with gun-toting policemen.

The cattle in this country nonchalantly stroll down busy streets. Like Nundi, they roll their big round eyes. Some watch the ticket counter at a movie theater, patrol the narrow passages of a bazaar, taste deep-fried snacks from streets stalls they pass, sweep up fallen leaves from roadside trees.

The people of this country share their lives with descendants of holy cattle. Setting the yoke. Letting them plow a vast field, tow a wagon. Or they milk a cow and drink. Dry shit for fuel. In just the way they have since the long gone days of Krishna.

At the
Foot of Mithuna

Here she combs her hair, here puts on makeup in a hand mirror. Another there with a backward glance, bending at the narrow waist, raises in her hand the sole of her foot. And then a letter is composed, jeweled garments glitter, instruments play. Each dances, each moves elegantly.

Here necks strain, arms extend, swollen breasts shake, bodies wriggle. There legs spread open, buttocks stick out, insteps arched; which hand belongs to which head is indistinguishable. They couple further, intertwine, lock in struggle.

In the midst of hunting, or while pulling a war carriage, he frolics with cattle, plays with elephants. Associating with horses, mating with lions, then sharing affection with God. Men to women. Women to men. Give their bodies to another, caress each other's skin, embrace, kiss, present a phallus, display a vulva, feign a coquettish air of ecstacy, hold a banquet full of joy.

It hardly appears to be sandstone. Scantily clad. Inundated in the light pouring from the raw blue sky of Khajuraho. Gods, incarnations, even beasts, form a mass of eros, burst from the wall; spurting, surging, twirling. Thrashing, until they come down crashing on the crown of my skull.

Taken
for A Ride

Clump, clump. Through an ancient pink city in India, taken for a ride atop an elephant's back, I slowly pass. The white-turbaned youth with a stubbly beard gives his whip a crack. The silent elephant moves her massive bulk and does not misbehave. Huge legs making long strides. The earth trembles beneath the weight. Trods on the street of reddish earth. Clump, clump. Feeling the female elephant's warm body alive beneath my crotch, my concealed lingam swinging, we make our way.

Under the cloudless blue sky, upon a throne that rides above the elephant's shoulders. I, the traveler, from behind the driver look up at the salmon pink, folding-screen-like palace. Even the maharajahs of this land (I imagine) used to take this sloping road, rocked upon a conveyance such as this. In the strong sunshine of Jaipur, on the verge of the desert, in the hollow of the dark gray elephant's forehead, the dry air is split. From somewhere, a high-pitched voice chants the Koran. A Hindu sutra reading echoes.

Swung, swung. Guided by the elephant-wise youth, I timidly look down at the main street bazaar. Tibetans displaying all manner of clothing rest at their street stalls. Women selling sari, primary colors embroidered with gold and silver thread. Men in kaffiyeh who seem to be itinerant merchants. Souvenir shops, jewelers, a cobra charmer, gypsies, circus acrobats, beggars, fruit shops and the like fill the road, along with auto rikshaws, scooters, bicycles, cars, oxcarts, horse-drawn carriages, camels, donkey trains. Swung, swung. Every time the giant elephant's hulky body slips by them, the view, fanned by the large ears, lurches aslant.

Clump, clump. Through an ancient Rajasthani city, taken for a ride upon a throne set atop an elephant's back, slowly I pass. Not as a maharajah, but as a stranger, blown by the wind of an ancient pink city. Snorting her trumpetlike trunk, I get the elephants rank breath full in my face. On the elephant's back riding above the shoulders. Swung, swung. My swinging lingam goes bulging along.

The Memory
of the Twilight

Yes. When was it that I saw this landscape? Drenched in the light of the descending sun, the village of low thatched roofs shines over there. Yellow rape blossoms sway in the field where camels persist in plowing up the garden patch, this side of which the cattle and the pigs are kept. A peafowl makes a rare stop on the footpath that runs through the field where, at the foot of a nearby banyan tree, the villagers relax. Children play around a well, pouring water over their naked bodies. In a scummy pool, the wet black skins of the water buffaloes shine. I've surely come across this scene somewhere.

The red ball of burning fire sets deep in the field. From the window of a speeding car, the smell of something burning drifts. The muddy river flows with the color of the earth as, crossing an old iron bridge, I see a spreading field of full grown Indian corn. It's grown dark, and soon, I alone will be swallowed by the gap between heaven and earth. Not far from here, small lights become twinkling stars. Oh, yes. This familiar scenery, I viewed it before I was born. A memory of something I witnessed generations and generations ago. Perhaps in a world on another planet.

Kathmandau

Upon turning a corner of the narrow labyrinth, from across the way young me comes running barefoot with a runny nose, wearing a pair of dirty shorts patched many times. Is the familiar smell in front of me fresh cowshit in an old shed? The nearly rotten ripe persimmons of the farmer next door? Or is it the scent of blood on the little finger cut by a sickle? With my ponderous noggin cocked, I slip past a boy with a monstrous head. Kathmandau.

I climb the steep trail leading to a blue sky which seems about to drop. Phantomlike, snow-capped mountains tower over me. Passing beyond a dazzling mountain pass leading to the northern sky, in reddish brown clouds of dust a town appears. In a highland basin a jostled row of faded red brick houses. On the fences and walls of those buildings, scratched in black, oblong kerosine lamps, large sickles and shining suns with rays of light. Like those I left behind when I was a naughty child.

Wheels
of Light

Down the dim street, muddled with sleepiness, resting my heavy head on the reclining seat back, I'm transported on wheels. In the still slumbering town, a stray dog wanders. A huge banyan tree forms a tunnel with its thick-grown leaves. I am certain that I left Madurai to watch the sun rise at Kanyakumari.

Deep behind closed eyelids, glaring, bright light spins. The windmill of the windpower station just passed comes spreading toward me, instantly shrinks and is transformed into a miniature silver light bulb. Where really am I from and where am I going? Who am I? Why am I here now? Rocked right and left, left and right, I put these questions to myself as a mandala appears floating before me.

In the speeding vehicle, I gaze upon a ring of light. Becoming a snake, it whirls up through my spine, ties something over my head. Silently I clasp my palms on my chest. Momentarily, twenty-four huge, bright, golden wheels revolve, confirming that the burning sun is running over the heavens.

Earth Spirit
Communion

In the darkness of a cave, the shadow of a figure stirs. Now barefoot, I approach a tiny, undulating flame. Unfamiliar words of prayer are repeated. I pass several odoriferous men and women amid the chilling spiritual air.

Someone in yellow clothes beckons with his hand. I move forward to the small shrine's inner sanctum, built of hewn oblong stones. Holding in his hand a fire wheel, he places his palm upon the palm of my hand. With his finger the man, still muttering his prayer, puts a smear of ash in the middle of my forehead. Places around my neck a white saffron flower garland, fragrant to the nose.

Near the ancient carved stone temple of Mahabalipuram. In the neighborhood of what remains of half-finished Dravidic Gods and giant elephants carved in granite. Beyond the weathered, readily collapsing ruins, the vast Bay of Bengal dazzlingly wavers.

II

The Electric
Travel Notes

Swaying, as if with vertigo
From the tender rain in the Place de l'Opéra
To St. Germain-en-Laye
I sat in a speeding subway car
Nobody, not even the tour conductor, was aware of
What I alone felt

From the thunderstorm in Frankfurt, by private bus
To Heidelberg University
On the deck of a large and luxurious boat that
Descended from Mainz to Koblenz
Even an expert guide would have missed it, but
I alone was inspired by it

Between seats in an alpine railway car
From snowy Kleine Scheideg to Jungfraujoch
At a window in the TGV running full speed to Paris from
Cornavin Station, where I went through immigration
I could not record it on video or audio tape
Neither could I talk about it in an international call

At the bow of an old gondola in a Venetian canal
In a taxi heading for Heulige village in the Vienna woods
In the rattling corner of a crowded metro in Madrid
In the seat of a jet landing at foggy Heathrow Airport
I felt it, but I could not find it in a guide book or memo
Neither could a satellite transmit it

I wandered around the continent
Swapping one means of transport for another
Meeting all kinds of people who speak different languages
Charged by some power from deep in the earth
That no map depicts, that has no form
My body is still vibrating

The
Pompeii Dog

Wagging its gray tail that dog
Followed me from the small museum in the ruins
Near the vicinity where the bodies were excavated
In the first century after Christ, the great eruption of Mount
    Vesuvius
Buried the city under volcanic ash, earth, and sand
A great many men and animals then breathed their last

Forearms twisted in pain
The ash-covered dog died in agony from the toxic gas
The writhing body might have come around
Abruptly gotten to its feet and followed
Behind me as I staggered from jet lag
Along the paving stones deeply rutted by horsedrawn carriages
Running up the sloping road paved with gleaming cat's-eyes

In the grand square fully paved with calcareous rock
Stood crumbling brick walls and gateposts
On three sides, a covered two-storied corridor
Once a perfect promenade for the citizens of this bustling society
A phantom city excavated from the eighteenth century
Tailed by the gray dog
I slowly make the rounds

Temple of Apollo, Temple of Jupiter,
Assembly, polling place, court, exchange,
Food market, treasure house, granary, school,
Grand theater, music hall, athletic field, colosseum,
Public bathhouse, whorehouse, public lavatory . . .
That unfettered dog breaks into a trot
Ever so curiously surveys the environs

With a map of the mazelike ruins in one hand
I navigate the crossroads of Orpheus
And again a bakery, saloon, fruit shop, inn,
Laundry, hardware store, leathercraft shop . . .
After passing through a district lined both sides with shops
Footsore, feeling fuzzy
I got lost and wandered into a residential area
At which time, at the entrance of a house facing the street
The dog suddenly pulls up and begins barking

On the brownish floor of that dead house
My dog companion's dark image is inlaid
Standing on firm hind legs, tail upright
About to spring on its opponent
On its toes, knees bending forward
There drawn in dark letters on the mosaic
"CAVE CANEM"
Needlelike
Pierces my eyes

To
Lake Luzern

I took a break from financial negotiations
At the HandelsBank in Zurich
To zip to Luzern in a rented car
Climbing from valley to valley
Patches of snow lay on the alpine meadows
And through the narrow opening in the window
The cold March wind beat my brow

Late last February
When I first visited this summer resort
The snow fell continuously on the Vierwalastattersee
Everything was buried in deep snow
The trolley ran from the park in front of the station
Across the bridge, under which large swans gathered
Shivering with cold

Now bathed in the bright sunlight
Swans spread their wings
Frolicking on excursions far out in the lake
I crossed the Spreuer Bridge with its rotting roof
Walls lined with medieval paintings
Elderly couples come to take in the sunshine
All around me on the shore of the off-season lake
Various couples whispering
Move away, gently arm in arm

Will I, a complete stranger, ever know a day
Free from the hustle and bustle of work
To visit lovely places like this
And enjoy myself, like the couples
And the swans?

I return to the driver's seat
Turn back for the bank in Zurich

Istanbul
Twilight

Near the boisterous Galata Bridge
I boarded the large white ferry
That crosses the choppy Bosphorus
All but a few of the passengers around me
Whose commotion I couldn't understand a word of
Work from morning in the city on the European side
Return to their homes in Uskudar
When the sun crosses to the West

As the setting sun, slipping behind clouds beyond
Thrace, dyes the sky blood red
A chilly March wind blows through
The deck that faces Asia
To my left, a line of high-rise buildings in the new town
I sit sneezing as in front of me
A young Turkish couple cuddle
On a poorly made bench
Conspire in lighthearted whispers
Oblivious to the changing scenes
All of a sudden, the engine's pitch rises under foot
As the ferry veers to starboard
Then the old town behind us like a small hill
A bruise rising up in the twilight

The silhouette of the Topkapi Palace, just beyond reach
Over it, the illuminated dome and six minarets
Of the mosque of Sultan Ahmet
Shine milky white
As the golden crescent moon shimmers
For an instant, time folds back
As I stand empty-headed
I glimpse the image of an ancient city

In Ottoman Turkey centuries before
Gathered on the ferry, several middle aged women
Scarves on their heads blown in the sea wind
Repeat words of worship
Echoing the faint cry of the muezzin
While the whistles of passing ships overdub on the opposite shore
The baroque Dolmabachce Palace
Floats white above the shoreline

Then, arriving at Uskudar on the opposite shore
Around the penumbral square
Stand houses with ancient bay windows of wood
And jumbled rows of street stalls serving food
At the invitation of a friendly young man with a mustache
Feeling a little hungry
I had a skewer of kebab
And took a sniff of the local *raku*
Which smells like crude medicine
And turns milky when mixed with water
Slowly lifting the glass to quench my thirst
When, from a monochrome photograph
In the corner of the simple stall
My eyes meet those of Ataturk
Looking down, fixed right on me

Dancing
Lady

One night in June, I was listening to the songs of a young couple from Chieng Mai. The dimly lit den was filled with some 40 people. While her tall, lean husband played guitar, the petite wife beat a drum and sang Thai folk songs.

The two of them were well matched. The handsome man's dark wet eyes glittered, his long mellow voice was resonant. The lithe woman wore a dress with an orchid embroidered on a purple ground. She talked to the audience a bit in English and had a lovely smile.

The audience sat around at antique tables drinking beer and juice, taking it easy, when from out of nowhere a little girl who appeared to be lost approached the couple in mid-performance and climbed up on the low stage. Fluttering her short pink skirt, the child toddled as if dancing to the melody. *Nueng song sam, nueng song sam . . .*

Was it last summer? From the Kuchan wharf in Bangkok, rocked on a small launch on the Chao Phraya River as I passed under the Taksin Bridge, then heading up a dark muddy canal. When I got off the launch near a marketplace where the black huts of people living on the water stood in rows, a garden of unfamiliar tropical flowers spread out before me. I thought I noticed a girl dancing amid the clustered plants. But what had seemed the fluttering of a miniature skirt in dance were the pink petals of the orchids.

On the stage the couple from Chieng Mai sing folk song after folk song, but the little girl is no longer to be seen. With her tiny fluttering skirt, from her parents' protection, where did she disappear? O little Dancing Lady. The sweet fragrance of that orchid hangs faintly in that June night den.

Drifting
in Indonesia

Nowhere in the streets of Batavia, Old Jakarta, could I find a bust of Pieter Erbervelt, a traitor under Dutch rule. A statue of the poet Chairil Anwar stands in Merdeka Square, not far from the National Monument.

They say there used to be many bats at sunset, before the flood of Japanese cars clogged the capital. Traffic is so congested people add the words "kira kira" when they're not sure they can be punctual for the appointments they make. When I visited the botanic gardens at Bogor, an eighty-four-year-old man acted as my guide. He'd been living there for forty years. He pointed out the rare 'Traveler's Tree,' and explained about a bat which had just been tagged in the shade of a tree, all in fluent Japanese which he learned when the country was under Japanese occupation.

Borobudur, the largest monument in the Buddhist world, is near the old city of Yogyakarta, in the center of the island. Today Indonesia is an Islamic country, but I happened to see a group of young girls from the country folding hands in prayer before a Buddhist image. Later, I visited the Hindu Temple of Prambanan, where performers still dance under the full moon, and I went to the banks of the Bengawa Solo, famous in folk songs.

In the eastern island of Bali, Hinduism is alive. Men gather outdoors in circles to dance the Keçak, rhythmically moving their arms to hoarse cries. Young girls dance in quick movements, exorcising sickness and death. When a person dies, their ashes are scattered to the waves in devotion. The people of the island still bear heavy loads on their heads.

Two Poems
about Guilin

1

Just a short walk around back, off
Brightly lit night on Zhongshan Boulevard
To a totally dark, inconspicuous toilet
Amid the faint sounds of water dropping
I felt some strange presence move

It's just a little different from
That darkness we experience when we enter a movie theater
I'm afraid but I try to see, stooping slightly, peering in
Though I know I can distinguish nothing
With my eyes unaccustomed to the black world

Soon, the small sounds of water cease
And soft steps
Silently pass by
As I hold my penis in my hands
I take a stance, as if to fire a pistol
In actuality, pissing in the darkness

A short walk, maybe ten steps
And I'm back on the main street
The free market is crowded with buyers and sellers
Shop lights, bare electric bulbs hanging in tents
Bright as day

"Wait a minute!"
The night rather bright, as I made my way back
These commanding words came flying in Japanese
From a busy crossing near the Yang bridge
Surprised by the familiar ring
I looked back and found
The young Zhuang girl whom I'd met when I set out

An oval-faced girl of fifteen or sixteen
With the same gesture she'd used before
Raised the bunches of plastic bags hanging
From her arms, standing on tiptoe to show
A variety of tea canisters and boxes for brushes
"Thousand yen, thousand yen.
This discount, not buy?"

Bu xie xie, bu xie xie
By repeating those brand new words of Chinese
I had barely succeeded in getting away last time
After that, I had a nice time
Looking around the art and craft shops
Shops selling a vast variety of goods
I had completely forgotten about her
By the time I was returning on Zhongshan Boulevard, when
"Thousand yen, thousand yen."
"This cheap. Buy, buy."

Here she was again, small statured
Babbling short broken commands
From her fair complexioned face
Raising her high-pitched voice to a scream
No matter how I waved her off, *bu xie xie*
She would not give up, just like that Zhuang boy Lolo
Who set out to find the brocade
Earnestly facing burning mountains and icy seas
She followed me around the corner of shadowy Shanhubei Street
Up to a point near my lodgings at the Li River Hotel
Repeating, "You buy. You buy."

Guilin Zaihui
The roughly finished bamboo wine cup
Still smells of lacquer
Four small cursive characters on its side, and scenery
From the Li River which I'd descended that morning
Drawn in three colors; black, green, and red
As I slowly pour *laojiu* into it, Lolo's face appears
Superimposed on the fair face of the young girl
Who succeeded in selling the cup

At the Foot of
the Statue of Natsagdorj

Bashful boy
Stand there at the foot of the dark blue statue
Nearly three times your size
Even standing on tiptoe
That massive lime colored pedestal
Imitating the mountain highlands
With your clear eyes
Look carefully at the great man with his pen in hand
Sitting steadily atop it
You can see the boot toe
Sticking out from under the skirt
Of Mongolian cloth he wears, his knee jutting skyward
He looks cheerful and seems about to start talking
If you know even a little about him
Won't you tell me?

That red pullover well suits
Your sunburnt face, your pageboy haircut
Boy, who looks so Japanese
But of course you can't understand Japanese
Can you tell me what the man beholds in the distance
With his eyes, his serene looks
Which I point at with an awkward gesture?
Is he seeing the high mountains covered with forest
In the north where he was born
Or the rise and fall of the sand dunes spreading south
From the country whose beauty he admired
Or the lovely Haraa River, as wide as an ocean
Flowing through the plain where he rode horses?
Tell me, if you can read, what meaning is expressed
By the five vertical lines of swept up gold letters

Carved in the wall
Near the pedestal you lean against

Little fellow, tilting your head
Giving me a peek of your white teeth
I don't suppose I'll forget the day
I met you, a stranger to me
And stopped for a while
At a corner in a square in Ulan Bator
To talk with you through gestures
Unable to make sense of each others' language
You too, someday remember
These moments I've captured on film
Who knows, we might even meet again
At the foot of the statue of Natsagdorj
Let's shake on it

Night
in the Gobi

Perhaps it is an illusion
The tense metallic hum
A vast number of large luminous points
Calling out to the dark plain
Standing there at the door of the yurt
Still full of the smell of fermented *kumis*
Above me to my right, far away
From north to south in the deepening blue sky
The glittering, silver sand-river flows
Those two stars could be Vega and Altair
Brightly lit, bigger than the others
Each on its side of this river of stars
Yes! I was no more than three
When timidly I peeped through the darkness
At that large cluster of stars
Held close to my mother's bosom
Grabbing her swollen breast
Bathing in silver quicksand
That swan, wings extended
Descending upon me more vividly than even that time before
Beating its wings before my eyes

Thousands of miles away
From this enormous land
How many wonderful summer night skies
Have I seen in the islands I come from?
A long time ago, on a night like this
I left a hut near the top of Mount Fuji, flashlight in hand
Approaching a sharp ridge in total darkness, I had the illusion I was
    ascending to the stars
As they fell from that sky
Sometime ago, in a valley above Lake Biwa

Attending a folk music festival
Camping out in a meadow to the music of a guitar, I
Looked up into a sky, tense with stars
Far away, I journeyed over the Hidaka mountains
Passing through Obihiro city and the town of Kami Shihoro
Led to a ranch in a wide plain, where I bedded down
In a pasture with the cows under a starry blue sky
When I was living alone on Shikoku
Walking just like this on the sand
From the dark tip of Cape Ashizuri
I saw stars scattered in that sky above the sea
Then on the Manzage beach
Around midnight, blown in the breeze of the semitropical sea
I came close to tears looking up into the shallow night
Still holding on to the waning light of day
As beautiful as these night skies were, nonetheless
None can touch the beauty of the sky I see tonight
From around Sagittarius
Which I find with some difficulty
The sounds of water descend faintly to the earth
From the flood of the Milky Way

As I near the yurt, hunched over
Overwhelmed by this sky of myriad stars
I spy a girl of the herdsman's family
Waving her hand
Beckoning "return"
The dim light smells slightly of milk
A flock of sheep returned from the pasture
Sleep quietly together on the wide grassy field
Under this tremendous starry sky
Let the family, sheep, and I
Rest silently

On the
Bank of the Angara

The setting sun is dazzling
Summertime past nine p.m.
On the Siberian Railway a long freight train
Echoing past on the opposite bank
Beyond, directly above a dark blue mountain range
Radiates the day's last warmth
Red, falling, pouring rays of light
Penetrate the stranger's eyes
That's right, some forty years ago
When a Japanese POW, having finished the day's labor
Washed the sweat off a body swollen from malnutrition
With cold water that flowed from the Baikal
Riding the ripples like a gorgeous golden kimono glittering
On the surface of the river floating, sinking, the midsummer sun
Refracted through drops of water still on the eyelids and tears
Must have been even more painfully brilliant than now
A blurred reflection in the eyes

Somewhere about the beginning of this century
Japanese soldiers were rounded up to come here
Leaving families beyond the sea
Remembering their faces
Floating up one by one in the mind
Soundlessly that flaming, expanding ball of fire
Approaching the Barguzin Mountains
Dyeing the surrounding clouds purple red
Moves closer, growing huge
Two centuries ago
Having drifted to the Aleutian Islands, sailors of Ise
Visited Kamchatka, Okhotsk
Yakutsk, Irkutsk
From the bank of this river watched the setting sun

(No station or white building to block the view)
The green expanse of taiga must have been more vividly
    illuminated
Now it's early August, 1986
Having returned from the forlorn Japanese cemetery
A small plot of land surrounded by a large forest
I have climbed a hillside in the suburbs of Irkutsk
Dumbly resting my bones on an old bench in a tiny park

The warmth of the blood red setting sun still lingers
Passing on the parched-white Gagarin road
People having finished work
Families, tourists, in twos and threes
Come to rest in the cool shade of the verdant trees
Looking back, the roof of the local museum
Rises obliquely to my right
From a nearby Intourist hotel
The manic dance of young men and women to
The raucous singing of rock and roll seeps
Into the dim darkness

Tagaytay,
South Luzon

To Fidel Rillo

"Masarap!"

The old woman with tangled salt-and-pepper hair
A rough old hatchet in her hand
Shouts suddenly at the little girl
With motions that seemed to scold her

They were squatting
The quartered remains of green coconuts at their feet
Her wrinkled old hand picked up one of the shells
That tourists had eaten
Then tossed away
She stuck it in the little girl's face

The girl grabs it in her bony hands
And quenches her thirst
Loudly slurping the juice from the little meat
That remained in the bottom of the shell
Her clear eyes shine like porcelain
From her sun-darkened face

The old woman stands up, the edge of the cliff behind her
The hatchet still in her hand
As some raucous, middle-aged, Japanese men walk by
She stares at their backs
Then glares beyond them to the north

"Ma . . . . Masarap?"

Under the sun in a land of everlasting summer
The murderous blade
Reflects the heat and glare
How far is it prepared to go
With a blinding flash?

Behind the woman bent with age
Taal volcano is mirrored in a wide lake
A gust of wind ripples the surface
The poor have left their homes and the hill
They used to live on
And migrated to Metro Manila to look for better lives
The ruins of fields and hamlets scattered about
Under a canopy of tall trees and plants

"Masarap!"

Suddenly
The girl's shrill voice echoes
She nibbles at the coconut flesh, then jumping to her feet
Looks up at her grandmother's fierce face
And gives her a toothy smile

Smokey
Mountain

An overpowering smell of ammonia
I instantly cover my nose with my hand
At the tip of my utterly dusty shoe
A slice of rotten durian lies
Swarming with buzzing bluebottle flies

Before my eyes a mountain of rubbish piled high
Here and there along a bending sloping path
Rows of flimsy huts thrown up, called 'barong barong'
Each wall stands beside another
Patched together with plywood
Tin, and vinyl sheets on three sides to form
A place more cramped than a horse's stable into which
A few members of a family invite me

In tropical sun and sudden downpours
Waste instantly goes bad, ferments
To a smolder from which thin smoke rises
At mid-slope on the artificial mountain
Men, women, old and young
Dig around the rubbish using sharpened sticks
Rummaging for something of value

Empty cans, empty bottles, vinyl bags
Fragments of glass, plastic containers
Assorted bones of chickens, cows, pigs . . .
They dig up anything near at hand
Throw them into their bamboo baskets and bags
Just then a garbage truck made-in-Japan
Pulls in heaped with garbage from Metro Manila
They madly rush over
To be the first to dig in

The Navotas River's muddy flow discharges
Near the gulf of gourd-shaped Cocomo Island
I look up and directly in front of me
Another smokey mountain rises high
Continues to smolder under a scorching sun
On that mountaintop a church door glows
Kept always closed

—O our father who art in heaven
The wretched people who live here, when
I wonder, will they be redeemed?

A strong, sharp smell of ammonia
The tears won't stop falling. I, the vagabond
Loiter on the smokey mountain, lost in a fog
From the depth of that awful vision
A boy appears wearing a dirty short-sleeve shirt
Gives me the V sign and a friendly smile
Draws near, transformed into an angel

Survival
Songs

1

Summer vacation is over, you know
Kanan kanan kanan kanan
An evening cicada, left alone in a tree on Yoshida Hill
Cries its last

Though it feels like only a few days ago that
A massive waterfall surged through the streets
Of the parched town in the ancient basin
Churning up water at a tremendous speed

People are doing a quick change
To finish homework left
For the end of the 20th century

Suppressing a yawn, the school term begins
Bamboo blinds and outdoor benches disappear
As the surviving insects start singing alone

2

Don't make fun of my bent neck
Don't make fun of my hunched back
Don't make fun of my crooked arms
Don't make fun of my twisted hips
Don't make fun of my bowed legs
Don't make fun of my whole body stooped

This neck's long distant past
A war behind this back
Luggage at the end of these arms
A family around this waist
A steep slope under these legs
A life dangling from this whole body

The neck now straightens out
The back now throws out its chest
The arms now swing alternately
The waist now stretches
The legs now stride forward
The whole body now breathes

Concerning
Decorations

Well, may I help you, sir?
You see, displayed in the show window are, sir
Genuine and true medals, sir
From small ones to large ones all certifying the owner's honor
So dazzling, sir
So blinding, sir

This, the Grand Cordon of the Supreme Order of the
    Chrysanthemum, established in the Meiji Era
As were the Orders of the Rising Sun, the Precious Crown, and the
    Sacred Treasure
Such and such are on the chests of members of the Imperial family
    and servicemen
Row row row your boat . . . those Taisho Era badgers, cunningly
    old
Gently down the stream . . . mesmerized by Imperial rescripts
Merrily, merrily, merrily . . . distinguished in battle
Decked out in medals and swords, astride horses
Hunt across Asia
Momentarily drop from sight after the Showa's defeat
Reappear in disguise from the First Class to the Eighth
Incorrigible faces redone
Shine sinisterly in the middle of town

Well, the latest good buys, sir
Grand Cordon of the Supreme Order of the Chrysanthemum, ten
    million yen, sir
The First Class Order of the Golden Pheasant, also ten million yen, sir
The Seventh Class Order of the Rising Sun, excellent condition in
    a box nine hundred thousand yen, sir
Excellent! The prewar, the midwar, and the postwar together
With the Order of Culture mixed in for good measure

Priced higher than rare memorial stamps and old coins
A few of the items might be assumed to be fakes, sir
Slightly wicked
Decoration inflation

Ludicrous and ridiculous, chagrined and galled
Such and such, and this and that force an unavoidable nuclear war
Can you really say that?
Bless you, bless you, sir
Decor ah-choo tions!

Legend

Once upon a time
About the time the continent of America was discovered
In Europe, the Kingdom of Spain
Assembled a fleet called the Invincible Armada
In time, ordered across the sea to conquer England
It was instead utterly defeated
A great many ships going down

Once upon a time
Before war broke out in the Pacific
The pride of the British fleet
The *Prince of Wales*
Had the world-renowned reputation of being unsinkable
In time, engaged by Japanese forces of that era
Rocked by profound fire the ship
Sank deep to the bottom of the South China Sea

Once upon a time
As World War II drew to an end
The Japanese Imperial Navy's battleship, *Yamato*
Was hailed as the greatest in the world
But in time, steaming to action in Okinawa
Was the victim of an intense assault by the U. S. Air Force
And vanished into Davy Jones's Locker

Once upon a time
About the time of the Cold War between the
    world's two superpowers
The brilliant U. S. Air Force
Built a base on land requisitioned in Okinawa
Called it an unsinkable flagship
Nevertheless, attacking North Vietnam across the sea

Many pilots who took off from that ship's deck
Never made it back

Once upon a time
But no! Stirring military marching music
Still pouring out of pachinko parlors all over town. Now
The Japanese prime minister visiting North America
Boasts that the islands extending
From north to south
Are an impregnable, unsinkable aircraft carrier
However, in time, a great earthquake
Occurring in the northern Japan Sea
Sends tidal waves surging toward the coast
In a wink
All the people swiftly swept away

Builder
of Bridges

Kenneth Rexroth died in California on June 6th, 1982, at the age of seventy-six. As he lay on his deathbed his head was pointed west toward Japan. This poem was read at a meeting in memory of Kenneth Rexroth held on October 2nd, 1982, at The American Center, Kyoto.

Bridges remain,
Connecting distant regions,
Though the builders' bodies disappear.

I saw him in Honyara-do, a coffee shop in Kyoto,
Where young people gathered
In dim light, so cosy
That our heads almost touched the ceiling.
I saw him on a Friday night, in a room on the second floor
Of a house belonging to a maker of homemade ice-cream
At Marutamachi and Shichihommatsu, where Cid Corman lived
His large frame shook, breathing,
His entire square face smiling.
Sprightly old Kenneth Rexroth.
We didn't speak the same language,
So an invisible curtain was often drawn between us.
I strained to catch
The tone of his voice, the light in his eyes;
Muscle movements, actions,
All slipping in through the skin.

Open-hearted Rexroth, on the verge of a drawl.
With the buoyant movement of his body,
He bridged Modernism and the Beats,
English and ancient oriental poems,
The American continent and Japan,
Crossing the vast Pacific many times.

Able now to lay aside the clouds of legend and venerable tales,
I feel even happier than the time
I felt extremely happy for the shortest of moments
In a very small corner of this huge universe,
To be able to communicate with a soul
Like a comet from far away.
Yes! The last time I met him was
(That narrator's voice reminds me)
The evening of April 21st, 1978,
Here, on the floor of this American Center
When seven young Japanese women poets,
Who could have been his grandchildren
Got up and read before him.
He read *The Love Poems of Marichiko*
Seemingly without stopping to breathe.
I wish I could relive that moment.

Dear Kenneth Rexroth, he was a kindred spirit.
The body vanishes, but surely
The bridge remains.

Remarks
on New York

Bathroom At Tiffany's

———

A skyscraper city
Two adjacent states
Three big airports
Four stadiums
Five boroughs
Six rivers flow
Spanned by seven bridges
South along Eighth Avenue
Greenwich Village around Ninth Street
Ten museums adjacent to Central Park

———

Run in Central Park
Cute squirrels during the day
Frightening muggers at night

———

On Broadway
At the Winter Garden
On moonlit nights stray cats congregate
Even the big stage is a small dump
They sing and dance merrily
A musical of apparitions
Possessed by the dead spirit of T. S. Eliot
Jellicle cats
Hoisted to the vast ceiling

———

An evening breeze blows on a night in early May
Around Forty-Second and Broadway
On the street neon signs shine in the dim of evening
Where the skull of the literati Kafu goes ahead of me
Dressed in old clothes and wearing a pair of wooden clogs
Clutching an umbrella

"I like your eyes, you're just my size,
I'd like you to like me as much as you like"

On the corner that leads to Sixth Avenue
A listless song sung by a blonde
Who may be getting sober or
Getting over a cold

"Just like a prayer, your voice can take me there,
Just like a muse to me"

An evening breeze blows on a night in early May
The skull ahead of me has already disappeared
A lone dashing yuppie
With a young blonde walks quickly by
In a fashionable suit wearing shiny black shoes
Carrying an attaché case

A Message
from the Unknown

I wish my shabby words
Could sail across the vast ocean
Reach the young girl who plows the earth
Dry her wet cheeks even slightly

I wish my feeble voice could
Soar over the mountains
Reach the boy who works the street
Stave off the hunger in his mind

Young friends from the continent
Please teach me, in your sweet native tongue
Accents that reach great distances
On the winds which seem to blow beyond these islands

———

Do you feel
Signals from the universe?
Can you write down
Inspirations from the world?

Through its temperature, a human body can
Transmit and receive words from the unknown, and
Surely, identify itself and communicate with others
Through a tender heart and
Gestures much quicker
Than those of cold computer terminals

While their hearts still beat
The greatest happiness
For the living here on earth
Is the sharing of spirit

With the energy that belongs to
Someone behind the universe

Can you give birth
To an object with fresh life
By communicating with someone beyond yourself?
Can you create
A self that stands splendidly alone
By sending out your own ideas?

III

Secret Passage
under the Capital

At the Vatican Embassy
In the front yard behind high fences
Hidden by leaves
Japanese cicada chirring
In the late afternoon, still hot from midday
At peak volume

Here in the middle of Chiyoda Ichibancho
In an underground room of a white high-rise
Opposite the embassy
A narrow one-way lane between them
With a pale smile on his whiskered face, a thin, old consultant
From the Institute of Distribution, Industry, and Economics
Informs me, down from Kyoto in my blue suit
Slowly in a low tone

"In this political deadlock,
The point may be
To find a way under
The thick wall that confronts us. . . ."

In the well air-conditioned room
I took my leave of the bureaucrat with the fine head of silver hair
Sitting in a swivel chair, he swiftly turned his back
And suddenly I found myself
Lost in a dark underground passage
I thought, there must be an exit somewhere
"Excuse me, . . . the exit?"
Wiping the sweat off my forehead with my hand, stuttering
Uncertain as I was of her nationality, I asked the way
Of a middle-aged woman who was passing by

The passageway probably led, in fact
From that dark spot to a dead end
Yet somehow I managed to slip
Out into the road, under the intense sun
Looking up, I saw thick leaves beyond the fences
Of a residential area, a few passing cars, as
Simultaneously, from the Vatican Embassy
The incessant chirring of the cicadas
Landed on my sweat-soaked back

Mount
Fuji

The light of flashlights
In darkness dots that connect to form the letter ⟨
Voices hushed
Slipped down a steep, scree slope
Skin ripped open by the slashing wind

In the spurt of hot blood
Caught the scent of volcanic ash
With my hand, covered the wound
Rock's sharp corner stabbing my chest
Dreary hardship of Sisyphus

One by one, the stars go out
Presently dawn will come
To check this impulse to vomit

Pigeons
of Hiroshima

Coo, coo, coo
Sky blue, blue, blue
From the pre-afternoon plaza
A flight of pigeons lift off *en masse*
Circle slowly over the Motoyasu River
A shimmering fountain, higher and higher
Blown straight up to the midsummer sky
A sultry breeze, more temperate
A stiff gust from the stagnant riverside
At the approach to Aioi Bridge
When lingering before the rustling weeping willow
That drapes the monument to Miekichi Suzuki
At a tilt even steeper than
The leaning wreck of the dome
On the verge of collapse
Lamenting, the numerous
Short shadows of the dead

What's this, an illusion?
Beyond the melting air
Loading immobile people
Second-hand streetcars displaying destinations in Kyoto
Gion, Nishijin, Ginkaku-ji
Above which wheels
A single flock of pigeons returning to the Moto River
Turning up into the tense blue sky
Louder than the giant cheer
Rising from the nearby baseball stadium, crying
Moan, moan, moan, moan, moan
Coo, coo, coo

Visions of
Flowers, Nagasaki

An endless drizzle falling on the roadside where
Clusters of hydrangeas globes waver

"We call them *'otakusa'* here."

A slender local girl
Halts before the blossoms blooming light purple
Half closes her eyes and casts them downward
Under the red umbrella, she smiled

I walk slowly through a cut
Up the wet stone-paved slope
Remembering the glistening surface of
A huge tortoiseshell I saw a little while ago

From a mission school atop the hill
Schoolgirls descending in twos and threes
Come by with light, flapping steps
Past an old Western-style house
Chatting about nothing to do with the rosary
On their way home in this world

"It is red . . ., it is red . . ."

The sing-song of the young lady acting as guide
Rings unexpectedly in my ears
After she'd moved by, returning to my senses
Beyond the red umbrella
The skyline of the war-ruined city of sloping streets
Came rising up red

Deep jagged bay
In a vision of the endless drizzle
Clusters of hydrangeas globes changing light pink
Faintly waver

A Night
in Okinawa

A white one, black one, yellow one
A big one, small one, fat one
A lean one, average one, tall one, short one
Male, woman, man, female, woman, male, male, male
Coming, coming, coming on
Grownups, children, youths
Old men, old ladies, the young and old, families
Soldiers, hostesses, dealers, waitresses
Tourists, riff-raff
Jumbled, mixed together
One after another spring up from the ground

It is still mid-February, but
A tepid springlike night breeze wafts
Here and there through subtropical darkness
Outnumbering their Japanese counterparts, non-Japanese
Streaming, streaming, streaming, streaming
This near the U.S. Air Force Base at Kadena
The Koza Naka-no-cho amusement area
Neon signs in English and Romaji
Mysteriously flash and blink
Cutting loose from the day's cares
Questions of whether nuclear weapons are here or there
Such monotonous issues are left behind
On the rhythm of amplified hard rock
Men and women with skin of different colors join the fray
Indecently dance like mad

Nevertheless this is Nippon
Unaccustomed to the *awamori*-and-water
I ordered one more
Suddenly I was drunk
Before my *Yamatonchu* eyes
From a movie billboard at the intersection
A dark skin beauty steps naked
Shaking her hair loose, she walks alone, and
Night on this island of military bases
Pitches into a leaning roll

A
Private Letter

Poetic Ramble is a gift from
An old friend in Tokyo;
A book made with style.
He left a small town in Yamaguchi, and
Rambled round Kansai through the hardships of youth,
Then flowed to the capital.
Me? for the time being I live in Iyo, separated
From Yamaguchi only by the Inland Sea.
He must be enjoying
The Rhetorical Present now.

In the meantime,
If I turn my eyes to the south,
Kochi—old Tosa—beyond
Sacred Mount Ishizuchi on Shikoku,
I see a drunken man shouting,
"This is exile of the first-degree!"
I could find him and start up a conversation,
Seeing how his voice reaches all the way here.
The cursing voice repeats itself,
Louder than the sound of the Pacific waves.

Well, let these things be.
For I, at my age, having been
Driven from the Kyoto life I was used to,
Came all the way here across the Inland Sea.
Although I have nothing to do with Taneda Santoka,
That pious Buddhist pilgrim begging alms,
What if from this moment I set my decadent self out
On a pilgrimage into areas unknown to me,
Perfectly aware of my peculiar appearance.

Murder
Method

Of all the nerve
Before my very eyes
A cockroach makes a quick run for it
Instantly taking aim
I snatch a beer cap lying within reach, raise it aloft
To hurl at the outlawlike intruder

In more warlike times, birds in flight were
Downed with stones flung by masters of the martial arts
I am not assuming to possess such mysterious prowess
The fatigue of a day's work
And the numbness induced by two or three glasses of beer
Have left me feeling slightly drunk
That my comfortless widower's life
Is momentarily relieved after supper
By this performance seems somewhat sad

I haven't got a drop of religious sentiment
I did not volunteer to love a cohabitating insect
Or maintain the magnamity to forgive
The fellow who feeds on other people's leftovers
Just before it reaches the cover
Of a dark part of the cluttered floor
Rapid fire I launch
Another cap at the hated enemy
After numerous attempts, one shot
By mere chance hits its mark
Knocked topsy-turvy
Ungracefully its fore and rear legs tread thin air, but
Finally cease to stir

Got it!
Coming close to observe
Its pitiful demise
Genuinely
Pumped up with pride over my success
A fiendish smile spreads to the corners of my mouth
Slowly and heavily I mutter
"It serves you right"

Puke

Twice, three times
I gagged on the vomit
Having gone out drinking this evening
I throw up the bowl of Chinese noodles
I ate on my way home drunk
Then a moment later
Up comes the *gomoku* rice I ate for supper

At noon, a load of work
Left no time to eat the obligatory *bento*
Without touching a bite of it, I brought it home
And ate it, which was probably a mistake
Unaccustomed to the degradations of single life
Cooking supper for myself is a pain in the ass
So being a confirmed sluggard
Has the fact that I've occasionally gone out to have a few drinks
Brought down this curse on me?

But, how many years has it been
Since something as unfortunate
As tasting the suffering of nausea
Has happened to me?
Once, when the war in Korea was still going on
On my way home from an evening part-time job
I ate some *shiokara* at a stall which hit me pretty hard
I guess that was the last time
In the middle of the night
Before the dirty toilet bowl
Rubbing my rotten belly
I bent over and thought
It's not like I'm trying to imitate those ancient Romans
Having eaten their fill of delicacies
Putting their fingers down their throats

To empty their stomachs, I am not attempting that
Even less do I resemble that French guy Roquentin
Who, seeing a horse chestnut before his eyes
Had the sudden impulse to vomit in disgust
That's not why I'm puking

Over and over
My stomach heaving
Repeatedly choking and throwing up, after which
I gargled to rinse the rancid taste from my mouth
Lying in my *futon* in the six-mat room
I feebly raise my head and
Look at the alarm clock by my pillow
It's already past two a. m.

Getting Worse
in A Hurry

These days
Everything I eat and drink
Seems bad for me without exception
Drinking the local sake by myself, it's nice to get tipsy
But, as it stays with me the next day
It's probably bad for my liver
When I cook myself dinner
Since I know what goes on behind the scenes
Whether or not the meal is good for my health
Is awfully uncertain, even chancy
Even bottled *shiokara* or *tsukudani*
Makes me feel somehow like I am pecking at a feeder
And then a tangerine for dessert
Though touched by ocean breezes and so tasty
Eaten before I go to bed
Will surely increase my blood sugar level

Breakfast I eat out
Seated on a stool and feeling comfy, but
Rats and cockroaches have the run of the place so
It must be unsanitary
The *bento* provided at noon
Appears quite sumptuous, therefore
Artificial flavors and colors must have been added
Even an omelet will increase my cholesterol, I guess
Though I don't smoke
The vitamin pills I take after meals
If they are so effective
They probably have side effects
And what's more, coffee is bad for the stomach

Past the age of fifty
An employee transferred away from home
Living alone in a place like this
Life deteriorates daily
I must be getting worse in a hurry
The nights with no one to talk with are dreary
In spite of myself, I frequent cheap pubs, get drunk
And return to this solitary cell-like room
Looking like a prisoner sentenced to life
If I keep this up it's curtains
Scared shitless by such a thought
Clenching both fists
Facing the mute wall
In a fit of madness I scream
"Uwahhhhhhhhhhh"

Ambulance
Avenue

Before dawn, as usual
I'm awakened by the siren of an ambulance
Pee pow, pee pow, pee pow
Coming from far off that sound
Like an alarm clock which I couldn't reach
Set for the wrong time
Turning at this cheap apartment house just around the corner
From a nighttime emergency hospital
Into which a few times every night
Victims get carted

The Second World War's
Ominous sirens were different
Not like this shuddering moan
This slightly stupid
Even somewhat humorous noise, so
I don't spring out of bed in alarm, but
In the hours before dawn, I sleep so lightly
Being woken unexpectedly is
Not a pleasant experience
Sometimes I can't fall straight back to sleep, then
I lie awake and think about my death

I'm sure it was seven or eight years ago
Near Kitayama Kinkakuji where Rengedani Road begins
There were always hearses going by
That bank where I was working at the corner
At worst I saw five or six of them a day
It was like a hearse grand prix
Because it was on the outskirts of Nishijin
In the neighborhood where the Kamiya River flows

The weavers there used to call it
Funeral road

On this street in Matsuyama where I'm living temporarily
People on the verge of death
Every so often
Come whistling by in ambulances
Men aren't made
To live forever
Pee pow, pee pow, pee pow
When did dawn's light overtake the night?
Living a single man's life, I
Who left my family across the sea
Try now to capture their vague faces
On the canvas of my mind
Pee pow, pee pow, pee pow

Date
with A Gun

"Today we got guns,
Pistols, wanna buy one?"
The lively young guy at the Dobashi Market
Hooking his right index finger round
Like he's pulling the trigger of a gun
In front of a shop, fresh fish on display
Above the chatter of customers all around
Loudly confronts me

A little fish for supper is just the thing
For the dreariness of single life
To treat myself to a thick fresh slice
I've come as usual on my way home from the factory
To have a look at what's in the shops
I'm well enough acquainted with
This young knife-wielding fellow, but
Is there any need for guns these days, or
Pistols, such dangerous
And questionable things?
With a dubious look on my face
I stop for a moment
"A shorefish, just caught, very fresh,
A relative of the shark," he says
"These are the ones that bite people."
Octopus, flatfish, mackerel, sea bream, and the like are on display
But as I peek my head in the window as I always do
The young guy, a towel wound tightly around his head
Effortlessly grabs the ferocious
Baby sharklike thing's head
With his bare hand
Shows me the sharp teeth in the side of its mouth
Thrust before my eyes

This reminds me, late the other night
In a narrow lane of the mazelike area behind the station
A gunfight broke out
An unidentified man in his early forties
Lying on his stomach bleeding from his left side
Just murdered
After that the police did a lot of legwork, but
The victim was never identified
It seemed unlikely the murderer would be caught
When it gets a little darker
Drunkards, streetwalkers, pimps and
Other suspicious looking people
Pop up all over this area, so . . .

"A four hundred yen gun
How about it for self-protection," he says, joking, as
Deftly with his well-honed knife he cuts
The soft-looking white meat
To give me one slice of sashimi
Placed on a styrofoam tray and
Wrapped smoothly with a sheet of newspaper
Just like the pistol he was talking about or the like
Holding it at my hip, bringing it back home
To relish it alone with warm sake
Toss it back raw in my mouth
Like the pleasant feeling of putting a weapon away
Straight from the numb tip of my tongue
Down the entire length of my body it penetrates
Hitting me with quite a wallop

IV

From
The Beginning of the End

1

Cut off the outside light
Move toward the darkness inside
Neither the light of early dawn
Nor twilight sorrow

Behind closed eyelids
A small universe
Makes standing ripples
Drifting aslant

No one says a word
Falling, nothing makes a sound
Not the faintest hum

Avoid all things
Touch the tip of the tongue to the gums above
And forget them all

4

Bend your legs
Keep thigh touching thigh
Rest your chin on your knees
Arms wrapped underneath

Face tilted slightly
Eyes looking the other way
I wonder what is being spoken
By lips half open

If one could flee oneself
Under these circumstances
With an attitude like this

Then put the question to the knees
Gently rubbing
The lengthy line of the shin

10

What was lost
Can never be replaced
Scattered fragments
Of what was once my illusion

There should never have been
Anything to lose, yet
There's useless fat
Padding the joints

Vanity
Whips stronger than the wind
Through the breast of youth

No simple despair
But an unrequited hollow
In the unheated darkness

11

I want nothing
Make the most of the moment
I want to do nothing
Surrender to this space

I moved too much, so
I sit here calmly
I talked too much, so
I do not open my mouth

Sudden attack
Teeth in pain
Deep in the gums

Look up and watch the upper sky
From a seat by the window
In the corridor of a tall building

29

It is to be neither decorated
Nor lauded

It would not be welcomed
Nor looked back upon

But it moves and
Breathes
Where none expect it
It responds

Little fish, you come up to the surface
Leaving little bubbles,
Go back underwater again

It's just fine, fine
To continue living
With no chance of fame

40

Nothing would happen
If someone did not go there
If someone did not come there
Nothing at all would happen

Yet since, for some reason
Someone did go there
Someone did come there, then
Maybe something happened

For a while, just a little while,
Lips to lips
Belly to belly

To truly know one another. Later
Facing the fading world, one shakes
One's head in denial
Nothing happened. Nothing

69

Amid the snowfall of petals
Tomorrow deserts me
Yesterday makes a frontal assault
And the present is terrible darkness

Having wasted
The time I was given
Left alone to wonder
Am I actually going to disappear

Into a hole scooped from the earth
And be buried by beasts
Like when I was born

Having lived
On a small planet
For a few short breaths

Siding with the minority
Standing there, obstinate
A solitary pole in the middle of the flood
Applauding myself

If my performance
Proves that I exist
I'll hold this pose forever
Never move

To be drowned
To be punished
Defeated in the end

Like an idiot
Aloof
And far from the ovations

Return to oneself
Face the enemy
Turning one's back on one's allies
The wind howling down

For the time being
Stand for the solitude of crowds
Noise as loud as
The sound of wheels

Been waiting a long, long time
But nothing has come
And probably nothing will

Keep getting up
Leaning on the wall
Plumbing the depths of drunkenness

107

Don't bother to welcome me
No need for greetings
No forced smiles
No preparations, none at all

Whenever, wherever the feeling moves me
I'll stay
Just a little space to lie down
Will suffice my heart

Somehow I'll end up dead
At the end of this short trip
Right now, I'm about halfway there

Don't bother to say hello
Just leave me be
To make the most of living now

117

Expose yourself to light of the sun
Head away from home
Raise your rakelike fingers
Toward the unreachable sky

Sparks are born and die
In utter darkness
With this hand reach down and yank
Guts inside out, melting into mush

Aged ideas make me want to vomit
I gasp for breath
But suffer the pain

Descending the stairs underground
Into the artificial eddies
As if being sucked down

From
From the Labyrinth

1

Stick that chin out
Let today's intentions spew forth
Lather up the light red soap
Give up yesterday's warped dream

The safety razor's edge
Reflects just a hint of the sword's brutal brilliance
From the mirror on the wall, blood
Spurts, suddenly

The radio airs jazz and incessant talk
Inescapable moments
Of really total drivel

Shaved off my beard
Exposing fresh bluish cheeks that
Smart in the early spring breeze

42

Moments of intimation
Will not occur again for aeons
Even if you express one in words
You'll never be able to convey it exactly

When a waterfowl flaps its wings
What is it trying to tell you?
When an animal howls
What appeal is it making?

It's like I've seen this landscape before
It's like I've heard this sound before
It's like I've felt the touch of this hand before

One day you're born
Until you breathe your last
Believe in the intimation that occurs but once

94

After the bitter defeat
Summer after summer has past
The wounded boy, dripping blood
Stands with his back to the shimmering hot air

That heavy low-hanging thing
Just barely resists being driven away
Thunderheads billow as if painted in the sky
The stifling stench of humid green grass

Undoubtedly myriad events have occurred
How many decades have, shall we say, flown by
How little indeed has the earth changed

Whether to expose the wound or to conceal it
Since either is detestable
Remain, standing quietly, as you are

That thing, rolling up and down
Stop it! Catch it!
Ever so busily
Leaping and bouncing

Its color, its odor
Its texture, its shape
No place to pin them down
What the hell is that thing?

By flexing the creaking body
Can I once more become
A tender youth?

The more arduously the clay is mixed
The more grandly the kneaded piece
Takes certain form

Capillary vessels burst in my eye
Dyeing the white of my eye bright red
In the peaceful mirror
Swelling up dreadfully

Even a gentle face
With just one such flaw
Can completely change
Instantaneously gain a fiendish look

I have become a tame man
Getting fat before I knew it, and
Huffing and puffing with each breath

I close my eye
Conceal the burning color
Yearning to have a dream like that of no other

166

Things on the verge of ruin
Don't admire them for their beauty
A pomegranate bursts open
Allowing a peek at the vermilion seeds

On the planet's final day
Even more profoundly than today
I imagine the sky will clear
The crystalline air trembling

Cirrus clouds transform
The seasons come and go. Most momentously
The world seems about to change

On a fine afternoon
Tossing my superfluous shadow to the floor
I lean back in a broken chair

177

Whom are you preparing to take on?
With that folded umbrella
Thrust out sinisterly
Amid the falling white powder

Carrying sheets of paper under your arm
Smelling of ink
Each morning already sold
Run until you reach the station!

Even an implement of defense may become
A weapon for attack
You need only change the way you hold it

Grabbing the handle
Swing your arm in a sweeping arc, crosswise
The sharp point will hit the heart

213

Sleep now, low row of houses
Even the rumble of a passing train, will not wake you
Hugged to the breast of deep blue mountains
Wash the dirt off your filthy roof tiles

Before long the day will be over
Intermittent explosions as well as
Lingering train whistles
Sucked deep into the darkness

Luggage of time past
Thrown up on the overhead rack
Just about to doze off

At a stop, like a will-o'-the-wisp
A bashful young boy comes leaping aboard
To speak in an unfamiliar dialect

From
White Night

1

Face flushed
From hours of sleep
Shaving away that warmth with a safety razor
I feel the morning chill

Out of the small radio on the dining table
Happy chatter and pop music flow
Exchanging a few short words with my unaffable wife
Over steam rising from morning soup

I leave home a minute later
Kick a rock on the pavement
And worry about the scuffmark on my shoe toe

Looking up at the gloomy sky
With a look of utterly bored displeasure on my face
I am dragged to the bus stop

22

Men and scenery roll
The floor goes up and the ceiling slips down
Dropping my cup the instant I got up
Supporting myself against the rocking wall with both arms

Space was as it usually is just a while ago, but
Suddenly it's warped grotesquely
The strength in my sturdy legs diminished
A weight descends upon my shoulders from above

While dancing madly my mind becomes obscure
My vision totally blurred
As if someone knocked me down

As the commotion and rock music recede
Falling to the slimy floor, my eyes closed
Lying there like a half-dead reptile

57

After getting perfectly intoxicated
Acting as if nothing happened
Those unmoving eyes are fixed
Beyond the rectangular metallic world

Lacking the budding vitality of trees and grass
Being petrified in this weakened stance
Lament what has gone so quickly
Fear what tomorrow will bring

No rhetoric can express the present moment
With a big gulp of air
Suppress the rising gorge

Search for evidence for living here and now
On the wall of the landing, reflected in a mirror
Glare eye to eye with that contorted face

Distant thunder
A flash of lightning zigzags
The quiet rustle of the trees
Transmitted to me through the earth

Covering my face with an old straw hat
I am lying in a field of grass bending to the wind
With sweaty fingers folded
Across my heaving abdomen

I neither know what I'm waiting for
Nor have an idea about what I'm hearing, but
Something is imminent

From the cloudy sky, a large, cold raindrop
Falls upon my chin, an inkling
Of the roaring assault yet to be endured

101

I hate beautiful landscapes
Autumn-tinted mountains
Pampas grass undulating on the highlands
The profoundly clear blue sky

A dilapidated brick station building
Silver birch leaves blown flickering in the breeze
The roof of a cottage viewed through boughs
Sharp peaks of distant mountains

At one time, in fields of swaying rice
Buffeted by hot wind laden with the smell of mud
Swinging a pick; never forget that time

Plow up this fraudulent homeland
Decorated with fragrant bourgeois fairy tales
I hate beautiful landscapes

129

A cutout past
Paste it on a piece of paper
A peeling, sepia colored
Photograph that will not stir

From the bottom of my almost totally erased memory
Something of uncertain date
Suddenly floats to the surface
Steadily rewinds time

A bundle of papers, carelessly thrown out
Pulled at random from the pile
The even more youthfully ferocious self

That's me someday, somewhere, cut out
Beautifully applied
But just a scrap

V

Transition

We are not planning any price increase at all.

We are not planning any price increases within the year.

We will not be considering a price increase for a while.

We hope to hold price increases down with all our capacity.

At present, we are planning to shelve price increases.

We will not permit immediate price increases.

If we do allow price increases, they will not take effect right now.

We would like to avoid price increases as much as we can.

There are those who say price increases are unnecessary, but we are giving consideration as to whether or not to allow them.

Price increases may be inevitable, but it is too early to know yet.

We'd like to give due consideration as to when we will increase prices.

We have not yet allowed price increases.

We do not want to allow any immediate price increases.

We are reluctant to allow price increases, but price increases within the year may be necessary.

Price increases in the near future may be necessary.

Price increases may be necessary.

Let's decide how much.

Meetings

To prepare for the main conference,
We have a steering committee.
Some arrive late.

For the steering committee,
We hold a special committee.
Some snooze.

For the special committee,
We hold a standing committee.
Some leave in the middle.

For the standing committee,
We hold a small committee.
Some say nothing.

For the small committee,
We hold a preparatory meeting.
Some don't show.

For sake of the preparatory meeting
We hold a banquet.
Some are full of spirit.

Japanese Flowers

Chrysanthemum

Chrysanthemum flowers bloom
In a person's face
Becoming pockmarks
From a distance
Like a pyrotechnical display
White, yellow
Drawing small circles

Chrysanthemum flowers arranged
As symbols of
A family crest
Emblems
Like chrysanthemum fossils pasted just as they are
On necklaces
For grand cordons

Just before they wither and die
Down and out flowers
Are admired
For their length
Gentlemen!
Deep fry those leaves
For a meal of *tempura*

Cherry Blossoms

In a rusty fishing village
An ancient cherry tree
Remained leaning
In full bloom
Petals
Of pink
Growing lighter
Coloring the neighborhood

In a dim
Corner of a bar
An old fisherman lifted his cup
Above his right arm
Exposed
On bareback skin
Tattooed
Cherry blossoms at full bloom
Suffusing an ubiquitous aroma

The
Famous Actress

She was swatting flies
In the tiny shop front of the pharmacy
With moves she would show the camera
Posing like she was on screen
Repeating each gesture
Smiling a professional smile
Even as mud splashed from cars
Stained her bright dress
She faced the people on the street

Honors and awards had once
Been heaped upon her as
The audience clapped its hands
There were no cameras now
Gone were the directors who had sung her praises
But even when the passersby dwindled
She threw all her spirit into the act
Snatching a commercial insecticide
To chase flies in a poster

Breaking
Up

Breaking up
Road repaved
Breaking up
Water pipes buried
Breaking up
Gas pipes replaced
Breaking up
Cables covered with dirt
Breaking up
Sewage laid
Breaking up
Subway built
Breaking up
Roads got muddy

The
Machine

A machine has done writing
A machine has done calculation
A machine has done copying
A machine has transmitted voices

A machine has made a machine
A machine has made a machine that makes a machine
A machine has produced a machine
And it operates a machine

A machine of a machine of a machine
A machine has maimed a man
A machine has liquidated a man
A machine of a machine of a machine of a machine

Song for
a Ten Yen Coin

Aiming a rifle that did not shoot
I shot a fierce animal
Riding a horse that did not run
I chased down a herd of buffalo

In only three minutes
I have driven from Kobe to Tokyo
Through a clearance two centimeters wide
I set out to explore Mars

I looked into the story of Snow White
I looked down at the town through a telescopic lens
I sprinkled fashionable perfume
I had my fortune told

Tiring, I asked vending machines
For juice to drink, for gum to chew
Listened to a song on a jukebox
I made a call on a public phone

Say, ten yen coins
Where have you gone with your tinkle?
If you hear me calling you
Get out through the hole you disappeared into

Forging
Money

I run a print shop
That counterfeits money
I buy bread, order my suits and
Pay my rent with my funny money

Nobody knows that I'm a forger
Even the Treasurer of the Bank of Japan
Pockets fakes with his cigarette change and
Buys gifts and presents for his wife or his boss
I run a print shop
That forges money
One day, because I'd been paying tax with fake money
The detectives came to my home

Under Article 148 of the criminal law
I was hauled into court. It came out at the trial
That the money I was using was real
Everyone else has the phony notes

Electrification
Boom

Home electrification
Beard shaved, bread toasted
Rooms cleaned, sewing machine started
At the touch of a switch
We can drink juice
While in the rush of events
Wives' electrification
Husbands twisted around
Wives' henpeckification
All at the touch of a switch

National electrification
Railways run, rumors run
The Self-Defence Force alerted, rockets launched
With the touch of a button
Nuclear reactors activated
While in the misunderstood events
The electrification of the masses
With the touch of a button
Young, old, men and women make hoopla
Crown Princification

Oh, Wonderful!

At the zoo
In front of a stork
A crowd forms
In a department store
Around a fashion model
Shoppers stop and stare
At a railway crossing
Over a body
People look
All along the river bank
Up at the fireworks
Summer vacationers shout

Oh wonderful!

And now
Standing on the sidewalks
Men and women being sentimental
Wave Rising Sun flags
At their old chieftain in a shabby suit

Sonnet on a Mustache

With their whiskers
Fur seals detect game in the sea
Giraffes' whiskers are for
Protecting their lips from acacia prickles

Thanks to whiskers
A hedgehog can walk a mountain trail
Leopards and lions know whether or not
They can get their bodies through

At the roots of animal whiskers
Sensitive nerves and muscles are provided
To move whiskers at will

At the root of a man's mustache
Nerves are provided to preserve appearances
Muscles to keep dignity

Home Ground

Long ago, Deguchi Wanisaburo
Dreamed a great dream in the ruins of a castle.
He bucked the authority of the time and
Foretold the ruin of the empire.
Long, long ago Akechi Mitsuhide
Assembled his soldiers there and
Advanced along the ridge from Oi-no-Saka
To attack Honnoji.
Long, long and even longer ago, Ashikaga Takauji
Revolted there against the military government.
Long, longer, and longer ago than that
Shuten Doji lived in the mountain
Together with demons.

Long, long,
Long ago in the long-distant past
Red water rippled there
All the time.
Even now when the area is flooded,
A lake is formed, as in ancient times,
With large whirlpools spun
In red deeper than rebel blood.

Rokuro
Neck

If tossed, it will fly back. If kicked, it comes hopping home. But this one ain't no rubber ball. In public, it ought to be curled up in the breast pocket, but is tempted to stick its funny face out. A real asshole, it is second to none at acting perverse. Collusion it flatly refuses; as for mischief, it will give tit for tat.

If you think it's cheerful and humming a tune, suddenly it gets hopping mad. While pretending to shrink away from an assignation, it gropes the luxurious breasts of an woman in ecstasy, and strangles on a chuckle. This one: eats only what it likes, laughs uproariously, jeers obstinately clapping its hands, even more selfish than a spoiled child, totally egotistical. If pressured, it will surely push back. If stamped down, it will certainly spring back.

When night falls, that which performs, without any gimmicks, the illusion of free elasticity; is it sticky chewing gum, or a chameleon tongue? No, no. Not a spring or a boomerang. Even now it carries its head for a lantern on a prowl in the dark. Its fate; to be one in two and being two, still be one. Purring in parchedness, till the break of day, it is looking for a game to quench its thirst.

Cactus

When Master Peyote lost his way . . .

Yes. Young Master Peyote, on a journey, could not continue on his way. This was in a large desert in the Central Highlands of Mexico and he was walking alone. He found that the ground was actually quicksand. He had, it seems, lost his way. Stamping around, he sank quickly to his waist. He was shocked, but he waved his arms and legs and raised clouds of sand and dust, trying to get out as quick as he could . . .

Was he saved? Negative. As he strained and struggled, his body sank deeper. Eventually he was buried with his backpack, up to his neck. Pained sounds came from his parched throat, as he yelped again and again. No one answered. There was only the sight of endless yellow sand and the sun, glaring down. "Ah, I remember these half-buried skeletons. . . ." He screwed up his pale face, muttering weakly and rolling out his hot tongue. His ceramic eyes slowly opened wider and wider in the hot air, shimmering over the sand.

Soon, his head stopped moving completely. It mutated into a green mass of flesh, rooted deep in the sand. But whenever the fiery wind blows, he dreams once more of the powerful flapping of Pegasus who once flew free in the sky.

Devilfish

Junk food was turning him into skin and bone, and even though there was no sign of polio or spinal caries, the youth's supple spine was forcibly removed from his body. Skilled army surgeons were called in to do the simple, drastic, unheard of operation, without anaesthetic. The body was hung on a butcher's hook by the scapula or a rib. Scalpels and forceps separated the muscles. The spine was taken out quickly; a spurting vein reconnected; the opening sewn with machinelike competence. What practiced hands!

Thirteen as I was, I fainted. When I came to, I lay dying on a bed, covered with blood, my teeth clenched. One after another, victims were carried in on stretchers. They groaned and moaned, they writhed, and worse, rolled back their eyes. They were at death's door, and some actually died. A military officer hovered among them, dispensing slaps instead of medicine, shouting to everyone within earshot ". . . Damn! Grab yourself a knife or an awl. Whatever you can lay your hands on. Slash the enemy. Smash him. . . ."

For the next ten years I somehow survived, with a long, narrow hollow space in my body, from my mollusc neck to my waist. How difficult it is to walk without a prop, like walking through the sea. There are American plaster casts, French crutches, and Russian metal walking sticks on the black-market. Legal, taxed imports or contraband, they are simply beyond my means. As for my spine; it was buried in an air-raid shelter along with scrapped swords and photos of the Emperor.

Now my back aches even more. Is that because my spine was re-moved, or because the long-secret munitions factories jacked up the casting of duralumin spines? Whatever caused this double strength wrath of mine, without me realizing it my form has mutated into one of those bodies with eight tentacles, and it is I directing those suckers toward the khaki casting machines.

In the
Locker Room

An umbrella, a bag
A jacket, a pair of sneakers
A cloth-wrapped bundle
And more, are stuffed in a jumble
Deep in my locker
No one knows I've hidden a small, concentrated explosive
Nitroglycerine!
No! More organic, more volatile
A grenade is not even in the same ballpark

Guided weapons are commonplace
These things, not trained on any target
Hurtle back at us
It's clearer than a litmus test
One morning, after a steady radioactive rain
I smuggled it into the old gray building
Concealed under my raincoat
Like carrying a dangerous object This Side Up

Unless someone sniffs out my secret
I am a free agent. I move easily
The odorless, colorless, transparent, flammable liquid
Swinging ominously
In its plastic cylinder
Checking it and
Flipping the combination lock
I secure the door with the only key
No matter how I pull, it won't move an inch

No one can say that no glowering eyes gleam
Betrayal at any time or place in the quiet rows of lockers
That hold the playthings of each person;
Bottles of perfume, whiskey, cameras
Weekly magazines, mah-jongg tiles and other stuff
If I got careless and it were found
It would be my neck! It would mean the electric chair!

In the corner of a dimly lit room
After ending work at midnight
Bathed in ominous, metallic light
I ready myself, secretly imagining
The moment I'll throw it down
Like I would a Molotov cocktail
Making it go off, blasting
The reinforced concrete walls into smithereens

Midnight
Rounds

Carrying a patrol clock on my shoulder
Relying only on the light of my flashlight
I set off in the middle of the night to inspect the building.
Linoleum spreads across
The ground floor business department.
Under the vast ceiling another floor above,
The long, narrow information counter
Glowing palely
Recalls the daytime bustle, then
Silhouettes of automatons
Herded among partitioned desks
Flit about uncannily,
Smoothly and incessantly meshing,
Rotated and controlled by who?
Having dropped in on that hideout
From the managers' lounge furnished with easy chairs
I count my way through a number of reception rooms to
Cut through the front entrance, the lobby, and the room where
    staff make tea.

An emergency exit, the night entrance,
I pass through the room for door-to-door salesmen, the mail room
Descending the dark stairs to
Reach the oppressing basement,
A completely wire-screened vault.
Swept deep within beyond the thick door
Cash, bank drafts, securities.
All that unreachable stuff!

Tut-tutting along alone
I turn the key in the hole of the patrol clock
Recording the irrefutable evidence.
Reconnoitering such areas as
The elevator room, the air-conditioning room,
The emergency power generation room, the boiler room, then
Reappearing on the ground floor,
The garage, a toilet, a small terrace,
Past the water feed and electricity distribution rooms and the
    employee dining room to
Climb the stairwell and
End up in front of the mezzanine floor warehouse.

The second floor; business promotion division.
Desks crowded with telephones
Sleeping colder than tombstones.
A number of rooms,
Quite a few lockers,
I pass these by, then
The Credit Supervision Division, the Accounting Division, and the
    Economic Research Division one after another,
The Managers' dining room, a small meeting room,
The nurse's office, the dark room, and the typing room in that
    order.
Automatic calculators, microfilms,
Intercoms, teletypes
In among all these things
Silhouetted
Automatons are crowded together, and dancing.
I climb more stairs and
Arrive at the fourth floor; the General Affairs Division.
Footsteps echo even more loudly
A large meeting room, the switchboard operator's room,

The Personnel Division, the Inspection Division, the Business
    Administration Division
I look into the private offices of individual directors
Finding my way at last to the president's office
To open the door with a powerful kick.
There another room suitable for protecting top secrets
Equipped with a soundproofing system
Reflected in the illuminated mirror.
Engaging large and small gears in the building,
That rotation and control device,
Where on earth is it if it is not here!

The fourth, fifth, and sixth floors,
The spiral staircase winds ever upward.
Walking in search of a secret hidden path
I slowly inspect every nook and cranny in the building.
Outside the glass window, the town fast asleep
Lit with innumerable lights like noctilucae.
In the ground floor night-duty room a short while ago,
Two guards, a former military police officer and a failed special
    agent,
Boozed it up, proudly laughed out loud
Reminiscing over slaughter and rape in the war
While I, carrying a patrol clock on my shoulder,
With only the light of a flashlight
Following the stairwell
Ascending ever upward to who knows where.

A
Comedy

The grayish brown skull grips a gun
Taking aim at its own heart

The creaking unoiled factory gears
Must work hard to keep up with the destruction and repair

Way off, hurrying from open sea to cove, sea birds warn
"The earth now suffers a severe case of leprosy"

Those who are clapping their hands to this bloody opera,
Are yahoos with cataracts, lured out by trumpets and orders

A Woman
from the Sea

She came from the sea. Her hair like seaweed. Coral in her mouth.
There was seawater in her womb, swishing. Water from her time of
birth. Pubic agar. Shells for her ears.

From the depths of the sea she escaped, whose inner memory has
known an extraordinary world of pressure, forever dark and cold. She
endured it for thousands of years, then came up to land. Leaving traces
of seawater perfume, her flesh shone the color of fish scales beneath
the burning sun. Our eyes paused on the remnant of regressed fin
behind her wasp waist.

Nuclear explosions and border lines are not recognized by the sea. I
found a newborn baby in her amniotic fluid. The very fluid she
brought with her to land.

The
Young Dead

The dead youth is young forever. As you sleep in the darkness of the classics of the past, you pass your wild energy on. It was a time of rootless vagrancy. We gathered, downing strong spirits, and sang peasant songs. A sudden rain pounded down upon our heads. Tense battles put an end to a young man's hope, buried in the darkness together with a multitude of dead bodies.

The shower abated. The incident became the stuff of legends. Routines and machines choke people. Look, he who betrayed you survived in vain. He has reached retirement age and is afraid of cancer. In a room far from the fires of war, a crazy record is stuck in a groove.

In
the Fog

I was born in a fog, brought up in a fog, and now, I live in a fog. A hollow land surrounded on all sides by mountains; in the deep fog, a barrier that has always blocked the view. It is my home, my fence, my embankment.

This weighed so heavily upon me, I hopped the local train arcing through the rice paddies, shook off this place and made for the sea. Suddenly it comes back to me; I'm just a boy standing down by the open sea, with faint ripples of the returning tide. Yet the sea horizon I expected is lost in the fog. Stepping into a hut beside a rock, I sit down beside a young fisherman to share a drink. He is tanned from the sun. The drink is pungent and clear. A few cups and we are singing.

The night was complete white darkness, like smoke enclosing all things. To the ears of my insomnia, sleepless nights always bring the rattle of a train emerging from among mountains, its whistle short and sharp. Such a strange place. Is this the seashore of my dreams, or the hollow I left behind? Standing on the bluff of the cape, I am in the fog, and all I can do is flicker like a lighthouse.

VII

My
Stamp

My flat nose
    like who
  or unlike who
    like mother
    two rabbits in the house

My flat foot
    like who
  or unlike who
    like father
    two lizards in the house

My protruding navel
    like who
  or unlike who
    my thing
    of me, by me, one stamp

Sneeze
Counting Song

The first means I am praised
    The second that I'm blamed
The third that I have caught a cold
    The fourth means it's a cough
The fifth means tonsillitis
    The sixth, it's complications
The seventh one says go to bed
    The eighth; the chest in pain
The ninth means I have asthma
    The tenth, alas, that I'm incurable

Haa
Too Too Too

Haa too too too
　　　haa too too
too too too
　　　haa too too
too too too
　　　too too too too

　　　haa too too
　　　too too too too
　　　haa too too

too too too too
　　　too too too
haa too too
　　　too too too
haa too too
　　　haa too too too

haa too too
too too too too
haa too too

Cicada

Me   me   me
     me   me   me
me   me   me
     me   me   me

Time   time   time
     time   time   time
time   time   time
     time   time   time

Free   free   free
     free   free   free
free   free   free
     free   free   free

Two
Pigeons

One pigeon
    died.
The other pigeon
    descended.

One pigeon
    died.
The other pigeon
    walked.

One pigeon
    died.
The other pigeon
    cried.

One pigeon
    died.
The other pigeon
    called.

One pigeon
    died.
The other pigeon
    left.

One pigeon
    died.
The other pigeon
    came.

O Little
Planet

Turn around and around.
O little planet.
Now I'm in the Middle East,
Somewhere in Arabia, somewhere in a desert.
No one knows where I am.
Animals are my good friends and I play with them.

Turn around and around.
O little planet.
Now I'm on
The North Pole.
No one knows where I am.
Ice is my friend and I sleep with it every night.

Turn around and around.
O little planet.
Now I'm in
A spacecraft.
No one knows where I am.
The universe is my friend and I swim in it.

Sounds
of Asia

In Japan dogs go "wan-wan."
Chinese dogs go "wan-wan."
Dogs of Vietnam go "gaw-gaw."
In the Philippines dogs go "baw-waw."
Indonesian dogs go "gug-gug."
Dogs of Mongolia go "hofu-hofu."
And Thai dogs go "hon-hon."

Please let me know how dogs go in your country.
Please let me feel the sounds of Asia all over Asia.

In Japan cats go "nyao."
Chinese cats go "miyao."
Cats of Vietnam go "mew-mew."
In the Philippines cats go "ngiaw."
Indonesian cats go "meiohg."
Cats of Mongolia go "myau."
And Thai cats go "meo-meo."

Please let me know how cats go in your country.
Please let me feel the sounds of Asia all over Asia.

In Japan cows go "mo."
Chinese cows go "ma."
Cows of Vietnam go "o-o."
In the Philippines cows go "ngna-ngna."
Indonesian cows go "em-em."

Cows of Mongolia go "umu-umu."
And Thai cows go "woa-woa."

Please let me know how cows go in your country.
Please let me feel the sounds of Asia all over Asia.

Notes on the Poems

I

Darkness Strange

Punjabi dress The native dress of Punjabi women in northwest India consists of a blouse and pants, and a scarf worn around neck.

Railroad Homeless

Hindi, Telugu, Bengali, etc. The Republic of India has 24 official languages, including Sanskrit.

Cattle in India

Shiva "The Destroyer," the third member of Trimurti in Hinduism. Believed to live on the Himalayan mountain Kailas. Shiva has a third eye in his forehead and carries a three-forked spear. Temples where Shiva is worshiped are denoted by a lingam (phallus).

Nundi Holy cattle. Shiva's vehicle.

Krishna A hero-god appearing in Indian myths. Born in Mathura, North India. One of the most popular of Indian deities. Seen in many miniatures playing with a cowherd girl. Also said to be an incarnation of Vishnu.

At the Foot of Mithuna

Mithuna Sexual intercourse.

Khajuraho A place in northern India. Carvings of mithuna and celestial maidens are seen on the outer walls of Hindu temples there.

Taken for a Ride

Jaipur The capital of Rajasthan, a desert state in northwest India. A maharajah in this district built Jaipur in the eighteenth century. The outer walls of the castle and many buildings in the city are constructed of rose pink sandstone, therefore it is known as the "Pink City."

Kathmandau

Kathmandu The capital of Nepal. Pronounced locally as *Kathmandau*. The city used to be called Kantipur.

Wheels of Light

Kanyakumari Cape Comorin. Located at the south tip of India. As the waters of the Bay of Bengal, the Indian Ocean and the Arabian Sea meet here, it is said to be a holy place. At this cape, the sun rises from the sea and sets in the sea.

Madurai A city in South India, the second largest city in the state of Tamil Nadu. The center of Dravidic culture.

Earth Spirit Communion

Mahabaliprum Also called Mamallapuram. Approximately 61 km south of Madras. Facing the Bay of Bengal, it prospered as an important port in the seventh century.

II

The Pompeii Dog

cave canem Latin for "Beware of the dog."

Dancing Lady

nueng-sung-sam "One, two, three," in Thai.

Drifting in Indonesia

Pieter Erbervelt Executed and gibbeted as a traitor for plotting a rebellion against Dutch rule in 1722 at Batavia. His cenotaph was destroyed by the Japanese during World War II.

C. Anwar Born in 1922 in Medan, Sumatra. A famous Indonesian poet, he was active in the fight for independence from Dutch colonialism. He died in Jakarta in 1949.

kira kira "about" in Indonesian.

Two Poems About Guilin

Lolo The young hero in the most famous folktale of the Zhuang tribe of southern China. He endures many adventures and hardships in the search for his grandmother's magic brocade.

At the Foot of the Statue of Natsagdorj

Natsagdorj (1906–1937) Descendant of a noble family. Considered the father of modern Mongolian literature. He wrote poems, novels, and plays.

Tagaytay, South Luzon

Masarap "delicious" in Tagalog.

Smokey Mountain

A dump near Manila which is continually smoking because of the heat released by the garbage decomposing under the hot sun.

barong barong Slang meaning "hut" in Tagalog.

Survival Songs

Yoshida Hill A hill in the city of Kyoto. Sight of many historical and legendary events.

Remarks on New York

**"I like your eyes, you're just my size,
I'd like you to like me as much as you like"**
From Ladies of the Night by Kafu Nagai

**"Just like a prayer, your voice can take me there,
Just like a muse to me"**
From Like a Prayer by Madonna

III

Secret Passage Under the Capital

Chiyoda Ichibancho A quarter in Chiyoda-ku. Chiyoda-ku is the ward where most of the central government office buildings are located in Tokyo.

Pigeons of Hiroshima

Miekichi Suzuki (1882–1936) A writer born in Hiroshima. He was the chief editor of the literary magazine *Akai Tori (Red Bird)* and the founder of a poetry reading movement.

Visions of Flowers, Nagasaki

"It is red . . . , it is red. . . ." A popular children's song in Nagasaki Prefecture traditionally sung during the New Year holidays. The verses tease a prostitute who wore silk garments given to her by a Dutchman when Japan was closed to the outside world.

A Night in Okinawa

Koza An amusement quarter in Okinawa. After World War II, American bases were built which are still operating today in Okinawa.

awamori A strong alcoholic spirit made in Okinawa by distillation of sugarcane.

Yamatonchu A somewhat derogatory term used by the native people of Okinawa to refer to Japanese from Honshu, the main island of Japan.

A Private Letter

The Rhetorical Present An influential essay by literature critic Ryumei Yoshimoto, who maintained that poetry after World War II was to be distinguished by its rhetorical quality.

Santoka Taneda (1882–1940) A famous free-verse Haiku poet who became a priest and lived the life of a wandering ascetic.

Puke

gomoku rice Japanese pilaf.

bento A traditional Japanese boxed lunch consisting of rice, small side dishes, and condiments.

shiokara Fish guts pickled in salt.

Roquentin The protagonist of J. P. Sartre's *Nausea*.

Getting Worse in a Hurry

tsukudani Fish or seaweed boiled in sugar and soy sauce.

Date with A Gun

sashimi Thick slice of fish consumed raw.

V

Home Ground

Wanisaburo Deguchi (1871–1948) A religious figure and leader of the Omoto sect of Shinto. He was imprisoned during the war for *lèse majesté* under the infamous Maintenance of the Public Order Act.

Akechi Mitsuhide (1528–1582) A famous warlord. In the Warring States period he launched a surprise attack on general Oda Nobunaga at Honnoji Temple, after which Oda was forced to commit suicide.

Ashikaga Takauji (1305–1358) The first Shogun of the Muromachi period.

Shuten Doji A mythical group of thieves disguised as goblins. They were said to have lived on Mount Oe, in northern Kyoto.

Red water ripples . . . The home ground of the title refers to the area where the poet grew up. The area, Kameoka, used to be called "Tamba" meaning "red ripples."

VI

Rokuro Neck

rokuro In general, refers to a pulley block, but in ancient Japanese ghost stories, *rokuro* is an apparition with an elastic neck which can be lengthened or shortened in the dead of night.

"to be one in two . . ." In Dante's *The Divine Comedy*, canto XXVIII, Dante meets Bertran de Born who has been condemned to carry his head as a lantern in the depths of hell for the crime of encouraging Prince Henry to rebel against his father, King Henry II. "Of his own self he made himself a light / and they were two in one and one in two" [translation, Mark Musa; Penguin Classics (1984)]

VII

Haa Too Too Too

is a chicken call (in Japanese, "too" pronounced as toe).

The Translators

The Electric Travel Notes, Drifting in Indonesia, At the Foot of the Statue of Natsagdorj, Night in the Gobi, Tagaytay, South Luzon, Survival Songs, Builder of Bridges, Secret Passage under the Capital, A Private Letter, Transition, Meetings, The Famous Actress, Breaking Up, The Machine, Song for a Ten Yen Coin, Forging Money, Electrification Boom, Oh, Wonderful!, Sonnet on a Moustache, Home Ground, Cactus, Devilfish, In the Locker Room, A Woman from the Sea, The Young Dead, In The Fog, My Stamp, Sneeze Counting Song, Haa Too Too Too, Cicada, Two Pigeons, O Little Planet, Sounds of Asia are taken from the volume *Selected Poems* by Takashi Arima, 1990, translated by Tadao Hikihara, John Kuzel, and Ian Perlman.

Cicada and My Stamp were translated by William Puette.

Two Pigeons was translated by Kiyomi Oi.

About
the Author

Born in Kyoto in 1931, Takashi Arima graduated from Doshisha University with a degree in economics. He began writing poetry after World War II, under the influence of Mitsuharu Kaneko, symbolist and translator of Rimbaud and Baudelaire. He became a member of the Modernist group in Kyoto and published many essays and poems in *Gendaishi (Contemporary Poetry)*.

When folk music became popular in Japan, many of Arima's satirical pieces were set to music, and are now available on records and CDs. His popularity was further increased through the "reading caravans" he organized to tour the country and present his works.

Widely published in several languages, Takashi Arima today continues to write poetry while teaching at the Osaka College of Literature and the Kyoto College of Arts. He is a member of the Japan Poets' Association, a representative of the Kyoto Contemporary Poetry Association, consulting editor to the magazine *Shi to Shiso (Poetry and Thought)*, and chairman of the Asian Center for Cultural Exchange in Kyoto.

Also by Takashi Arima

POETRY

Metamorphoses, Cosmos-sha (1957).
The Twilight Wall, Eureka (1959).
Forging Money, Shicho-sha (1963).
A Woman from the Sea, Shicho-sha (1967).
Repetition, Ashi-shobo (1971).
The Beginning of the End, Kokubun-sha (1973).
The Poetry of Takashi Arima, Honyarado (In English, 1976).
From the Labyrinth, Kokubun-sha (1977).
White Night, Hakuchi-sha (1981).
Parody Fool, Kindai Bungei-sha (1982).
Islands, Sunagoya-shobo (1982).
Mongolian Horses, Sojin-sha (1988).
Takashi Arima: Selected Poems, Vol. 31 of the series
    Contemporary Japanese Poetry, Doyo Bijutsu-sha (1988).
Stranger's Songs, Noa Henshu Kobo (1989).
Selected Poems, Doyo Bijutsu-sha (In English, 1990).
North, South, East, and West, Noa Henshu Kobo (1991).
The Memory of India, Kashin-sha (1992).

SONGS FOR CHILDREN

New Children's Songs, Self-Published (1963).
My Stamp, Guerrilla-no-Kai (1966).
My Promise, Guerrilla-no-Kai (1966).
Haa Too Too Too, Kyoto Folk Song Association (1969).
Kyoto Children, Oral-ha (1974).
Rakuchu, Rakugai, Rakugaki, Mito-no-Kai (1975).
Thanks, Riron-sha (1981) (Awarded the 29th Sankei Prize for
    Children's Publications, and Recommended for the Culture Prize)
O Little Planet, Doyo Bijutsu-sha (1983).

The "Weathermark" identifies this book as a production of Weatherhill, Inc., publishers of fine books on Asia and the Pacific. Book design and typography by Liz Trovato. Typesetting by Trufont Typographers, Inc., Hicksville, New York. Printing and binding by R.R. Donnelley. The typeface used is Weiss Roman.